MUIRHEAD LIBRARY OF PHILOSOPHY

An admirable statement of the aims of the Library of Philosophy was provided by the first editor, the late Professor J. H. Muirhead, in his description of the original programme printed in Erdmann's *History of Philosophy* under the date 1890. This was slightly modified in subsequent volumes to take the form of the following statement:

'The Muirhead Library of Philosophy was designed as a contribution to the History of Modern Philosophy under the heads: first of Different Schools of Thought—Sensationalist, Realist, Idealist, Intuitivist; secondly of different Subjects—Psychology, Ethics, Aesthetics, Political Philosophy, Theology. While much had been done in England in tracing the course of evolution in nature, history, economics, morals and religion, little had been done in tracing the development of thought on these subjects. Yet "the evolution of opinion is part of the whole evolution".

'By the co-operation of different writers in carrying out this plan it was hoped that a thoroughness and completeness of treatment, otherwise unattainable, might be secured. It was believed also that from writers mainly British and American fuller consideration of English Philosophy than it had hitherto received might be looked for. In the earlier series of books containing, among others, Bosanquet's *History of Aesthetic*, Pfleiderer's *Rational Theology since Kant*, Albee's *History of English Utilitarianism*, Bonar's *Philosophy and Political Economy*, Brett's *History of Psychology*, Ritchie's *Natural Rights*, these objects were to a large extent effected.

'In the meantime original work of a high order was being produced both in England and America by such writers as Bradley, Stout, Bertrand Russell, Baldwin, Urban, Montague, and others, and a new interest in foreign works, German, French and Italian, which had either become classical or were attracting public attention, had developed. The scope of the Library thus became extended into something more international, and it is entering on the fifth decade of its existence in the hope that it may contribute to that mutual understanding between countries which is so pressing a need of the present time.'

The need which Professor Muirhead stressed is no less pressing today, and few will deny that philosophy has much to do with enabling us to meet it, although no one, least of all Muirhead himself, would regard that as the sole, or even the main, object of philosophy. As Professor Muirhead continues to lend the distinction of his name to the Library of Philosophy it seemed not inappropriate to allow him to recall us to these aims in his own words. The emphasis on the history of thought also seemed to me very timely; and the number of important works promised for the Library in the very near future augur well for the continued fulfilment, in this and other ways, of the expectations of the original editor.

H. D. LEWIS

MUIRHEAD LIBRARY OF PHILOSOPHY

General Editor: H. D. Lewis
Professor of History and Philosophy of Religion in the University of London

Action by SIR MALCOLM KNOX

The Analysis of Mind by BERTRAND RUSSELL

Belief by H. H. PRICE

Brett's History of Psychology edited by R. S. PETERS

Clarity is Not Enough by H. D. LEWIS

Coleridge as a Philosopher by J. H. MUIRHEAD

The Commonplace Book of G. E. Moore edited by C. LEWY

Contemporary American Philosophy edited by G. P. ADAMS and W. P. MONTAGUE

Contemporary British Philosophy first and second Series edited by J. H. MUIRHEAD

Contemporary British Philosophy third Series edited by H. D. LEWIS

Contemporary Indian Philosophy edited by RADHAKRISHNAN and J. H. MUIRHEAD 2nd edition

The Discipline of the Cave by J. N. FINDLAY

Doctrine and Argument in Indian Philosophy by NINIAN SMART

Essays in Analysis by ALICE AMBROSE

Ethics by NICOLAI HARTMANN translated by STANTON COIT 3 vols

The Foundations of Metaphysics in Science by ERROL E. HARRIS

Freedom and History by H. D. LEWIS

The Good Will: A Study in the Coherence Theory of Goodness by H. J. PATON

Hegel: A Re-examination by J. N. FINLAY

Hegel's Science of Logic translated by W. H. JOHNSTON and L. G. STRUTHERS 2 vols

History of Aesthetic by B. BOSANQUET 2nd edition

History of English Utilitarianism by E. ALBEE

History of Psychology by G. S. BRETT edited by R. S. PETERS abridged in one volume, 2nd edition

Human Knowledge by BERTRAND RUSSELL

A Hundred Years of British Philosophy by RUDOLF METZ translated by J. H. HARVEY, T. E. JESSOP, HENRY STURT

Ideas: A General Introduction to Pure Phenomenology by EDMUND HUSSERL translated by W. R. BOYCE GIBSON

Identity and Reality by EMILE MEYERSON

Imagination by E. J. FURLONG

𝔐uírheaὸ 𝔏íbrarg of 𝔓bílosopbg

EDITED BY H. D. LEWIS

CONTEMPORARY PHILOSOPHY IN AUSTRALIA

CONTEMPORARY PHILOSOPHY IN AUSTRALIA

EDITED BY

ROBERT BROWN

AND

C. D. ROLLINS

LONDON · GEORGE ALLEN & UNWIN LTD
NEW YORK · HUMANITIES PRESS

PRINTED IN GREAT BRITAIN
in 11 on 12 point Imprint type
BY UNWIN BROTHERS LIMITED
WOKING AND LONDON

ACKNOWLEDGEMENTS

Many philosophers not represented in this collection have helped to make it possible. First and foremost, we are grateful to all those who by offering papers for inclusion gave us the opportunities of choice. There are, of course, a number of Australian philosophers we should have liked to include. But for various reasons, personal or academic, they were unable to contribute. Secondly, we are indebted for aid, encouragement, and many other signs of goodwill, to the following: Mr David Bostock, Mr John Clendinnen, Dr Edward Curley, Professor Quentin Gibson, Professor Grover Maxwell, Dr J. E. McGechie, Professor Graham Nerlich, Professor C. F. Presley, Professor Michael Shorter, Professor J. J. C. Smart, and Mr David Stove.

Thirdly, we should like to thank Mrs Helena Michel and Mrs Glenda McIntyre for their typing of what often must have seemed an irreducible manuscript, and Mrs Elizabeth Short for making our task easier by helping us with the reading of proofs and the preparation of the index.

ROBERT BROWN
C. D. ROLLINS

CONTENTS

INTRODUCTION

In preparing this volume for publication, the editors decided to invite an expatriate Australian philosopher to contribute some observations about the development of philosophy in Australia during recent years. They suggested that I compare philosophy in Australia as I knew it, with what the essays they have selected show it now to be. Except for fifteen months in the mid-fifties, I have not been in Australia since 1951; and it has been since then that Australian philosophy passed from tutelage to full citizenship in the international republic of letters.

Australian philosophy in 1951 was still dominated by the schools of Sydney and Melbourne. Although P. H. Partridge, as Professor of Social Philosophy, was insinuating the subject into the Australian National University, and although J. J. C. Smart had been installed in the Chair at Adelaide, their work had only begun. Of the two dominant schools, Sydney alone had a thoroughly elaborated doctrine. This was the work of the late John Anderson, whose position may be studied in his posthumous *Studies in Empirical Philosophy* (Sydney 1962), which contains an introductory essay by Professor J. A. Passmore. Anderson maintained that, since genuine philosophical and scientific inquiry is disinterested, notions like the obligatory, the useful (for whatever end), and the common good have no place in philosophical ethics, and that their appearance there is symptomatic of corruption. As guardians of the intellectual tradition, the Universities, as Anderson conceived them, are beset by temptations and threats to compromise with one interest or another; and he won his enormous moral authority by the splendid dignity with which he fought for intellectual liberty and seriousness against clerical and political attacks, which few of his colleagues wished to oppose.

Anderson was chiefly occupied with philosophical logic, his central contention being, in Passmore's words, that 'the logical form of any statement will reveal it to be asserting some matter of fact (whether truly or falsely)', making such an assertion being identified with 'giving a description . . . of a certain sort of thing'.[1] Along with this 'actualism' (to adapt a term of Nelson Goodman)

---

[1] J. A. Passmore, 'John Anderson and Twentieth Century Philosophy', in John Anderson, *Studies in Empirical Philosophy*, Sydney, 1962, p. xix.

went a characteristic development of William James's radical empiricism. Everything about which an assertion can be made is complex. There are neither logical atoms nor a logical absolute. In this respect a knower does not differ from things known. Persons and minds are not transcendental unities, but complexes of feelings conceived as objective structures.

The influence of Anderson is plain in Professor Passmore's demonstration, in his essay in this volume, 'Russell and Bradley', that Russell's logical atoms stand in a relation of *coincidentia oppositorum* to Bradley's absolute. Anderson's rejection of logically ultimate subjects was clearly prophetic, but Passmore hints at a stronger claim. If the individuals over which the variables of quantification theory range are not logical atoms, what are they? Although most logicians hold that this semantical question can be satisfactorily answered in one way or another, the last paragraph of Passmore's essay intimates that he is not satisfied.

Another side of philosophy which Anderson encouraged, but which cannot be described as 'Andersonian', is also exhibited in Passmore's essay: namely, an interest in the history of philosophy that is both historically and philosophically serious. Passmore's own *Ralph Cudworth* and *A Hundred Years of Philosophy* are well known; Professor S. A. Grave's *The Scottish Philosophy of Common Sense* and Professor D. H. Monro's *Godwin's Moral Philosophy* rather less so. In this volume, Professor Monro's 'Mill's Third Howler' is a good example of the *genre*. Monro confirms a persuasive defence of J. S. Mill against G. E. Moore's charge that he confounded a means to happiness with a part of happiness, by exploring Mill's use of some ideas from Hartley's psychology that are by no means obsolete. Monro's ultimate aim is philosophical rather than historical: to urge that to the question, 'Why should I be moral?' a solution along Mill's general lines is 'at least as promising as any other as yet put forward'.

Melbourne, the second of the schools that dominated Australian philosophy in 1951, is harder to describe. Owing to the teaching there of G. A. Paul during the war, and of Douglas Gasking and A. C. Jackson after it, the strongest influence was the oral Wittgensteinian tradition, supplemented in the late forties by typescripts of *The Blue and the Brown Books*. Although there was no distinctive Melbourne Wittgensteinian position, as there was an Andersonian position, most outsiders qualified to judge agreed that there was a Melbourne Wittgensteinian style. Moreover, the spirit of philosophy at Melbourne was antithetical to that at Sydney in two respects. First, most Melbourne philosophers were moralists, and in politics approved the establishment of the Welfare State, which Anderson scorned as 'melioristic'. An Andersonian who dabbled in left-wing politics had Sorel's *Reflections on Violence* in his pocket; a Melburnian did so in the faith of the pre-war Popular Front. Secondly, although most Melbourne philosophers were not Christian, they could acknowledge the possible legitimacy of Christian and Jewish theology, since comparatively few of them agreed with Anderson in rejecting total schemes and ultimate objectives in philosophy as a matter of principle. It is not an accident that, in Australian philosophy, most attempts to establish an objective foundation for morality (e.g. in the work of Kurt Baier and H. J. McCloskey), or to solve problems in philosophical theology in conformity with a religious tradition (e.g. in the work of A. Boyce Gibson, M. J. Charlesworth, Eric D'Arcy, and G. Schlesinger) have roots in Melbourne.

The essays in this volume show that the schools of Sydney and Melbourne are no longer pre-eminent; and, even more important, that they are no longer clearly distinct. Certain views of Anderson are worthy of defence, and still defended; but Sydney is no longer Andersonian. Although Professor D. M. Armstrong, who at present occupies Anderson's Chair, has claimed Anderson as an ancestor of his materialist theory of mind, the influence of J. J. C. Smart and U. T. Place is plainly more direct and immediate, and in large part derives from the work of Gilbert Ryle. Armstrong's colleague at Sydney, Professor C. B. Martin, who has worked at Cambridge with John Wisdom and also at Oxford, is equally independent; as witness his forcible and refreshing essay on P. F. Strawson's theory of persons. As for the Wittgensteinian tradition at Melbourne, superficially it has left no trace in this volume at all. No doubt it has borne fruit, as in the essay by Professor Peter Herbst; but it has done so like the grain of wheat in the Scriptures, by falling to the ground and dying.

Have the essays in this volume any characteristics that distinguish them as Australian? Let us consider some of them.

Under the name 'Central State Materialism', one form of the thesis that the human mind and the human body are synthetically identical has been sturdily defended in Australia by J. J. C. Smart, D. M. Armstrong, and others. Mr M. C. Bradley has contributed to this volume a careful study, 'Two Arguments against the

B

Identity Thesis', in which Central State Materialism is defended against one objection, but held to succumb to another. The objection Bradley considers fatal may be sketched as follows: since many (not all) bodily sensations are at the places they appear to their possessors to occupy, and since those places are often remote from those occupied by their possessors' central nervous systems, at least some bodily sensations cannot be at the same place as the states of the central nervous system with which, according to Central State Materialism, they are identical. The chief interest of Bradley's essay, of course, is not in this skeleton argument, but in his reasons for its premises, and in his rebuttals of objections to them. These, while original and admirable, do not seem to me to be recognizable as distinctively Australian. Presented with Bradley's paper, a reader who had not read other work by him, and did not know his name, would have no way of telling that it was not written by an American or a British philosopher.

This is also true of the four essays on philosophical logic: Professor Max Deutscher's 'A Causal Account of Inferring', Professor Brian Ellis's 'An Epistemological Conception of Truth', Professor L. Goddard's 'The Existence of Universals', and Professor Peter Herbst's 'Fact, Form, and Intensionality'. All are strongly individual, but none is distinctively Australian.

D. M. Armstrong's 'Colour Realism and the Argument from Microscopes', and Keith Campbell's 'Colours' share a characteristic that is more common in Australia than elsewhere. In continental Europe as well as in Britain and the United States, science is commonly held to contradict much that is implicit in what we ordinarily say and presumably think[1] about the things we encounter. Of those who take such a view, some maintain that what is implicit in our speech is true, and that science is merely instrumental. The *Lebenswelt* is the real world. Others insist that scientific theories, even though they will be superseded, nevertheless have a better claim to be considered true than anything pre-scientific. On both sides it is agreed that what Wilfrid Sellars has called 'the scientific image' of man is incompatible with the 'manifest image' of pre-scientific thought.

Both Armstrong and Campbell reject this. They do not deny that some things implicit in what we ordinarily say are false: thus Armstrong holds that a red object under a mercury vapour lamp does not merely look brown, but *is* (transiently) brown. Yet both

[1] The phrase is from J. L. Austin, *Philosophical Papers*, London, 1961, p. 179.

contend that the common view of colours as properties of physical existents is both true and reconcilable with the findings of science. Treating what we ordinarily say as in large measure scientifically neutral, they conclude that such philosophical questions as, 'Is the colour of a surface identical with the light-waves emitted or reflected from it?' cannot be properly answered without considering scientific results.

The doctrine that what we ordinarily say about the things we encounter in the world is in general compatible with the results of science cannot, however, be described as characteristically Australian. As Sellars has pointed out, G. E. Moore held it, even though he did not always appreciate the philosophical bearing of scientific results. Nor can the plain, downright style in which these essays are written be ascribed to a national temper: its models, chiefly British, are familiar.

Contemporary Philosophy in Australia is a happy title for the volume; for philosophy is a cosmopolitan subject, and its contents are cosmopolitan.

ALAN DONAGAN

Professor of Philosophy, University of Illinois.

JOHN PASSMORE

RUSSELL AND BRADLEY

Few men who have been disciples are left unaffected by their discipleship, however sharply they may break with their former masters. If they cease to be disciples, they have a strong tendency to swing to what the world regards as 'the opposite extreme' from the doctrines their masters had taught them. But furthermore, the 'opposite extreme' they choose turns out very often, on closer examination, to be not so 'opposite' as at first sight appears. So a former Communist is not uncommonly converted into an anti-Communist of quite exceptional virulence, who continues to deploy in the interests of his new cause the controversial reckless-ness, the paranoid suspiciousness, which he learnt from his earlier teachers. He may become a convert to a more bigoted sort of Roman Catholicism but will seldom end his days as a model of tolerance and liberality.

It is important to remember just how ardently the young Ber-trand Russell espoused Hegelianism, as he makes perfectly clear in *My Philosophical Development*.[1] In 1898—i.e. at the age of twenty-six—Russell was still trying to write a dialectical philosophy of nature. Of course, we have to ask ourselves in what his Hegelian-ism consisted. Like a great many creative thinkers, Russell has never been particularly good at understanding other philosophers, even when, as in the case of Frege or Meinong, he greatly admired their work. And the situation in regard to Hegel is complicated by the fact that he had British representatives, or what were commonly supposed to be such. There was McTaggart: the most idio-syncratic of disciples, unusual amongst British Hegelians, however, in taking Hegel's dialectic as seriously as the young Russell himself did. And then there was Bradley. No Hegelian certainly, but com-monly described as one, he had sufficient in common with Hegel

---

[1] London, 1959. Before he understood the formal study of philosophy, however, he had been an adherent of a Mill-type empiricism. This he fell back on after his disenchantment with 'Hegelianism', but in a way much modified by his Hegelian experience.

to attract the admiration of Hegel's disciples. The 'Hegel' against whom the young Russell reacted was in all probability not Hegel himself but McTaggart, with regard to the dialectic, and Bradley as to monism. These, there can be little doubt, are the philosophers he referred to in 'The Philosophy of Logical Atomism'[1] as 'the people who more or less follow Hegel'.[2] My present concern is with Bradley.

We can sum up Bradley's main—and so far Hegelian—thesis as being that 'The truth is the whole'. The further our judgments are from the whole, according to Bradley, the less of truth there is in them. No judgment is wholly satisfactory; this is a consequence of the fact that to judge is to distinguish subject from predicate and thus to mutilate the unity of the whole. ('I accepted', writes Russell of his early philosophical beliefs, 'the Hegelian view that none of the sciences is quite true, since all depend on some abstraction and every abstraction leads, sooner or later, to contradictions.')[3] But of all judgments the least true, because the most remote from the whole, is the singular judgment. And of all singular judgments the poorest, the least true, is a judgment of the form 'That is red', assigning a sensory predicate to a merely designated subject. No judgment could less effectively represent, according to Bradley, the total system of reality. It is more, not less, 'abstract' than, let us say, 'All whales are mammals', for this judgment at least draws our attention to the systematic interconnection of properties in Reality—the properties of 'being a whale' and 'being a mammal'—whereas 'This is red' does not even serve that very limited purpose.

In his *My Philosophical Development* Russell tells us that when he broke with Hegelianism his initial tendency was to accept as real everything which Hegel had denied to be real. 'In my first rebellion against Hegel, I believed that a thing must exist if Hegel's proof that it cannot is invalid'; 'this gave me a very full universe.'[4] To this it can be added, I think, that Russell came to believe that the most satisfactory of all propositions must be what Bradley took to be the least satisfactory—propositions like 'This is red'. For Bradley, judgments are true only in so far as they point towards the total system of reality. The tendency in Russell's

[1] First published in *The Monist*, 1918–19, reprinted in B. Russell, *Logic and Knowledge*, ed. R. C. Marsh, London, 1956, pp. 175–282.

[2] In *My Philosophical Development*, he particularly expresses his indebtedness to McTaggart, but Bradley—along with G. F. Stout—appears as an Hegelian.

[3] *Ibid.*, p. 42.   [4] *Ibid.*, p. 62.

philosophy is in the opposite direction, to argue that—at least so far as empirical propositions are concerned—the truth of a proposition resides in its being analysable into propositions truly asserting facts which are absolutely independent of one another.

Russell does not commit himself to this conclusion quite wholeheartedly; it was left to his pupil, Wittgenstein, to take the final steps. But it is certainly the direction in which Russell moved, towards a logical atomism only slightly mitigated, in the interests of induction, by an occasional exception. 'It used to be thought', Russell writes in *My Philosophical Development*, 'that one fact could be logically dependent upon another. This can only be the case if one of the facts is really two facts put together. From "A and B are men" it follows logically that A is a man but that is because "A and B are men" *is really two propositions put together.*'[1] So whereas for Bradley every judgment was a representative, however unworthy, of Reality as a whole, for Russell an atomic proposition represented nothing but a single atomic fact: 'All atomic propositions are mutually independent.'[2] If such an atomic proposition is rejected as false, its rejection would have no other effect except that this particular proposition no longer forms part of the totality of true propositions. Everything else would be exactly as it was before. To put the point metaphorically, for Russell for such a proposition to be proved false, would be as if an anonymous friendless stranger were to die alone, remote from human habitation, affecting by his death nobody but himself; for Bradley it would be as if a child, however imperfect, were to die in the midst of his family circle, inevitably affecting the general character of that circle by his death.

One of Bradley's difficulties, as we have already seen, is that no judgment can adequately represent the Absolute. It is impossible to nominate an example of a true judgment because any judgment in some measure falsifies, merely in virtue of the fact that it distinguishes subject from predicate. So the standard of comparison by reference to which a judgment is (relatively) to be condemned as unworthily representing the Absolute is not a perfectly true judgment but only a judgment which, so it has to be supposed, comes close to the truth. Russell's problem (and Wittgenstein's) lay in precisely the reverse direction, but led to the same 'unspeakable' conclusion. No proposition which it is possible to nominate has the degree of independence they ascribed to an

---

[1] *My Philosophical Development*, p. 119, my italics.   [2] *Ibid.*, p. 119.

atomic fact; this, Bradley might say, is a consequence of the fact that propositions *have* predicates and are, so far, not wholly atomic—predicates introduce into them an element of generality. For Bradley every judgment is too independent to represent the Absolute; for Russell and Wittgenstein no proposition is independent enough to be atomic.

Consider, for example, 'This is red'. If we reject this proposition, we may also have to reject such propositions as 'This will suit Mary's complexion', 'This will look well in my room', 'This is bright', 'This is the same colour as that object over there'. So it is not a wholly independent, atomic, proposition. As Wittgenstein recognized in the *Tractatus*, an atomic proposition would have to consist of logically proper names in immediate combination; nothing less will suffice. But then the problem is that 'logically proper names' are as elusive as the Absolute.

Russell himself defines logical atomism much less rigidly when, as in 'The Philosophy of Logical Atomism' he has in mind the contrast between himself and Bradley. 'The logic which I shall advocate', he says, 'is atomistic as opposed to the monistic logic of the people who more or less follow Hegel. When I say that my logic is atomistic I mean that I share the common-sense belief that there are many separate things; I do not regard the apparent multiplicity of the world as consisting merely in phases and unreal divisions of a single indivisible Reality.'[1]

The word 'separate' is here the rub. William James had drawn attention to a phenomenon he called 'vicious intellectualism'; this consists in supposing that what is distinct cannot be related and what is related cannot be distinct. 'It really seems "weird",' he wrote, 'to have to argue (as I am forced now to do) for the notion that it is one sheet of paper (with its two surfaces and all that lies between) which is both under my pen and on the table while I write—the "claim" that it is two sheets seems so brazen. Yet I sometimes suspect the absolutists of sincerity!'[2] It is no less 'weird' to have to argue that there is not just one fact but a whole set of facts in 'This is red'—or for that matter, in 'Socrates is mortal' or 'All men are mortal'. If it is taken at the commonsense level, of course, the assertion that 'There are many separate

[1] *Logic and Knowledge*, p. 178. Monism was to Russell the great enemy; he distinguishes his own reaction against Hegel from G. E. Moore's because Moore, Russell says, was mainly concerned to reject idealism, he himself to reject monism. (*My Philosophical Development*, p. 54.)

[2] *A Pluralistic Universe*, London, 1909, note on p. 357.

things' is a mere commonplace. Indeed—since any assertion consists of a set of separate words and so does its negation—it would be 'pragmatically self-refuting' to try to deny that there are separate things.[1] But it by no means follows that there are *particulars*, defined as Russell defines them, particulars which have the peculiarity that 'each of them stands entirely alone and is completely self-subsistent'.[2] Particulars, in this sense, are as mythical as Bradley's Absolute. Instead of rejecting the whole concept of 'what stands alone' and 'the self-subsistent', what Russell has done is to transfer these properties from Bradley's Absolute to atomic particulars.

Why does Russell set up this queer sort of metaphysics? Well for one thing, as comes out in a good many places in his writings, Russell imagines it to be the only alternative to monism. It is not, as it were, 'safe' to stop anywhere short of the pure particular; if we do, then before we know where we are we shall be back in the embraces of Bradley's Absolute. We can protect ourselves against such conclusions as that 'The truth is the whole' or that 'There is no Reality short of the Absolute', so Russell thought, only by asserting that there are propositions whose truth cannot possibly consist in the contribution they make to a total system. For we see that they make *no* contribution to it and that there are entities from whose existence the existence of the Absolute cannot possibly be deduced, because it is their nature to exist in entire independence of the existence of anything else. From the fact that they exist, that is, *nothing* can be deduced.

There need be, Russell argues, only one particular. So it is logically impossible to conclude from the existence of a particular to the existence of an Absolute. It is striking testimony to the power of Hegelianism that Russell does not feel safe against it except by affirming a more than Humean looseness and separateness.

The fact that since particulars are indescribable it is impossible to nominate examples of them will not, he says, worry him, any more than it worries Bradley that he cannot describe the Absolute. Russell, like Bradley, is content to say that the existence of his ultimate metaphysical entities is a necessity of logical analysis and that we can, at least, get sufficiently near to them to see what kind of thing they would be. So in 'The Philosophy of Logical Atomism' he writes that 'The whole question of what particulars you

---

[1] See J. A. Passmore, *Philosophical Reasoning*, London, 1961, for 'pragmatically self-refuting' propositions.   [2] *Logic and Knowledge*, p. 201.

actually find in the real world is a purely empirical one which does not interest the logician as such'.[1]

One does, however, more than suspect Wittgenstein's influence at this point. At other times what Russell calls his 'robust sense of reality' leaves him uneasy about his inability to give examples of atomic propositions, just as it made him uneasy about Meinong's 'objects'. So he tries, by falling back on the British empiricist tradition, to identify particulars with 'objects of sense'. For Bradley, mind and God, in the capacity of unifying systems, give us a glimpse of the Absolute; we can imagine them being converted after 'supplementation' into the Absolute. For Russell, sense data give us a glimpse of particulars; with further analysis we could imagine them being converted into particulars

Russell was led to the doctrine of pure particulars, however, by still another route, and this time with more positive help from Bradley's logical analysis. Oddly enough, in *My Philosophical Development*—although not, for example, in the essay 'On Denoting'[2]—he ignores Bradley's influence; he writes as if his analysis of the proposition had derived solely from Peano and the mathematical logicians. He made progress in logic, he says, once he sharply distinguished between the two propositional forms represented in 'Socrates is mortal' and in 'All Greeks are mortal'. As he rightly says, traditional logic identified these forms for most logical purposes, on the ground that the validity of a syllogism is unaffected if a singular proposition replaces a universal proposition. But in fact, so Russell argues, these propositions are completely different in logical form. Whereas 'Socrates is a mortal' ascribes a predicate to a named subject, 'All Greeks are mortal' relates the predicates 'Greek' and 'mortal'. Whereas 'Socrates is mortal' gives us information about a particular person, namely the person to whom we give the proper name 'Socrates', 'All Greeks are mortal' does not give us information about Greeks. 'The statement "All Greeks are mortal" says nothing about Greeks in particular.'[3]

Now, admittedly, Russell did not learn from Bradley to distinguish the singular from the universal form. Bradley accepted, and indeed developed, the view that the correct analysis of a singular proposition would reveal it to be a universal, and he rejected

[1] *Logic and Knowledge*, p. 199.
[2] First published in *Mind*, Vol. XIV, 1905, reprinted in *Logic and Knowledge*, pp. 39–56. See the footnote on p. 43 of that volume.
[3] *My Philosophical Development*, p. 66.

outright the conception of 'names' which are purely denoting and
have no connotation. But the view that 'All Greeks are mortal' is
not, appearances to the contrary notwithstanding, 'really about'
Greeks is characteristic of the Idealist logicians. Then what, if
not Greeks, is 'All Greeks are mortal' about? To this question
Russell and Bradley give the same answer: it is about 'everything'.
Where they differ is in the interpretation they give of 'everything'.
For the monist Bradley, 'everything' has to be read as the name of
an entity; it means the total system, the Absolute. For the atomist
Russell it has to be read distributively, it means 'each and every
particular'.

Mill had sometimes suggested—in one of the several analyses of
universal propositions which he offers—that 'All Greeks are
mortal' is 'really about' Socrates, Plato, Aristophanes, etc.
Socrates, Plato and Aristophanes are, for Mill, examples of
particulars. This is undoubtedly the presumption from which
Russell set out. Wherever he offers his readers a preliminary or
informal exposition of his views, proper names like 'Socrates' are
taken to stand for particulars. So, as we have already seen, he
contrasts 'Socrates is a man' and 'All Greeks are men' by arguing
that 'Socrates', unlike 'Greeks', is a *name*. Even in 'The Philosophy
of Logical Atomism' he begins by treating Socrates as a particular
although a footnote warns the reader that this view will later be
questioned.[1]

As part of that later questioning, he makes the distinctly odd
remark that 'What pass for names in language like "Socrates",
"Plato" and so forth, *were originally intended to fulfil this function
of standing for particulars,*'[2] and admits that in ordinary life, we
fully accept them as such. But to do so, he came to think, is metaphysically dangerous. For the particulars named by 'Socrates' and
'Plato' are, on the face of it, 'complex systems bound together into
some kind of a unity', and it is, Russell thinks, 'the contemplation
of this sort of apparent unity which has very largely led to the
philosophy of monism'.[3] We are not really safe from Hegelianism,
it seems, so long as he still thinks of 'Socrates' and 'Plato' as names.

So Russell rejects the view that 'Socrates' and 'Plato' are names;
they are, he says, 'really descriptions'. This has the effect, incidentally, that Bradley was right after all in supposing 'Socrates is
mortal' to be identical in form with 'All Greeks are mortal';

[1] *Logic and Knowledge*, p. 182.   [2] *Ibid.*, p. 200 (my italics).
[3] *Ibid.*, p. 190.

'Socrates is mortal' must now be taken to mean something like 'For all *x*, if *x* is Plato's teacher, *x* is mortal'. It, too, is 'really about everything', not about Socrates. If the Idealist logicians were mistaken, it is only in failing to recognize that there are 'ultimate' singular propositions which cannot be thus read as universal hypotheticals. It is important to recognize that Russell's initial criticisms of traditional, and Idealist, logic rest on the presumption that 'Socrates', 'Plato', etc., *are* names of particulars; and it is distinctly unfortunate that, when at a later stage in his argument, this assumption is abandoned, he did not go back to take a second look at the initial stages of his criticisms and the effect his new view would have upon them. Indeed, he still continues to speak of 'Socrates' as a name whenever he has the task of introducing to his reader the distinction between 'names' and 'predicates'. Nor is this an accident.

For what, if not 'Socrates', *does* serve to name a particular? What acts as the subject, that is, in a *genuinely* singular proposition? It is, Russell says, 'very difficult to get any instance of a name at all in the proper strict logical sense of the word'.[1] The only example he can give is a demonstrative like 'this' or 'that'. But it is easy to understand why he does not, in first introducing the concept of a 'name', give 'this' as his example. Nothing could be less like what is ordinarily meant by a 'name'. And even these words, if they are to be taken as the names of particulars, cannot be read as we ordinarily read them. For if anybody holds up a book and says: 'This is my new book' we normally take it that 'this' is equivalent to 'this book'. And 'this book' is not, on Russell's view, a name. So we have to suppose that what the speaker is really talking about is some kind of sense-datum—Russell calls it 'an actual object of sense';[2] something, incidentally, which we cannot observe at all. (So 'this' is converted into a demonstrative which does not, and cannot, point to anything—a pointless pointer!) 'What solipsism *means*', wrote Wittgenstein in the *Tractatus*, 'is quite correct; only it cannot be *said*, but it shows itself. . . . The world is *my* world.'[3] Russell would be forced to this same conclusion. We can never know the atomic facts that anybody else knows because what they are about is something which he alone knows. A speaker's 'This is red' communicates nothing, if we are not allowed to interpret his 'this' as 'this *thing*'. But if we do so

[1] *Logic and Knowledge*, p. 201.   [2] *Ibid.*
[3] L. Wittgenstein, *Tractatus Logico-philosophicus*, London, 1922, 5.62 (p. 151).

interpret it, then we no longer interpret his statement as the atomic proposition which it 'really is'.

It is logically impossible, then, to 'give an example of' an atomic fact or, in consequence, an example of a particular. '"This",' as Russell puts it, 'has a very odd property for a proper name, namely that it seldom means the same thing two moments running and does not mean the same thing to the speaker and to the hearer.'[1] So we are back at the unspeakable, the incommunicable. Propositions are not 'really' about an indescribable Absolute, definable only as that to which predicates ultimately apply; they are 'really' about indescribable 'objects of sense', definable only as that to which predicates ultimately apply.

Even leaving this special doctrine about sense data aside, however, logical atomism ends up by being a kind of diffracted image of Bradley. The Absolute splits up into particulars, each of which, like the Absolute, 'stands entirely alone and is completely self-subsistent'; these are the 'ultimate' subjects of all propositions; what we ordinarily take to be subjects are all of them actually descriptions; the only true subject is 'everything'; 'everything' is quite indescribable.

No wonder, in his *An Inquiry into Meaning and Truth*, Russell revolted against so transcendental a metaphysics. In 'The Philosophy of Logical Atomism' he had, correctly, pointed out that his particulars have 'that sort of self-subsistence that used to belong to substance',[2] but it took him a surprisingly long time to arrive at the conclusion he finally drew in *Meaning and Truth*, that if this is so they must also share with substance the property of being an 'unknowable something'.[3] But we shall certainly have to look again at Russell's logical analysis of propositions if it be indeed true, as he argues in *Meaning and Truth*, that 'This is red' is not a subject-predicate proposition but is of the form 'redness is here'[4]—that 'red' is a name, not a predicate.

Something has obviously gone wrong. And what has gone wrong, I have been suggesting, is that Russell shares with Bradley the assumption that there must be an 'ultimate subject'. Whether there be one, or a finite number, or an infinite number, of ultimate subjects is a relatively unimportant question; what really matters is whether we accept, or reject, the view that there are such ultimate subjects. Ultimate subjects are logically necessary in the Bradley-

---

[1] *Logic and Knowledge*, p. 201.
[2] *Ibid.*, p. 202.
[3] *Meaning and Truth*, p. 97.
[4] *Ibid.*, p. 97.

Russell analysis of the proposition because otherwise all propositions would be merely hypothetical connections of predicates; only *via* its indirect reference to the Absolute, or to particulars, does a proposition achieve categoricity, succeed in saying something which is *not* hypothetical.

The decisive step is taken once it is denied that 'All Greeks are mortal' is 'really about' Greeks. For if there is any good reason for denying that 'All Greeks are mortals' is 'really about' Greeks, then there will be really the same reason for denying that 'Socrates is mortal' is 'really about' Socrates, or generally that 'X is Y' is 'really about' X wherever 'X' is a subject for which it is logically possible to substitute a description. So we are inevitably led to the conclusion that the 'real subject' of propositions must be an indescribable somewhat.

2

L. GODDARD

THE EXISTENCE OF UNIVERSALS

Various classical arguments have been advanced in support of the conclusion that universals exist, but there are two main general types: the argument from meaning, derived from puzzles of the sort 'How can general words mean?' or 'Why are we able to name things as we do?'; and the argument from predication, derived from puzzles such as 'How can two different things possibly be the same?' or 'Why are things what they are?' I want to show that these arguments have to be taken together, that when combined they do lead to the conclusion that there are universals, but that the existence so demonstrated is independent of any particular thesis about their nature, and is neutral, too, with respect to traditional naming theories of meaning. This leaves it open that universals can be identified as rules for the use of words, so that an acceptance of their existence is not incompatible with recent theories of meaning.

D. F. Pears says,[1]

'"Because universals exist" is the answer to at least two general questions: "Why are things what they are?" and "Why are we able to name things as we do?" Though Plato and Aristotle sometimes distinguished these two questions, it was characteristic of Greek thought to confuse them. Yet they can be clearly distinguished, the first requiring a dynamic answer from scientists, and the second a static answer from logicians.'

It is true that these two questions have often been confused, and sometimes even identified; and it is true that they can be distinguished and that they are different. But the confusion has its origins in what seems to be a clear insight, namely that the two questions, though different, are so related that whatever counts as an answer to one will count as an answer to the other. For when-

---

[1] 'Universals', *Philosophical Quarterly*, Vol. 3, 1951. Reprinted in Antony Flew, ed., *Logic and Language*. Series II, Oxford, 1953.

ever several different things have the same property, are the same kind, or of the same material, the same word names, or denotes,[1] each of them. If x_1 and x_2 are red then the word 'red' denotes them, and if the word 'red' denotes each of them then they are both red. That is,

$$x_1, x_2, \ldots \text{ are red} \equiv \text{the word 'red' denotes } x_1, x_2, \ldots;$$

or more generally,

$$(1) \quad x_1, x_2, \ldots \text{ are } \phi \equiv \text{the word } qu(\phi) \text{ denotes } x_1, x_2, \ldots {}^2$$

This being so, if we raise a puzzle about sameness of property, kind or material, i.e. a puzzle about predication, by asking Pears' first question, then we automatically raise his second question, and hence a puzzle about denotation; and conversely. To suggest, therefore, that 'because universals exist' is an answer to each of Pears' two questions is at least to recognize condition (1) whatever other defects the answer might have, and from this point of view it is a logically respectable answer even though one accepts that the two questions are different.

It might however be thought that though there is some such equivalence as that intended by (1), it is there incorrectly represented. For it depends on the assumption that there is a curious language-world linking relation of denoting when in fact what we have is the use of a word to denote. From this point of view, it might be said, (1) should be expressed as,

$$(1a) \quad x_1, x_2, \ldots \text{ are } \phi \equiv \text{the word } qu(\phi) \text{ is (or can be) used to denote } x_1, x_2, \ldots$$

But there is of course a distinction to be made between the (correct) use of a word to denote and the fact that it does (truly)

---

[1] I shall depart from Pears' terminology by using the word 'denotes' instead of 'names' as a blanket term to cover the relation between a general word and those things which have the property indicated (named) by the word, though it is obviously not a happy term in the case of verbs, prepositions and even adjectives (where 'describes' would be better). I reserve the word 'names' for the relation between a proper name and its referent.

[2] 'qu' is a quotation function which has as its values the quotation-mark names of the values given to its argument. Thus if $\phi = $ red then $qu(\phi) = $ 'red'. The function is necessary if we wish to generalize by using variables in a quotation context. We cannot so use ordinary quote marks since, e.g. ' "ϕ" denotes $x_1, x_2, \ldots$ ' expresses the false proposition that the Greek letter phi denotes $x_1, x_2, \ldots$ For a detailed discussion of various types of quotation function see L. Goddard and R. Routley, 'Use, Mention & Quotation', *Australasian Journal of Philosophy*, Vol. 44, May 1966.

denote a given particular or particulars. For we may use, say, the word 'blue' to denote a red object (as in a statement of the sort 'This is blue') and such a use would be perfectly correct though it would issue in a false statement. This being so, however, we may affirm that a word $qu(\phi)$ is or can be used to denote, say, x, even though we cannot affirm that x is ϕ and the equivalence in the form $(1a)$ fails.

The equivalence (1) is thus intended to express the fact that a word $qu(\phi)$ can be said to denote a particular x when, and only when, it is true that x is ϕ. That is, $x_1, x_2, \ldots$ are ϕ if, and only if, they constitute the denotation of the word $qu(\phi)$, in Mill's sense of 'denotation'. It is this sense which I wish to give to the word 'denotes' in (1). By contrast, the use of a word to denote, if it is identified with meaning, is closer to Mill's concept of connotation.

So we might best capture the intended use of 'denotes' by expressing (1) as,

$$x_1, x_2, \ldots \text{ are } \phi \equiv x_1, x_2, \ldots \epsilon Den(qu(\phi))$$

where 'Den' abbreviates the phrase 'the denotation of the word . . .' and 'ϵ' designates the membership relation. In this form it is simply a variation of the standard abstraction thesis,

$$\phi_x \equiv x\epsilon\hat{z}(\phi z)$$

since $\hat{z}(\phi z)$, the class determined by the property ϕ (or as Russell puts it, the class determined by the propositional function ϕx), just is the denotation of the word $qu(\phi)$. That is, we may affirm,

$$x\epsilon\hat{z}(\phi z) \equiv x\epsilon Den(qu(\phi))$$

and so derive the abstraction thesis from (1).[1]

---

[1] In view of what has been said, a more appropriate formulation of (1) would make explicit use of the operator 'it is true that . . .' ('T') as in:
$$T(x_1, x_2, \ldots \text{ are } \phi) \equiv x_1, x_2, \ldots \varepsilon\ Den(qu(\phi))$$
or, more simply,
$$T\phi x \equiv x\varepsilon\ Den(qu(\phi)).$$
Then, using,
$$x\varepsilon\hat{z}(\phi z) \equiv x\varepsilon\ Den(qu(\phi))$$
we should obtain the abstraction thesis in the form,
$$T\phi x \equiv x\varepsilon\hat{z}(\phi z).$$
So formulated the thesis has many advantages, and in particular enables us to distinguish significant and non-significant uses of predicative sentences and so to develop a formal theory of categories. (See my 'Predicates, Relations and Categories', *Australasian Journal of Philosophy*, Vol. 44, 1966.) However the introduction of 'T' makes for a good deal of formal complication and I omit it here for the sake of simplicity.

It thus appears that the compulsion to give the same answer to Pears' two questions derives its strength from the fact that we do commonly accept the abstraction thesis, since it implicitly expresses a relation between predication, on the one hand, and denoting, on the other (or explicitly so when formulated as (1)). And it seems in general that any theory of universals, to be consistent with (1), must stand as a single theory which explains both predication and denoting.

It is now interesting to see that traditional theories of universals culminated in analyses of predicative sentences which not only satisfied condition (1), or were consistent with it, but which implied it and so could be said to stand as explanations of it.

For suppose we ask how one word can be used to denote many different things. The word is one in the sense that it has one and the same meaning on different occasions of its use and independently of the objects which it is used to denote. What has to be explained, therefore, is how the one meaning is related to many different particulars; we have to explain denoting in terms of meaning, not vice versa. For if not, and we seek to explain meaning in terms of denoting, we shall be unable to account for the fact that two words may have different meanings yet the same denotation (cf. 'fairy' and 'unicorn'), or for the fact that the denotation class of a word may change even though its meaning does not (we might paint a black object yellow, so changing the denotations, but certainly not the meanings, of 'black' and 'yellow'). But sameness or constancy of meaning can only be explained by reference to something which itself does not change. This something we may call a universal, and by analogy with the situation which seems to prevail in the case of proper names, we may say that the word means because it names a universal.

I shall call this the argument from meaning. But it is not yet complete. For as it stands, it still tells us nothing about denoting. That a word means by naming a universal is an explanation which so far is independent of the fact that it denotes a given set of particulars, unless the universal is itself related to those particulars. For though the word gets its meaning by naming a universal there is as yet no reason why it denotes this set of particulars rather than that. And we can only provide the link between the word and the objects by providing a link between that which the word names and the objects; that is, by saying something about predication. In order to solve one problem we have to solve both.

Considerations of this sort seem to force us towards the familiar type of analysis: to say that $x_1, x_2, \ldots$ are ϕ is to say that there is an entity α such that the word $qu(\phi)$ stands in some constant relation R to α (usually taken to be the relation of naming) and α stands in some constant relation S to $x_1, x_2, \ldots$; i.e.,

$$(2)\ x_1, x_2, \ldots \text{ are } \phi \equiv (E\alpha)(qu(\phi)R\alpha \cdot \alpha Sx_1, x_2, \ldots)$$

Now the right-hand side of this equivalence defines a new relation R/S which is the relative product of R and S, for in general,

$$x(R/S)y \equiv (Ez)(xRz \cdot zSy)$$

Thus we have,

$$(E\alpha)(qu(\phi)R\alpha \cdot \alpha Sx_1, x_2, \ldots) \equiv qu(\phi)R/Sx_1, x_2, \ldots;$$

and since R/S directly relates the word $qu(\phi)$ to the objects $x_1, x_2, \ldots$, it may be taken to be the relation of denoting. That is,

$$
\begin{aligned}
x_1, x_2, \ldots \text{ are } \phi &\equiv (E\alpha)(qu(\phi)R\alpha \cdot \alpha Sx_1, x_2, \ldots) \\
&\equiv qu(\phi)R/Sx_1, x_2, \ldots \\
&\equiv qu(\phi) \text{ denotes } x_1, x_2, \ldots
\end{aligned}
$$

The proposed analysis (2) thus implies the original condition (1), and it is for this reason that traditional theories of universals could claim to stand as unified theories of predication and meaning which provided an explanation of the link between language and the world.

So although one might accept with Pears that the two *questions* which lead to the problem of universals have often been confused, it would be a mistake to conclude from this that theories of universals which seek to provide one *answer* to both questions are somehow improper because of this. On the contrary, traditional theories which culminated in analyses of the kind described above, however confused, and whatever epistemological or ontological difficulties they encountered, were logically acceptable just because they gave an answer to both questions. And in general it seems to be a necessary condition for any satisfactory theory of either meaning or predication that it should explain both.

To take the argument from meaning in this way is therefore to regard it as leading to a general condition which must be satisfied by any cogent theory of meaning. When so taken, however, though it is consistent with all traditional theories of universals, it is independent of any given one. That is, the proposed analysans of predicative sentences,

$$(3)\ (E\alpha)(qu(\phi)R\alpha\ .\ \alpha Sx_1, x_2, \ldots)$$

is neutral with respect to the nature of the universal whose existence is being affirmed. For we may take α to be a form, a common property, an abstract idea, a concept, a Russellian class or a paradigmatic particular and still satisfy the required condition. Of course the cash value we give to α will determine the cash value we give to S. If α is a Platonic form, then S is the converse of the relation of participation or imitation; if a common property, then S is 'is shared by'; if a Lockean abstract idea, then S is 'is abstracted from'; if a concept, then the relation of comprehension; if a Russellian class, then the converse of the relation of membership; if a paradigmatic particular, then the relation of similarity; and so on.

In some cases the details of the proposed nature of the universal may be more complicated than this, but even so the general structure of condition (3) is satisfied. If, for example, we take a more complicated version of the theory to be found in Locke, namely that a general word stands for a nominal essence and that individuals of a given kind have a real essence in common (which we cannot ever know, except in the case of mathematical objects), then the relation S is in effect resolved into two relations S_1 and S_2 and Locke is putting up some such analysis as the following:

$$x_1, x_2, \ldots \text{ are } \phi$$
$$\equiv (E\alpha)[qu(\phi)R\alpha\ .\ (E\beta)(\alpha S_1\beta\ .\ \beta S_2 x_1, x_2, \ldots)]$$

where α is the nominal essence, β the real essence, and S_1 some relation (not specified) between them. The relation of denoting is then defined by $R/(S_1/S_2)$. Russell's theory, too, involves complications of a similar kind. For though he might be taken initially to be proposing a simple form of (2), namely,

$$x_1, x_2, \ldots \text{ are } \phi \equiv (Ec)(qu(\phi)Rc\ .\ c\overset{\smile}{\in}x_1, x_2, \ldots)$$

as an analysis of predicative sentences, where c is a class and $\overset{\smile}{\in}$ the converse of the relation of membership, he was concerned also to analyse the notion of membership in terms of paradigmatic particulars and the relation of similarity (cf. the definition of number). In order to take this into account, use has to be made also of the further equivalence:

$$x_1, x_2, \ldots \in c \equiv (Ey)(y\epsilon c\ .\ x_1, x_2, \ldots Sy)$$

where y is the standard particular and S is the relation of similarity. Thus we have a Lockean-type theory:

$$x_1, x_2, \ldots \text{ are } \phi$$
$$\equiv (Ec)[qu(\phi)Rc \cdot (Ey)(c\check{\epsilon}y \cdot ySx_1, x_2, \ldots)]$$

The relation of denoting is then defined by $R/(\check{\epsilon}/S)$. In the special case of the definition of number, $x_1, x_2, \ldots$ are particular classes, c a class of classes, y the 'given' class and S the relation of 1-1 correspondence.

The reason why condition (3) is neutral with respect to any particular traditional theory arises from the fact that the argument from meaning, in terms of which it is established, is transcendental. For the point of the argument is to establish what must be so in order that the facts be as they are. The conclusion, that there are universals which relate words to things, stands as an explanation of the fact that several different things are ϕ if, and only if, the word $qu(\phi)$ denotes them. So the conclusion (2) accounts for the *possibility* of the fact (1). Or equivalently, the assertion that there are universals is an answer to each of the questions 'How can things possibly be as they are?' (or more particularly 'How can two different things possibly be the same?') and 'How can we possibly name (denote) things as we do?' These are not quite as Pears expresses them, though his formulation of the second is similar.

Now if we have an agreed fact X and ask 'How can it possibly be?' we are in effect looking for premises from which it can be deduced. The transcendental argument takes the form: X is so, but could not be so unless Y were so; so that Y, the conclusion of the transcendental argument then functions as a premise, or set of premises, which imply X. Hence one test of the value of a transcendental argument is to see whether or not its conclusion Y does in fact imply X. This test, as we have seen, is satisfied by the conclusion (2) of the argument from meaning since it does imply the fact (1) which we are seeking to explain. There is nevertheless an openness which remains characteristic of any transcendental argument even though it satisfies this test.

Suppose, for example, we have an agreed fact X expressed by a sentence of the form 'Some S are P', say 'Some cats are black', and we ask how this can possibly be, i.e. what accounts for it. The natural way would be to look for evidence by empirical investigation. But we might simply look for premises Y from which it can be deduced and offer: all creatures with a given genetic structure are black and some cats have the required genetic structure. We are now in a position to explain the black colour of some cats. But from a purely logical point of view the phrase 'genetic structure' has no content. Any premise of the form 'all creatures with feature α are black and some cats have feature α' would yield 'Some cats are black' as a conclusion. Hence if our task is simply to find premises, and there are as yet no empirical considerations which enable us to determine a cash value for α, we may simply reply, 'Because there are alphas' in answer to the question 'How can cats possibly be black?', intending this as an abbreviation for 'Because there is an α such that all αs are black and some cats are αs'. And even if we introduce a word such as 'gene', which because of its etymology has apparent content, and reply 'Because there are genes', we have *so far* not given any interpretation to the word. It is a theoretical concept with no empirical content in spite of its occurrence in an existential assertion. The existence which has been established by the transcendental argument is simply its existence as a theoretical concept and not yet as an identifiable item of experience. For it is postulated on the basis of a logical need only, namely that of standing as a deductive link, and not an empirical one. It is thus in the general nature of a transcendental theory that the argument which is held to establish the existence of a theoretical concept should be independent of any particular interpretation of that theory in terms of which the concept is cashed. In accepting (2), therefore, as an explanation of (1), we are not yet committed to the existence of universals as identifiable items of experience (or thought) any more than the theoretical physicist who accepts the mathematical theory of elementary quantum mechanics, and thereby the existence of quanta, is committed to identifying the theoretical quantum as a wave or a particle.[1]

This openness thus accounts for the possibility of competing theories at the level of interpretation and explains the neutrality of the conclusion (2). The conclusion is independent of all particular traditional theories simply because it is characteristic of all transcendental arguments that they should be open in this way.

---

[1] It is perhaps worth noting that the proposal to solve the problem of interpreting elementary quantum mechanics by postulating wavicles (wave/particles) is no solution at all but simply an affirmation that 'quantum' is a theoretical concept which can be interpreted in two different ways.

This means, therefore, that the conclusion of the argument from meaning is independent of all traditional theories of *predication*. For it is independent of the nature of the universal and it is this which determines the nature of predication. It may yet be said, however, that the conclusion is not independent of traditional theories of *meaning*, since it is not independent of the kind of theory of which traditional theories are examples. For however (3) may be particularized, by giving different cash values to α and S, this does not affect the cash value given to R. In all such theories, R stands as the relation of naming.

It thus seems that there is still a case to be made for the view that the answers to Pears' two questions are independent. In spite of what has been said, it remains possible to argue that it is a mistake to look for one theory which answers both questions, and to claim instead that they call for different kinds of answers: the problem of predication calls for a dynamic answer from scientists; the problem of meaning, a static answer from logicians. For in terms of what has been said, we may give the static answer 'Because general words name universals' to the question 'Why are we able to name (denote) things as we do?' while remaining uncommitted with respect to any particular theory of predication. The two questions may therefore be independent, and it is possible that the question 'Why are things what they are?' should be answered by scientists or someone else independently of whatever philosophers may say about language.

But to push the argument this far is to push it too far. For though it is true that all traditional theories of universals are consistent with a naming theory of *meaning*, this does not imply that the problem of predication is independent of the problem of *denoting* in the sense that we could, consistently with a traditional theory, give an answer to one without giving an answer to the other or that we could answer them separately by two separate lines of inquiry. In fact, the assertion 'Because general words name universals' is an answer to the question 'Why do general words mean?' and not at all an answer to Pears' quite different question 'Why are we able to name (denote) things as we do?' It only seems to be so if we are misled into thinking that the general thesis Meaning-is-Naming is itself a complete explanation of denoting, requiring no further elucidation; while the general thesis that particulars are related to universals is not yet an explanation of predication and can therefore be filled out independently. But if the argument from meaning is accepted, then however the universal is specified it must be such as can stand in place of α and satisfy condition (3). It has to be the sort of thing which, because it stands in relations to both words and things, accounts for both meaning and predication. It has to be the sort of thing which can stand in a constant relation to words and a constant relation to particulars. If this is so, however, and if the scientist does answer the question, 'Why are things what they are?' he thereby answers the question 'How are we able to name (denote) things as we do?' and the problem of meaning as well as the problem of predication gets solved by the scientists. If Pears really wants to say that these two questions can be answered independently by two separate lines of inquiry, then he is committed to the rejection of '$(E\alpha)(qu(\phi)$ $R\alpha . \alpha Sx_1, x_2, \ldots)$' as an analysis of predicative sentences, no matter how it may be cashed.

Now he may of course be very willing to accept this outcome, since he may wish to reject a naming theory of meaning and claim that all traditional theories were misplaced because they depended on it. But I now want to extend the point by suggesting that condition (3) is independent of every particular theory of meaning just as it is independent of every particular theory of predication, and further, that it is a condition which any logically satisfactory explanation of denoting must satisfy. I want, that is, to claim that the argument from meaning is acceptable, but that its acceptability is independent of the kind of theory of which traditional theories are examples, as it is already independent of every particular traditional theory. And this is so even though, as given, it may be taken to stand as a typical version of a *unum-nomen-unum-nominatum* argument.

It has to be recognized, however, that in arguing for the acceptability of a transcendental argument, one can never expect to show that it is conclusive, only that it is persuasive. The reason for this is that such arguments, besides being open in the way described, are open in a second way.

This second kind of openness arises because in general, Y, the set of premises which imply the agreed fact X, is not unique; other sets of premises may imply X. When we argue in the ordinary way from premises to conclusion there is usually only one possible conclusion; but when we begin with a conclusion X and look for premises Y there may be several possible sets which will stand in the relation of implication to X. Thus, for example, many different sets of premises will imply 'Some cats are black' so that the proposal to take Y as 'All creatures with feature α are black and some creatures with feature α are cats' cannot be regarded as a conclusive explanation. This fact accounts for the possibility of competing theories at the theoretical level and is exemplified by the Keplerian and epicyclic theories of planetary motion, the caloric and energy theories of heat, the big bang and continuous creation theories of the origin of the universe, and Newtonian and Einsteinian theories of gravitation.

Now although the first kind of openness does not present a problem if we are interested in discovering the general logical conditions which any particular theory of universals must satisfy, and indeed is an advantage, this second kind of openness is a serious difficulty. For unless there are conclusive reasons for accepting (2) it always remains open that there is some quite different theory, independent of (2), which will provide a logically satisfactory explanation of predicating and denoting. In the case of competing scientific theories there are of course standard ways of deciding such issues in terms of crucial experiments. If two theories Y and Z both imply an accepted fact X_1 but only Y implies a second accepted fact X_2 then Y is a better theory than Z; if, further, Z implies not-X_2 then Z is an incorrect theory. But such criteria are not in point in the case of competing philosophical theories. Here, the only criterion for determining whether or not Y is the best or only theory is the transcendental argument itself. If, therefore, one wishes to make the general point that (3), which is the meat of (2), is a condition which any satisfactory theory of universals must satisfy, it has to be shown that the premises of the transcendental argument from which (2) is derived are unexceptionable. And this has to be shown even though, as we have seen, (2) implies (1) and so can be said to stand as an explanation of it, for that only establishes (2) as one possible explanation, not as the only one.

The general position which has to be evaluated is therefore as follows:

We have an agreed fact (1) for which (2) is offered as the explanation. And since (2) implies (1) we may say that it does indeed stand as *an* explanation. Now (2) is not offered *ad hoc*; reasons are given for it. But it is only if these reasons are conclusive that (2) can be said to be *the* explanation of (1). On the other hand, if it can be shown that they are convincing, then (2) will not be established as the only explanation but it will be established as an important one. It must always remain logically possible that there are other quite different explanations just because transcendental arguments are as they are and because, in this case, there are no empirical criteria in terms of which other explanations can be rejected. Given, however, that the premises which establish (2) are compelling, then the second kind of openness is reduced and alternatives remain simply as logical possibilities rather than practical ones.

I want, therefore, to look rather more closely at the premises of the argument from meaning and to examine various possible objections to them in order to assess its value. In so doing I shall reject one of them as unnecessary. This move does not destroy the conclusion but merely increases its generality and makes it independent of the naming theory of meaning.

There are four steps to the argument:

(*a*) That in asking how one word can denote different things we are asking how one meaning can be related to different things; and implicit in this is the assumption: one word, one meaning.

(*b*) That constancy of meaning can only be accounted for by reference to something which is constant; and implicit in this are two assumptions: (i) that the meaning does remain constant on the different occasions that the word is used to denote different particulars, and (ii) that constancy or sameness (of meaning) cannot be accounted for except by reference to sameness.

(*c*) That the something which remains constant should be identified as the unique referent of the general word and that word has meaning by naming this referent.

(*d*) That sameness of meaning does not account for the fact that a particular word denotes some objects rather than others and, therefore, that the something which accounts for constancy of meaning is related to the objects.

That the form of the conclusion is independent of the naming theory of meaning follows immediately. For if we are concerned to use the argument simply to establish the conclusion,

$$x_1, x_2, \ldots \text{ are } \phi \equiv (E\alpha)(qu(\phi)R\alpha \cdot \alpha Sx_1, x_2, \ldots)$$

where R is a constant relation but not otherwise specified, then
(c) is an irrelevant premise. For the conclusion that there are
universals which stand in a constant relation to words, i.e. that
$(E\alpha)(qu(\phi)R\alpha)$ follows from (a) and (b), alone and by itself
accounts for constancy of meaning, however R is cashed, provided
R is identified as a constant relation. We thus account for the fact
that the meaning of $qu(\phi)$ is constant by postulating that it stands
in a constant relation to a constant; and it is this, and only this,
which is necessary to the argument. We may therefore reject (c),
since all that the rejection amounts to is that we refuse to specify
R; it does not destroy the form of the conclusion. The *unum-
nomen-unum-nominatum* thesis is a proposal to cash R and so to
explain sameness of meaning by postulating sameness of reference,
and though this is a possible explanation it is not necessary. R can
be cashed in other ways.

The acceptability of the argument, therefore, depends only on
(a), (b) and (d).

Consider first (a). There are various objections which might be
made here. It might be said that the implicit assumption, one
word, one meaning, is false because words are often ambiguous
and often have several meanings. But to meet this, one need only
restrict the argument to unambiguous words or even to the unambiguous uses of a word, and though we might in this way limit
the generality of the conclusion we do not thereby remove it.

Or again, it might be said that the meaning of a word is different
for different users and it is therefore false to say that the meaning
is constant. So to object, however, is to focus attention on a sense
of 'meaning' which, if not independent of the fact that a word
denotes, is irrelevant to it. For though the pragmatic meaning of a
word may vary from person to person, each will use it to denote
the same particulars or, if this is not generally so, we may restrict
the argument to those cases for which this holds.

A third objection might consist in pointing out that the meaning
of a word changes over a period of time, so that, again, it is not
true to say: one word, one meaning. Moreover, given that a word
does change its meaning, then its meaning cannot be explained by
reference to the fact that it stands in a constant relation to an unchanging constant. So (b), too, is false since b(i) is false. To meet
this, we may say either that the universal does not remain constant
but changes slowly and over a period of time, and then explain this,
or we may once more limit the application of the argument. For

if there is only one case of a word which is used on two different occasions to denote the same set of different particulars, then we may raise the problem of denoting for that case and take the argument as applying to it alone.

Such objections as these, therefore, might cause us to limit the generality of the conclusion but would not make it essential for us to give it up. If we take them seriously, however, they point to the fact that the concept of a universal as a fixed, unchanging constant is unnecessarily restrictive. For what the objections show is that it is not constancy of meaning which has to be accounted for but relative constancy. If, however, we can account for relative constancy by loosening up the universal in such a way that it enables us to explain ambiguity, pragmatic meaning and change of meaning, then (*a*) may stand in an amended form and the conclusion remain without limitation.

There is, however, a further quite different objection to (*a*) made by J. L. Austin.[1] This is, that we do not use one word on different occasions to denote different particulars; instead we use different (though similar) marks and noises (tokens) on different occasions to denote different (though similar) particulars. And this is true. If, therefore, we identify a word with a noise, then in this sense of 'word' we do not use the same word to denote two different individuals on different occasions;[2] we use different words. It thus seems to be a mistake to ask 'How can we use the same word with the same meaning to denote different individuals?' because we never do use the same word twice. But though words in this sense (tokens) are different individuals they are nevertheless the same in the sense that they are tokens of the same type; and they are the same, too, in that they have the same meaning and the same denotation. This being so, we may simply rephrase the question to ask 'How can we use different tokens of the same type with the same meaning to denote different individuals?' That is, 'How can two different tokens have the same meaning when not only are they used to denote different things but are themselves different things?' And we might add the supplementary question 'How can two different tokens be of the same type?' In this form the question is much tougher than it was but it still brings up

---

[1] 'Are There *A Priori* Concepts?' *Proceedings of the Aristotelian Society, Supplementary Vol. XVIII*, 1939. Reprinted in his *Philosophical Papers*, ed, by J. O. Urmson and G. J. Warnock, Oxford, 1961.

[2] Though we could: e.g. by cutting out a printed token and putting it into a different sentence. See Goddard and Routley, *op. cit.* (footnote on p. 32 above).

the same problem of how we can account for sameness of meaning in diversity. What has happened, only, is that the diversity is more complex. We have now to explain how the many tokens are related to one type, how the one type is related to one meaning and how the one meaning is related to many different individuals. But this is to complicate the problem, not to remove it, since the central puzzle, how the one meaning is related to many different individuals, still remains to be explained. And because this central issue is still the same, so the same sort of answer is relevant; namely that the different tokens of a given type each stand in some constant relation to a constant, which in turn is related to the many different individuals.

From this point of view, therefore, the condition, $(E\alpha)(qu(\phi)$ $R\alpha . \alpha Sx_1, x_2, \ldots)$, is over-simple because the equivalence from which we began, namely

(1) $x_1, x_2, \ldots$ are $\phi \equiv$ the word $qu(\phi)$ denotes $x_1, x_2, \ldots$

is over-simple. We should instead begin from the fact that

(1.1) Any token of the type $qu(\phi)$ denotes $x_1, x_2, \ldots$ if and only if, $x_1, x_2, \ldots$ are ϕ;

that, for example, if 'red$_1$' is a token of the type 'red' then 'red$_1$' denotes $x_1, x_2, \ldots$, if, and only if, $x_1, x_2, \ldots$ are red. This we can generalize if we introduce 'ϵ' to abbreviate 'is a token of the type' and introduce a further quotation function 'tqu' which takes as values the quotation-mark names of tokens. Thus,

(1.2) $[tqu(\phi)\epsilon qu(\phi)] \supset [tqu(\phi)$ denotes $x_1, x_2, \ldots$
$\equiv x_1, x_2, \ldots$ are $\phi]$.

This yields special cases of the sort,

If 'red$_1$' is a token of the type 'red' then ('red$_1$' denotes $x_1, x_2, \ldots \equiv x_1, x_2, \ldots$ are red)

If 'red$_2$' is a token of the type 'red' then ('red$_2$' denotes $x_1, x_2, \ldots \equiv x_1, x_2, \ldots$ are red)

If 'blue$_1$' is a token of the type 'blue' then ('blue$_1$' denotes $x_1, x_2, \ldots \equiv x_1, x_2, \ldots$ are blue)

etc. And we can generalize further to permit of cases in which the token is not of the required type, e.g. cases such as,

If 'blue$_1$' is a token of the type 'red' then ('blue$_1$' denotes $x_1, x_2, \ldots \equiv x_1, x_2, \ldots$ are red).

For here, though we allow the generation of hypotheticals with false antecedents, no harm comes of this since we cannot detach and so draw false conclusions of the sort,

'blue$_1$' denotes $x_1, x_2, \ldots \equiv x_1, x_2, \ldots$ are red.

In this form the general condition is,

(1.3) $[tqu(\psi)\epsilon qu(\phi)] \supset [tqu(\psi)$ denotes $x_1, x_2, \ldots$
$\equiv x_1, x_2, \ldots$ are $\phi]$.

Some simplification resulting from a more frugal use of quotation marks can now be achieved if we suppose that individual word tokens can be given proper names 'Tom', 'Dick', 'Harry', etc., and introduce a variable to range over such names. We then have,

(1.4) $[w\epsilon qu(\phi)] \supset [w$ denotes $x_1, x_2, \ldots \equiv x_1, x_2, \ldots$ are $\phi]$
special cases of which are, for example:

If Tom is a token of the type 'red' then (Tom denotes
$x_1, x_2, \ldots \equiv x_1, x_2, \ldots$ are red)
If Harry is a token of the type 'red' then (Harry denotes
$x_1, x_2, \ldots \equiv x_1, x_2, \ldots$ are red)
If Dick is a token of the type 'blue' then (Dick denotes
$x_1, x_2, \ldots \equiv x_1, x_2, \ldots$ are blue)

and though we may generate cases which have false antecedents no problem arises from this.

But however we express the condition (1) formally in order to take into account Austin's point, it should be clear that complications of this sort do not in any way lead to a rejection of the premise (a), or indeed of (b) or (d). For the consequents of these hypotheticals are, with slight differences, of the same form as (1) itself and what has to be explained is just such equivalences. Thus we now have to provide an analysis of

$tqu(\phi)$ denotes $x_1, x_2, \ldots \equiv x_1, x_2, \ldots$ are ϕ

rather than of

$qu(\phi)$ denotes $x_1, x_2, \ldots \equiv x_1, x_2, \ldots$ are ϕ

and so modify (a), (b) and (d) accordingly. But though Austin's objection causes us to modify (a), (b) and (d) by substituting 'token' for 'word' this will only affect the conclusion to the extent that it now takes the form

$x_1, x_2, \ldots$ are $\phi \equiv (E\alpha)(tqu(\phi)R\alpha . \alpha Sx_1, x_2, \ldots)$

instead of

$$x_1, x_2, \ldots \text{ are } \phi \equiv (E\alpha)(qu(\phi)R\alpha \cdot \alpha Sx_1, x_2, \ldots),$$

and the general form of the problem remains. In what follows, therefore, I shall continue to speak of the word as one; that is, I shall focus attention on the one type rather than the many tokens both because it is simpler to do so and because the logic of the problem is the same.[1]

Consider, now, (b). One might raise an objection to b(i) in terms of the fact that the meaning of a word does not remain constant but changes over a period of time. But this has been considered. The crucial assumption in (b) is b(ii): that constancy or sameness of meaning cannot be accounted for except by reference to sameness; and one might simply ask 'Why not?' Why can we not explain sameness in terms of difference? There are, however, some things to be wary of here. We must not make the mistake of supposing, when it is said that sameness of meaning can only be accounted for by reference to sameness, that it is being said that the sameness of meaning arises from the fact that the *reference of the word* is the same on different occasions of its use. That assumption is the premise (c) which has been rejected. Nor must it be supposed that we manage to explain sameness in terms of difference if we make an appeal to similarity, for an appeal to similarity is an appeal to sameness as an intermediate step. We have to say that two things are similar in the *same* respect; or that they are similar because both are similar to the *same* one paradigmatic particular. And if we rid ourselves of these distractions then it is difficult to see what support could be given to the view that sameness, whether of meaning or anything else, can be accounted for by difference. At any rate the onus of proof seems to be on those who might wish to make the claim, and in this connection it is perhaps worth noting that the assumption expressed by b(ii) is not peculiar to naming theories of meaning. If it is said, for example, that the meaning of a word is given by the rules for its use, what is being said is that a word means the same on different occasions of its use because it is used in accordance with the *same*

---

[1] So far as it has been described. But there is of course the further problem, deliberately left on one side, which arises if we ask 'How can two tokens be of the same type?' For example, how can two different noises have a feature in common? This is to raise the problem of universals at a different level and an answer to it would amount to an analysis of 'ε' and should be taken into account in any full explanation of meaning. One thing at a time however.

rules. I shall, therefore, accept (*b*) subject to its being expressed in terms of relative constancy rather than constancy; and I accept (*a*) subject to such modifications as are necessary to recognize the fact of ambiguity and the fact that, in a sense of 'meaning' which is not crucial to the sense which is required to explain denoting, the same word may mean differently for different people.

Consider, finally, (*d*). It is clear that (*d*) is quite crucial to the argument. We can indeed draw from (*a*) and (*b*) alone the conclusion that there are universals in the sense that there is a relatively constant something-or-other which stands in a constant relation to a given general word, i.e. $(E\alpha)(qu(\phi)R\alpha)$, and thereby account for its relative constancy of meaning on different occasions of its use. But if this were all that there is to the argument, then the existence of universals quite fails to explain denoting and so fails as a solution of the problem from which we began. For the problem is not a problem of meaning or even constancy of meaning but the problem of denoting (which involves sameness of meaning). We ask 'How are we able to name (denote) things as we do?' and the premise (*d*) provides the essential link between the one word *qua* one meaning and the several different things which it denotes.

Exactly the same difficulty would occur if instead of beginning with the problem of denoting we began with the problem of predication and asked, 'Why are things what they are?' or more generally, 'How can different things be the same?' We might again make the assumption in (*b*) that sameness cannot be accounted for except by reference to sameness and conclude that the many different things are each related to the same one thing, a universal. That is, we conclude $(E\beta)$ $(\beta Sx_1, x_2, \ldots)$. But if we take only this much of the argument, then, as Austin points out,[1] there is nothing to say that the β of this conclusion is the same as the α of the conclusion $(E\alpha)(qu(\phi)R\alpha)$, which follows from (*a*) and (*b*). We have to go on to account for the fact that if $x_1, x_2, \ldots$ are the same in some respect then the same word can be used to denote them. So just as (*d*) is an essential premise in the argument from meaning, so it or something like it is an essential premise in the argument from predication. The question is, however, whether it is true; and this question, in turn, is the question whether the condition

(1) $x_1, x_2, \ldots$ are $\phi \equiv qu(\phi)$ denotes $x_1, x_2, \ldots$

is true. For (*d*) simply affirms that what has to be explained is not

[1] *Op. cit.*

simply the fact that one word denotes several different particulars, nor yet the fact that several different particulars have the same property, but the further fact that these two are equivalent when the particulars are the same. It is this which constitutes the third, linking, premise which is expressed by (d) and which identifies the universals whose existence is established by the argument from meaning conceived as (a) and (b) only—and those whose existence is established by the argument from predication. If we are prepared to accept (1), therefore, (d) must be accepted; but if we reject (1) then we simply dismiss the problem a priori, for it is is only because (1) seems to be a fact of life, or a fact of language, or more correctly a fact which links the two, that there is need of any explanation at all.

I want to conclude, therefore, that there is a problem of universals, and a genuine problem, and that traditional arguments designed to show this were good arguments. They only seemed to be less good than they were because they were packed around with assumptions about meaning and naming which were irrelevant to the point at issue. Such arguments, whether from meaning or from predication, when stripped of their historical allegiance to naming theories are, I want to claim, valid: for all that they amount to in the end is that in order to explain the fact of sameness in diversity, reference must be made to some relative constant. And just because it is the case that many individuals are ϕ if, and only if, the word $qu(\phi)$ denotes them, so the constant in terms of which the explanation is made must stand in relations to both words and things.

What universals do is to stand as stable elements in diversity, in much the same way, logically speaking, as a co-ordinate system does this on a geometrical plane. In a sense, they bring order out of chaos. That there are universals, therefore, in this sense of 'universal' seems to me to be unexceptionable; but in saying this I want it to be clear what I am not saying, and in particular that I am not backing the realists against the nominalists. For, as I have argued, in neither the argument from meaning, as so given, nor in the argument from predication, as it could be given, does the word 'universal' have a content. It is a that-which, not yet a this. Accordingly, the conclusion is neutral with respect to all traditional theories, and α and S can be cashed in different ways.

The second point I wish to emphasize is that if we reject the premise (c), as we may, then the conclusion is also neutral with

D

respect to various theories of meaning and R may therefore be cashed independently. So the conclusion (2) does not, as it stands, provide us with any explanation at all of either meaning or predication. It provides us only with an explanation of the possibility of denoting and the possibility of predication in terms of a constancy which has yet to be determined. And until it is determined we know nothing whatever about either meaning or predication. I wish therefore to take the argument as establishing only that '$(E\alpha)(qu(\phi)R\alpha \cdot \alpha Sx_1, x_2, \ldots)$' (or '$(E\alpha)(tqu(\phi)R\alpha \cdot \alpha Sx_1, x_2, \ldots)$') is a necessary condition which any account of meaning or predication (hence both) must satisfy. Given this, then the problem which remains, the problem of universals, is how we may cash R, α and S. If we take R to be naming then we are committed to some sort of traditional theory. But what I should want to show is that we may instead take R to be the relation between a word and the rules governing its use and α as the set of rules for the use of a word.[1] Such an explanation has certain advantages. It removes, or at least seems to remove, the mystery from the universal, and it does explain the fact, which traditional theories failed to explain, that it is not absolute constancy of meaning which has to be accounted for, but relative constancy. For a set of rules may change its membership and so give rise to change of meaning. Particular rules need not change, but if more rules are added or some removed, then the set changes and so qualifies further, or less, the meaning of the word.[2] Besides, we can explain ambiguity in terms of rules which are themselves ambiguous or inconclusive (though this needs to be spelt out), and we can explain, too, how it is that the same word may mean different things for different

[1] The sort of theory I have in mind is that indicated by Ryle in 'The Theory of Meaning' in *British Philosophy in Mid-Century*, ed. C. A. Mace, London, 1957; reprinted in *The Importance of Language*, ed. Max Black, Englewood Cliffs, New Jersey, 1962: 'To know what an expression means involves knowing what can (logically) be said with it and what cannot (logically) be said with it. It involves knowing a set of bans, fiats and obligations, or, in a word, it is to know the rules of the employment of that expression.'

[2] Cf. L. J. Cohen, *The Diversity of Meaning*, London, 1962, Chs. I and II. One of Cohen's objections to the thesis that the meaning of a word is given by the rules for its use is based on the fact that meanings change. For 'if an activity is thought to be governed by rules, any change in it is *prima facie* evidence that a rule has been broken . . .', yet when the meaning of a word changes we do not look to see what rule has been violated. But this objection neglects the fact that meaning is not given by one rule but by a set, and that a set may change its membership without any one being broken. In this way the meaning of a word may change even though it is rule-governed.

people and yet denote the same particulars, for they may not know exactly the same set of rules even though the sets overlap. But there remain difficulties, especially with regard to predication.

I have wanted to insist that the condition (3) must be satisfied not simply to make a point against Pears—by denying the independence of the two questions he considers—but rather to show that a rule theory of *meaning* which stands in opposition to a naming theory must commit us to some account of *predication*, though not necessarily a traditional account.

3

BRIAN ELLIS

AN EPISTEMOLOGICAL CONCEPT OF TRUTH

The point of this paper is to prepare the ground for the acceptance of a unified system of truth and probability logic of the kind envisaged by Reichenbach.[1] In this system truth and falsity are regarded as limiting probability values. The first section of the paper will contain a brief sketch of the programme. But the main part of it will be concerned with removing what I take to be a general objection to the programme's feasibility, viz. that truth and probability are essentially different kinds of concepts, and that, consequently, it is absurd to regard truth as a limiting probability value.

I. TRUTH AND PROBABILITY LOGIC

It is possible to prove that the propositional calculus of Whitehead and Russell can be derived from any reasonable axiomatization of the probability calculus by restricting the range of probability values to 1 and 0.[2] In making the derivation the conjunction axiom, i.e.

$$P(p \cdot q) = P(p) \times P(q/p)$$

proves to be superfluous, and the 'given' operator occurring in the expression 'q/p' has no role in the derivation. The propositional calculus is thus a degenerate case of the probability calculus.

It can furthermore be shown that if the *full* probability calculus is used, and 'q/p' is written as '$p \longrightarrow q$' and interpreted as 'if p then q', then an implication system can also be derived. This implication system, which I shall call 'probability logic', turns out to have several unique and interesting properties. It differs from every

---

[1] H. Reichenbach, *Theory of Probability*, Tr. by E. H. Hutten and Maria Reichenbach, Berkeley and Los Angeles, 1949, Ch. 10, pp. 387–426.

[2] The proof will be published separately.

other implication system in common use (including all of Lewis' systems) and it yields convincing and novel solutions to some of the classical problems of implication and contraposition.[1]

It appears that there are no insuperable formal difficulties in regarding truth logic as a special case of probability logic. The question at issue is whether we can give an independent justification for treating truth and falsity claims as limiting cases of probability claims.

The sense in which I shall say that a proposition is probable is that which I have explained elsewhere.[2] As probability is here explained, it is both a relative and an epistemological concept. Truth, on the other hand, is always considered to be an absolute concept, not relative to anything, and having nothing to do with our state of knowledge of the world. There is thus an asymmetry between our concepts of truth and probability. While we may accept that the probability of a proposition may change as a result of new observations or discoveries, we should not accept that the truth value of a proposition may change. Every proposition is timelessly either true or false. Hence, so long as we retain these concepts of truth and probability, probability values cannot be regarded as intermediate truth values, and truth logic cannot be regarded as a special case of probability logic, even though, formally, a satisfactory system is derivable from it.

This is why truth logic has always been seen to be independent of probability theory. They are seen as being concerned with different kinds of discourse. If a system of truth logic could be derived from the full probability calculus by restricting the probability values which propositions may have to o and 1, then the system would be just one among many possible systems of truth logic. The fact that it was derived from the probability calculus would not give it any special claim to acceptance.

To argue against this general objection to the programme, I will try to show:

(a) that the absolute concept of truth, which both the correspondence and coherence theories have tried to capture, is a metaphysical concept in the sense that its use turns every truth claim into a metaphysical claim.

(b) that the absolute concept of truth is not required for communicating any items of knowledge or belief that we

---

[1] These points will be discussed elsewhere.
[2] B. D. Ellis, *Basic Concepts of Measurement*, Cambridge, 1966, Ch. XI.

may in fact possess. For this purpose an epistemological concept of truth would serve just as well. For, to every absolute truth claim that we can ever be in a position to make, there is a corresponding epistemological truth claim that we would be justified in making which contains precisely the same information.

(c) that since the purpose of arguments is the adjustment of our system of beliefs (which is an epistemological function) no concept of truth other than the epistemological one should ever be used in their rational assessment.

It follows that for the purposes of logic the epistemological concept of truth is all that is required. And this is a concept which would allow us to regard probability values as intermediate truth values.

2. TARSKI'S SEMANTIC DEFINITION OF TRUTH

It is important to show that Tarski's definition of 'true sentence' for the calculus of classes (and also his method of defining 'true sentence' for any formalized language of finite order) does not, as Popper claims it does, 're-establish a correspondence theory of absolute or objective truth'. Nor does it leave us 'free to use the intuitive idea of truth as correspondence with the facts.'[1]

First, Tarski's definition of 'true sentence' for a semantically interpreted formalized language (in the first instance, for the calculus of classes), would have no application if the language in question were a purely formal system. Tarski himself says that for 'sciences, to the signs and expressions of which no material sense is attached . . . the problem here discussed has no relevance, it is not even meaningful'.[2] Nor would it have any application to a non-formalized or colloquial language. For such a language, says Tarski, 'not only does the definition of truth seem to be impossible but even the consistent use of this concept in conformity with the laws of logic'.[3] I am not concerned to evaluate these statements here, but they do seem to show that Tarski himself would not have claimed to have re-established a correspondence theory of absolute or objective truth.

This becomes more evident when we examine the details of

---

[1] K. R. Popper, *Conjectures and Refutations*, London, 1963, p. 223.
[2] A. Tarski, *Logic, Semantics and Metamathematics*. Tr. by J. H. Woodger, Oxford, 1956, p. 166.   [3] *Ibid.*, p. 153.

Tarski's definition of 'true sentence' for the calculus of classes, and consider what his objectives were. They were to give a 'materially adequate' and 'formally correct' definition of 'true sentence' for a particular semantically interpreted formal system (the calculus of classes) and to determine the class of formalized languages for which such definitions are possible.

Let S be the class of well-formed formulae without free variables (hereafter called 'sentences') of the calculus of classes. Let Tr be the class of true sentences and F the class of false sentences. Then, in order that the definition of 'true sentence' be materially adequate and formally correct, it is required (in accordance with tenets of classical two-valued logic) that

   (i) Every member of Tr and of F is a sentence.

  (ii) Every sentence is a member of Tr or F.

 (iii) No sentence is a member of both Tr and of F.

 (iv) Every provable formula (Pr) is a member of Tr.

  (v) Every member of Tr, when semantically interpreted, is a true statement.

The conditions (i) to (iv) are those for formal correctness. The condition (v) is that for material adequacy.

A formally correct and materially adequate definition of 'true sentence' is achieved in the end by relying on the notion of the satisfaction of a 'sentential function', and by the trick of regarding a *sentence* as a sentential function of a special kind, viz. as one that has no free variables. Thus, it is explained that 'for every a, we have a satisfies the sentential function "x is white" if and only if a is white'.[1] And for a sentence (i.e. a sentential function with no free variables) we get 'for every a, a satisfies the sentence "b is white" if and only if b is white'. Now, since it is assumed that every statement must be either true or false, and that every sentence in the calculus of classes, when semantically interpreted, yields a statement, it follows that every sentence is either satisfied by everything or else it is satisfied by nothing. Accordingly, Tarski arrived at this now famous definition of 'true sentence' for the calculus of classes:

> x is a true sentence—in symbols $x \epsilon Tr$—if and only if $x \epsilon S$ [i.e. x is a sentence] and every infinite sequence of classes satisfies x.[2]

[1] A. Tarski, *Logic, Semantics and Metamathematics*, p. 190.
[2] *Ibid.*, p. 195. Brackets are mine.

He then went on to show the formal correctness of this definition, and to show how similar definitions of 'true sentence' could
be offered for any formalized language of finite order.

This, of course, is something of a caricature of Tarski's work,
and Tarski's real achievement in constructing a definition of a
'true sentence' for the calculus of classes and demonstrating its
formal correctness and material adequacy is both extremely
interesting and important. Nevertheless, the essential structure of
the argument is as I have presented it, and from this it should be
quite clear how absurd it is to claim that Tarski has 're-established
a correspondence theory of absolute or objective truth'. 'True
sentence' is openly and almost blatantly defined in terms of 'true
statement'. Saying that the sentence 'a is white' is satisfied by
every infinite sequence of objects is only a thin disguise for saying
that the sentence 'a is white', when semantically interpreted,
expresses a true proposition. Tarski has not, therefore, solved the
philosophical problem of truth. His eventual conclusion may be
allowed to stand unquestioned:

'For every formalized language of finite order a formally correct
and materially adequate definition of true sentence can be constructed in the metalanguage, making use only of expressions of
a general logical kind [e.g. satisfies the sentence 'ϕa'], expressions
of the language itself as well as terms belonging to the morphology
of language, i.e. names of linguistic expressions and of the struc-
tural relations existing between them.'[1]

But the philosophical problem of truth arises in natural languages which are neither formalized nor of finite order. And, even if
they were both formalized and of finite order, Tarski would still
not have solved the philosophical problem of truth. For this is not
a problem which can be conveniently shelved by forming a metalanguage.

3. THE CORRESPONDENCE THEORY OF TRUTH

The central thesis of the correspondence theory of truth is that a
proposition is true if and only if it corresponds to the facts. Difficulties with this theory arise as soon as we begin to probe the

[1] A. Tarski, *Logic, Semantics and Metamathematics*,. p. 265. Brackets are mine.

nature and terms of this relationship. There are many difficulties in the traditional concept of a proposition, but our main concern must be with facts. The most defensible, because least specific, answer that can be given to the question 'What are facts?' is that facts are whatever make propositions true. This answer is unexceptionable, but empty. For it seems that the only general filling that we can provide for the hole left by the 'whatever' in the phrase 'whatever makes the proposition that-p true' is the tautological 'Its being the case that-p'. If we are asked 'What makes the proposition that this figure is triangular true?', it is quite uninformative to answer: 'Its being triangular'. For the figure's being triangular is quite obviously a logically necessary and sufficient condition for the truth of the proposition, and it does not, therefore, in any ordinary sense, explain why the proposition is true, or say what makes it true.

It is not explanatory in the sense of fitting what is known into a wider pattern of knowledge. It makes no links with anything else that is independently known or knowable. The fact of A's being B is not something which can be ascertained independently of the truth of the proposition that A is B. The explanation therefore must be metaphysical, if it is any explanation at all. That is, if it is not a mere tautological transposition, like that from triangular to three-angled, it must be a linking of the assumed known (that-p is true) with the unknown and unknowable (its being, in reality, the case that-p).

The status of the correspondence theory of truth is not improved if more specific answers are given to the question: 'What are facts?' Either it becomes plainly false, or trivially tautological, or else it remains metaphysical. For example, it is sometimes said that facts are such things as objects or occurrences. For such things, we often want to say, may make propositions true. It is plausible, for example, to claim that it was the elephant which made it true that there was an elephant in this room or that it was the occurrence of the sun setting which made it true that the sun set last night. Elephants and sunsets thus appear to be the sorts of things that can make propositions true. Facts may, therefore, be things like these.

But in what sense did the elephant make it true that there was an elephant in this room? Did he cause it to become true, e.g. by coming into the room of his own accord, or was it his *being* in the room that made it true? If the former, the sense in which the elephant made it true that there was an elephant in the room is the same as that in which the elephant's keeper might have made it true by herding the elephant into the room. But no one, I imagine, would be happy to say that the elephant's keeper (or his action) could be the fact which corresponds with the true proposition that there was an elephant in this room. 'What made it true', has to be distinguished from 'What makes it (timelessly) true'. If, however it was the elephant's *being in the room* that made it true that the elephant was in the room, then the case is exactly like that of the figure's *being triangular* making it true that the figure is triangular. The putative explanation, if not false, is either a trivial verbal transposition or else metaphysical.

Also, consider the claim that it was last night's sunset which made it true that the sun set last night. There are at least two ways in which this claim may be understood. Firstly, 'made it true' may be understood to mean 'caused it to become true'. But in this sense the claim is obviously false. Last night's sunset did not cause the sun to set last night. It may have caused the birds to stop singing. But then no one would say that last night's sunset was the fact with which the true proposition that the birds stopped singing last night corresponds. As before, we have to distinguish between what makes a proposition (timelessly) true from what made it (causally) become true. Secondly, the claim may be understood to mean that the occurrence of a sunset last night is what makes it true that the sun set last night in the sense that it is a logically necessary and sufficient condition for the truth of this proposition. But once again, if this account is meant to be explanatory, and not a mere verbal rephrasing, then it is a metaphysical account. For the explanation is not achieved by setting what is known into a wider context of knowledge. We cannot ascertain that an occurrence of the kind in question did in fact occur, without, at the same time, ascertaining the truth of the proposition. There is only the one process. The supposed correspondence, therefore, can at best be a metaphysical one.

Difficulties with the correspondence theory of truth begin to multiply as soon as we stray from the field of observation statements. For it is not even very plausible to say that hypotheticals, laws, theories, and logical and mathematical propositions are true if and only if they correspond to the facts. Even if we allowed that in reality there are facts corresponding to true observation statements, facts whose existence metaphysically explains the truth of those statements, most philosophers would be reluctant to believe that reality also contains sets of hypothetical, nomological, theoretical, logical and mathematical facts.

Thus, unless we are Platonists, each of these classes of propositions provides a set of *prima facie* counter-examples to the correspondence theory of truth. To defend the correspondence theory, therefore, it has been felt to be necessary to show either:

(*a*) that despite first appearances, these propositions really are true because they correspond to the facts (in the sort of way that true observational statements may be supposed to), or

(*b*) that they are not really true or false, and hence not propositions, and hence not genuine counter-examples.

The first of these kinds of defensive reactions has been described by Lakatos as monster-adjusting and the second as monster-barring.[1] There is, of course, nothing irrational or improper about either of these reactions. But if they have to be used too often, or their use proves not to be very successful, then at least we should question whether the original thesis is worth defending.

Let us consider the true hypothetical proposition that if A had occurred, B would have occurred. With what part of reality may we suppose this true hypothetical to correspond? The hypothetical may certainly be true if neither A nor B had occurred. If there is a correspondence, therefore, in virtue of which this proposition is true, it cannot be a correspondence with the putative subject matter of the assertion, unless we are prepared to admit a world of potentialities, in addition to the world of actualities, and consider the former to be part of reality along with the latter.

Some have held out the hope that a satisfactory truth functional analysis of hypotheticals (including counter-factual conditional propositions) would one day be offered, which would enable us to treat hypotheticals as truth functional compounds of propositions whose truth values can be understood in terms of correspondence with reality. But this hope must now seem a very slender one. After fifty years of effort, no one is any nearer to achieving such an analysis.

A second kind of reaction has been to deny that hypotheticals are genuine propositions, or at least to say that such propositions are not true in the ordinary (correspondence) sense of 'true'. Thus,

[1] I. Lakatos, 'Proofs and Refutations', *British Journal of the Philosophy of Science*, Vol. 14 (1963).

it has been said that hypotheticals are really inference licences, or condensed arguments and as such are, strictly speaking, neither true nor false. They may be accepted and used, and because of this, we may say metaphorically that they are true. But here the word 'true' does not mean 'correspond with reality' in the sense in which we might half-plausibly say that observation statements correspond with reality. Hypotheticals are true in an utterly different sense of 'true'. Monster adjustment by the truth-functional analysis of hypotheticals having failed, it seems that the correspondence theory of truth is to be saved by the process of monster-barring!

Consider also the statement of any law of nature. If a law were simply an accidental universal then its truth might perhaps be understood in terms of correspondence with reality. But if anything can be taken to have been established in philosophy of science in the past twenty years it is that laws are not accidental universals. Firstly, laws support subjunctive conditionals (usually of the form 'If anything were an A it would be a B'), while accidental universals do not. Secondly, the antecedents of these conditionals are almost never satisfied by any real object; usually there are no As. That being so, the law that all As are Bs can hardly be a generalization about As that can simply be understood in terms of correspondence with reality.

Many attempts have been made to find an extensional analysis of laws which might enable their truth to be understood in terms of such a correspondence. But statements of laws (including statements of causal connections) have stoutly resisted such analysis. In every case, either the truth conditions of the analysans are manifestly different from those of the analysandum (the law), or the analysans itself contains statements asserting nomological connections and thus does not constitute an extensional analysis. Many philosophers have therefore come to the conclusion that laws are not genuine propositions, but rather are disguised statements of rules or 'inference licences'. As rules, however, they are neither true or false, but only more or less useful. Hence, they are considered not to constitute genuine counter-examples to the correspondence theory of truth.

In recent years, theories, also, have come to present a major difficulty for the correspondence theory of truth. In the last century it was widely held that theories are true if and only if they describe the reality which lies behind observable physical processes.

But with the development of quantum mechanics, this is not so easy to maintain, for no one has yet been able to describe any underlying physical processes which could possibly account for the range of quantum phenomena,[1] and many physicists believe that no such description is possible.

Even before the development of quantum mechanics, however, philosophers like Mach and Duhem were unwilling to allow that we could ever be justified in claiming that a theory was true or false. For the correspondence of theoretical statements with reality could never be observed in the way that they believed (wrongly) the correspondence of observation statements could be. Hence they considered truth claims for theories to be essentially metaphysical claims.

In response to the work of Mach and Duhem, the attempt was made to reduce theories to sets of observation statements, in order that their meaning could be understood in terms of what they supposed to be non-metaphysical truth conditions. If this positivist programme had been successful, then the truth of theories could have been understood in terms of the correspondence of these sets of observation statements with reality. But the programme was not successful, and the problem of truth for theories remained unsolved.

All attempts at monster adjustment with theories having failed, many philosophers have resorted to monster-barring. Theories, they say, are neither true nor false (at any rate, not in the correspondence sense of truth). Theories may be accepted and used, and we may believe that they will always be used. But they should be regarded as instruments rather than truth claims, since the sole criterion for their acceptability is their power as instruments for prediction—not their truth. If it is insisted that theories can nevertheless be true or false, then (so the argument goes) 'true' in this context must be understood to mean something like 'ultimately acceptable'. Thus theories cannot be said to be true or false in any correspondence sense of truth.

Again, propositions about mathematical entities have long presented a serious difficulty for the correspondence theory of truth. Consider the proposition that seventeen is a prime number. Undoubtedly we want to say that this proposition is true. But the number seventeen does not appear to be part of reality, nor

---

[1] H. Putnam, 'A Philosopher Looks at Quantum Mechanics', in *Beyond the Edge of Certainty*, ed. by R. G. Colodny, Englewood Cliffs, New Jersey, 1965, pp. 75–101.

primeness a property that could be possessed by anything that really exists. It is unnatural here to speak of correspondence with reality.

To overcome this difficulty, various views have historically been proposed. The first was to maintain that mathematical entities like numbers are really part of a higher kind of reality which cannot be discovered by the methods of empirical science (Plato). But this is to turn every assertion about mathematical entities into a claim which is more or less metaphysical, and few philosophers or mathematicians nowadays would be prepared to accept this. A second kind of reaction has been to hold that propositions about numbers are not really about such abstract entities as they appear to be. Really they are universal propositions about groups of objects (Mill), or particular propositions about the use of words in the English language (Dugald Stewart), or propositions about the positions that can be reached in a certain formal game (the early Wittgenstein). But for well-known reasons, none of these attempts at monster-adjustment were successful, and the problem of explaining the sense in which propositions about mathematical entities could be said to be true or false remained unsolved.

In the early years of this century, the attempt was made to reduce mathematics to logic so that mathematical truth could be explained as a species of logical truth. But logical truths themselves presented a major difficulty for the correspondence theory. For logical truths were supposed to hold whatever the world is like, and hence it seemed that their truth could not be explained by any correspondence with the world as it is. To overcome this difficulty, philosophers have argued that logical and analytic truths are really truths about the use of language. Such truth, it is said, depends upon the meanings of the various logical connectives in the various colloquial languages in the case of formal tautologies, and upon the meaning of other terms as well in the case of other analytic truths. But if this is so, and if a non-metaphysical account of analytic truth can be given in correspondence terms, then we ought to be able to point to the observable facts about a language or its use which make analytic propositions analytically true.

However, in view of Quine's arguments,[1] no such account seems to be possible. We might be able to define analyticity in terms of synonymy, or self-contradictoriness, but these terms are not observational terms, and the truth conditions for statements

[1] W. V. O. Quine, *From a Logical Point of View*, Cambridge, Mass., 1953, Ch. 2, 'Two Dogmas of Empiricism'.

involving them cannot, apparently, be spelled out in such terms. Consequently, no positivistic reduction of analytic statements to sets of observation statements about linguistic performance appears to be possible. Therefore, we cannot very well allow that the truth of analytic statements be understood in correspondence terms.

Hence, even if the logicist programme of reducing mathematics to logic were successful, there would still be apparently insuperable difficulties in understanding mathematical truths according to the correspondence theory of truth. Some philosophers have accordingly denied that logical or mathematical propositions are genuinely either true or false. According to Wittgenstein in his later works, for example, logical and mathematical propositions are not really propositions at all, but rules. And if we say that they are true, we mean only that we accept and use them, and insist upon others using them. Once again, the failure of monster-adjustment has led to the process of monster-barring.

For all these reasons, and others connected with moral and aesthetic judgments that have not been considered here, the correspondence theory of truth must be judged to be inadequate. Indeed, much of the history of philosophy over the past fifty years may be seen as one attempt after another to save the correspondence theory of truth in the face of its apparent shortcomings. The result seems to be that most of the things that logicians would wish to call propositions, when applying their various calculi, should not, if the correspondence theory is to be held, be regarded as propositions at all. For they are neither true nor false in the correspondence sense of truth.

The absurdity of concluding that these things are not genuine propositions demands that the correspondence theory be rejected. In Kuhn's sense, the correspondence theory of truth has been one of the major paradigms determining the nature and direction of philosophical inquiry. For it is this theory which has raised a great many of the questions with which philosophy has been concerned, and it is this theory which has determined what constitutes an acceptable answer. What seems most urgently to be needed now is a new paradigm.

4.   THE COHERENCE THEORIES OF TRUTH

The essence of the coherence theories of truth is the thesis that the truth is that which enables us to organize most coherently and comprehensively the whole of experience, including not only sense-experience and memory, but also moral, aesthetic, religious and imaginative experience. It is not maintained by any philosophers, so far as I know, that mere consistency is a sufficient condition for truth. F. H. Bradley, for example, specifically rejects such a criterion. 'Coherence apart from comprehensiveness', he says, 'is not for me the test of truth or reality.'[1] What may be lacking in any arbitrarily selected set of mutually consistent propositions is the element of comprehensiveness, and if this element is lacking, the propositions in question cannot be said to be true.

What is it, first, to organize most coherently and comprehensively our own experience? It is to arrive at a comprehensive and coherent system of beliefs about the world, ourselves, and our relationship to it.

It must be coherent in the sense that our beliefs are mutually consistent logically and hang together theoretically; and it must be comprehensive in the sense that it includes everything to be gained from sense experience and memory as well as moral, aesthetic, religious and imaginative experience. Indeed, the making of these classifications of experience is itself part of the process of organizing coherently and comprehensively our total experience.

Why, then, can I not imagine any consistent world I please, and call all else illusion or imagination? Would this not satisfy the criteria of coherence and comprehensiveness? To this Bradley answers:

'. . . you cannot confine yourself within the limits of this or that fancied world, as suits your pleasure or private convenience. You are bound to recognise and to include the opposite fancy . . . The fancied world not only has opposed to it the world of perception. It also has against it any opposite arrangement or any contrary part which I can fancy . . . Nothing, therefore, will be left to outweigh the world as perceived, and the imaginary hypothesis will be condemned by our criterion.'[2]

The criterion of comprehensiveness thus assigns a special role to perception in the quest for truth. And this is just because we are not free to perceive whatever we like.

[1] F. H. Bradley, *Essays on Truth and Reality*, Oxford, 1914, p. 203.
[2] *Ibid.*, pp. 214–15.

But Bradley denies that any or all of our perceptual judgments are infallible. For him, there is no solid foundation of knowledge upon which all else is constructed. He agrees with the empiricists in maintaining that no knowledge is independent of sense experience or memory, but he denies that there are any items of knowledge to be gained through perception and memory which cannot in principle be erroneous. He points out that all attempts to identify such truths have failed to yield anything upon which anything could be constructed, and that in any case these supposedly indubitable truths are only indubitable in the sense that we cannot doubt them without doubting a great deal else of what we think we know, and denying our otherwise coherent and comprehensive world picture. Moreover, he points out that it is not necessary to assume the existence of such truths in order to avoid scepticism. That we may reasonably doubt anything does not imply that we may reasonably doubt everything. Bradley concludes, therefore, that:

'. . . there is no single fact which in the end can be called fundamental absolutely. It is all a question of relative contribution to my world order.

"Then no judgment of perception will be more than probable?" Certainly, that is my contention.'[1]

To illustrate this, he says:

'If the observed fact is too much contrary to our arranged world, provisionally we reject it. We eventually accept the fact when after confirmation the hypothesis of its error becomes still more ruinous.'[2]

Now, all of this sounds reasonable enough, and much of it would be accepted by many philosophers today. For this much of Bradley's theory is consistent with a correspondence theory of truth. What I have set out here is only an epistemology of truth claims, not an analysis of their meaning. It may be agreed, for example, that all truth claims are in principle revisable, and that the criteria we actually use for deciding what truth claims we shall make are adequately characterized by coherence and comprehensiveness. But it may still be maintained that a proposition is true if and only if it corresponds with reality.

[1] F. H. Bradley, *Essays on Truth and Reality*, Oxford, 1914, p. 211.
[2] *Ibid.*, p. 212.

E

It is obvious, in any case, that if this were all there were to Bradley's theory, it would not provide an adequate explication of the concept of truth. Consider, for example, the proposition that as Caesar crossed the Rubicon a dog sneezed in Moscow. With whose experience would either the assertion or the denial of this proposition cohere in the relevant sense? Neither mine, nor Caesar's, nor the dog's. Yet Bradley, like everyone else, wants to say that a proposition like this is either true or false. To overcome this difficulty, Bradley introduced the concept of Absolute Experience of which the total experience of human race (and hence the experience of any individual, which he describes as a 'finite centre of experience') may be only a part. Truth is then defined as that which organizes most coherently and comprehensively such Experience. Truth is thus an ideal to which we finite beings can hardly aspire. We have to be content with our own limited experience and the partial truths that arise through the attempt to organize it in the way that to us is most coherent and comprehensive.

Now this concept of truth is not so very different from the concept that is sometimes supposed to apply to laws and theories, viz. that truth is ultimate acceptability. For it cannot be maintained that the truth of a law or theory is its ultimate acceptability to the human race. Humanity could be annihilated tomorrow. But it would hardly follow from this that all laws and theories that we now accept are true. To make the concept of ultimate acceptability coincide with our concept of truth, the former has to be made relative to some experience that transcends all human experience. And this is exactly what Bradley maintains, the only difference being that Bradley consistently applies his coherence concept of truth to all propositions.

It is not really necessary to argue for the metaphysical character of such a coherence theory of truth. To say that a proposition is true if and only if it is ultimately acceptable, i.e. that it would be accepted by a fully rational being whose experience transcends all human experience, who in fact experiences everything there is to be experienced, and who organizes his experience most coherently and comprehensively, is obviously to make a rather extravagant metaphysical claim. It is no wonder that the correspondence theory of truth, for all its shortcomings, has enjoyed such relative popularity. The coherence theory of truth does, however, provide us, at least in outline, with a satisfactory epistemology of truth, and we may expect to find this preserved in any more satisfactory theory.

5. THE EPISTEMOLOGICAL CONCEPT OF TRUTH

It has been shown that no attempt to give a non-metaphysical account of the absolute concept of truth of ordinary language has been successful, and we may reasonably suppose that no such account is possible. That being so, we may question whether we need such a concept at all, or whether we could get along equally well using a different kind of concept of truth. I shall argue that this is in fact the case, and that for all purposes of human communication we could just as well use an epistemological concept of truth which is a special concept of probability. It will also be argued that this is the concept that we should use when assessing the validity of arguments, and consequently, that for the purposes of logic, all truth claims should be represented as epistemological truth claims. This will allow us to regard probability values as intermediate truth values, and hence justify the use of the system of probability logic for the formal analysis of arguments.

To introduce the epistemological concept of truth, it is necessary to distinguish between a proposition and a truth claim. A proposition, as the term is here understood, is something that can be either asserted or denied (or perhaps considered without being asserted or denied). A truth claim on the other hand, is already strictly speaking an assertion, and is therefore not something that can be either asserted or denied (although it can be reaffirmed or contradicted). In traditional logic, this distinction is not commonly made, and every proposition is regarded simply as an assertion or statement.

Both concepts of proposition have a basis in ordinary language. When one person asserts that a certain proposition p is true, and another claims that-p is false, we oscillate between thinking:

(a) that there are *two* modes of assertion (viz. asserting and denying) but only *one* proposition (viz. p) that is being either asserted or denied, and

(b) that there is only *one* mode of assertion (viz. just assertion), but *two* different propositions (viz. p and $\sim p$) being asserted.

It is important for the understanding of what follows that the word 'proposition' should be understood in the sense (a), and that the truth claim that-p and the falsity claim that-p should be regarded as two different kinds of claims related to the one proposition. For this will allow us to regard a probability claim that-p as being yet another kind of claim related to this proposition.

Let us consider more carefully what is involved in making truth and probability claims. Firstly, the various truth and probability claims that we make are made in various contexts of observation and investigation. And within these contexts we may single out certain groups of observers or investigators who may be said to form a consensus. They form a consensus in the sense that there is agreement amongst them about what constitutes a conclusive case or proof, and about what is the relevance of evidence to particular propositions. They also form a consensus in the sense that, working independently of each other, they tend to reach non-collusive agreement in the probability and truth assessments they make.

Now when a man makes a truth or probability claim concerning some proposition p, he may either:

(i) commit himself before the consensus to which he considers himself answerable (e.g. by staking his reputation for rationality or theoretical competence) to the making of certain truth or probability assessments concerning other propositions, propositions which would be agreed by that consensus to be logically or theoretically connected with p; or, if he would not accept such a commitment, then to construct or defend an alternative logical or theoretical system and explain its detailed application, or

(ii) commit himself (e.g. by staking his reputation for honesty, competence as an observer and as a language user) to establishing to the satisfaction of his audience, if they are members of the consensus of competent observers and language users, to the following:

(a) that he was in a position to make the claim that he did,
(b) that he knew what he was saying, and
(c) that he believed what he was saying.

Normally, both kinds of commitments are involved, directly or indirectly, in making any truth or probability claim. In the case of observation statements and introspective reports, the commitments are primarily of the second kind, although a man's reputation for rationality or logical consistency is always at stake. But if there are other observers, or if other evidence relevant to the claim that has been made is available, then he is also committed to justifying his claim in the light of, or in the face of, this evidence.

In terms of the commitments incurred, what distinguishes a truth from a probability claim is the kind of backing one is committed to providing. In the case of a truth claim, one is committed to arguing that the grounds for claiming that-p are conclusive in the sense that:

(a) there are excellent grounds for asserting the proposition and no good grounds (judged in relation to the grounds for asserting it) for denying the proposition, and

(b) there is no need for further inquiry concerning the proposition.

In the case of a probability claim, however, one is not normally committed to arguing either of these. Usually it is sufficient to justify a probability claim that-p to argue successfully that the case for asserting that-p is stronger than the case for denying that-p. In some cases, however, the probability claim that-p may involve a commitment to conclusiveness in the sense of (b). If, for example, I were to claim that there is a probability of $\frac{1}{2}$ that if I had tossed this coin on to this table an hour ago (which I did not) it would have landed heads, then I would be committed to arguing that:

(b) there is no need for further inquiry concerning the proposition, but

(c) the grounds for asserting the proposition are as strong as those for denying it.

In other cases, there is commitment to conclusiveness in the sense of (a), but no commitment to conclusiveness in the sense of (b). This is the kind of case where we should be inclined to say 'It appears to be true that . . .' or 'It looks very likely that . . .', and then go on to say, '. . . but of course there is other evidence that must be considered'.

We have therefore distinguished three different kinds of probability claims which, in terms of the commitments incurred in making them, are obviously related to truth claims. But from this epistemological analysis, we have failed to discover any reason for not considering truth claims to be a special class of probability claims.

If this analysis of the logic of truth and probability claims were complete, however, then we should not be able to say that a proposition must be either true or false, although we do not know which. For what commitment would be made by saying 'It is either true or false that p'? Clearly, we should not be committed to arguing that either the grounds for asserting that-p or the grounds for denying that-p are conclusive in the senses of (a) and (b). We may well believe that there are no grounds for asserting that-p and none for denying that-p. What we should be committed to arguing is that the disjunctive proposition that either p or not p is true. Accordingly, if we were to use the word 'true' in a way that is consistent with this epistemological analysis, we should reject the principle of bivalence (that every proposition is either true or false) but accept the law of the excluded middle (that for every proposition p, it is true that either p or $\sim p$).

Consider the proposition that Caesar winked as he crossed the Rubicon. If we say that this proposition is either true or false, then if 'true' and 'false' were merely assertion and denial operators, we must as a result incur a kind of disjunctive commitment. That is, we should be committed to arguing either that the case for asserting or the case for denying that Caesar winked as he crossed the Rubicon is conclusive in the required senses. But clearly we make no such commitments when we say that this proposition is either true or false. We are simply committed to supporting the claim that the disjunctive proposition that Caesar either did or did not wink as he crossed the Rubicon is true—a claim which would be adequately supported by saying 'Well, what else could have happened?'

The trouble is that the words 'true' and 'false' have a dual role in ordinary language. On the one hand, they are used as assertion and denial operators, and this is the use that we have investigated. On the other hand they are used as predicate expressions, and the problem of truth has been seen to be that of saying what is predicated of what when we say that-p is true. We must conclude, therefore, that the analysis of truth claims that we have given does not give a complete account of the concept of truth of ordinary language. To complete it, we should at best have to give an account of what it is for a truth claim to be *correct*. Obviously, its defensibility does not make it correct, or its indefensibility make it incorrect. Yet, when I make a truth claim, it is hard to see how I could possibly be committed to anything more than defending it adequately. What more is involved must therefore be a kind of metaphysical commitment—which in an important sense is no commitment at all, since it is one that I can never be required to meet. Hence no sufficient non-metaphysical conditions for the truth of any proposition or the correctness of any truth claim can ever be given. Hence no non-metaphysical account of the absolute concept of truth of ordinary language is possible.

Two important questions arise from this conclusion:

(a) Do we need the absolute or metaphysical concept of truth at all for any purpose of human communication?

(b) Is the absolute concept of truth the one that we require for the analysis of arguments?

The answer to the first question appears to be 'No!' If we wish to claim that-p is true, then we can incur exactly the same (non-metaphysical) commitments by claiming that-p is certain or virtually certain. For it is a (pragmatic) contradiction to claim that-p is certain or virtually certain but that nevertheless p is not true. And it is also a (pragmatic) contradiction to claim that-p is true, but that nevertheless p is not certain or virtually certain. We could therefore get along perfectly well in the business of communicating information if we were to agree to use the words 'It is true that' to mean what we now mean by the phrase 'it is certain or almost certain that'. This would involve a radical linguistic revision, but there are no claims, other than metaphysical ones, that we could not make by using such a concept. If we call this concept the epistemological concept of truth, then nothing more than this epistemological concept can ever be necessary for any purpose of communicating information.

The answer to the second question also appears to be 'No!' For the purpose of arguing is to adjust our systems of beliefs, and this clearly is an epistemological function. It is to adjust the sets of commitments that we would be prepared to make. That being so, for the purposes of logic all truth claims should be regarded as epistemological truth claims, and the conclusions that should be drawn from arguments should be determined by applying a system of logic which is designed for handling such claims. The system of logic that we require is therefore one of probability logic.

Finally, it will be objected that our concepts of probability and epistemological truth both depend upon the absolute concept of truth. For (so it might be thought) 'it is probable that' just means 'it is probably true that', and 'it is epistemologically true that' just means 'it is certainly or almost certainly true that'. Hence, it will be said, we have not eliminated the need for the absolute concept of truth.

This objection is easily countered. From the fact that the sentences 'He is happy' and 'He is a happy soul' have the same empirical function it does not follow that the concept of a soul is presupposed by the concept of happiness. On the contrary, if it makes no sense to claim that he is happy but has an unhappy soul, or that he has a happy soul but is unhappy, then the use of the word 'soul' in this context can be little more than a redundant archaism.

4

PETER HERBST

FACT, FORM, AND INTENSIONALITY[1]

I

Strawson, arguing against Austin on Truth,[2] put forward a view about the nature of facts which has come to be widely accepted. My chief purpose here is to criticize and, if possible, to replace this view.[3]

Strawson offers the definition: 'A fact is what a true statement states.' He holds that there is no real difference between calling a statement true and saying that it states a fact. Both locutions are to be regarded as devices of assertion. Statements are of two kinds, episodic and non-episodic. Non-episodic statements are what I say; episodic statements are my saying of it. In the definition of facts the word 'statement' refers to the non-episodic kind.

Strawson's account of non-episodic or type statements has two legs:

(1) A statement is what I say or state.
(2) A statement is what is said to be true or false.

When statements are what persons state, the stating of statements is a kind of speech act, a human function. Statements thus understood call for an illocutionary account in Austinian terms. But according to Strawson, statements as well as persons state things. For the kind of statings which have statements as their logical subjects, an illocutionary account is clearly out of place. Also, it seems that the logical accusatives of stating by statements cannot

[1] In this article intensionality is spelt with an s. It is generally so spelt by those who treat it as a logical concept. Those who think that there is an irreducibly psychological concept, distinct from logical intensionality, generally spell it with a t. The spelling here is in accordance with the account which is given.

[2] *Proceedings of the Aristotelian Society, Supplementary Vol. XXIV*, London, 1950, pp. 111–56.

[3] In criticizing Strawson's theory, I also criticize my own former view in 'The Nature of Facts', *Australasian Journal of Philosophy*, Vol. 30, 1952. Reprinted in: *Essays in Conceptual Analysis*, ed. by Antony Flew, London, 1956.

be the same as those of stating by persons. 'Persons state statements' is an innocuous locution, if we mean that persons deliver themselves of statements and that the type of speech act which they perform on such occasions is called 'stating'. But are we really prepared to say that *statements* state statements? If not, what shall we regard as the accusatives of stating when *statements* are the logical subjects?

According to Strawson, statements—when true—state facts. Thus facts are a *possible* accusative of non-illocutionary stating. But presumably not all statements state facts, because not all statements are true. What do false statements state? What do statements state when they are neither true nor false? The answer in Strawsonian terms is not clear. Strawson suggests no general type or genus for the accusative of non-illocutionary stating. We only know that the class of things which statements state, must contain facts as a sub-class.

The argument of this paper is to hinge largely on the conception of reliance on fact. We rely on facts for many of our views and opinions, and also for our claims to knowledge. We rely on facts in our actions, and for our policies and decisions. Reliance on facts seems to be one of our most pervasive and deeply entrenched ideas, and although I can understand that philosophers with extensionalist preconceptions may wish to subject this idea to reductive analysis, I do not think that it can be side-stepped. I will regard it as a task for any intended theory of fact to explain what it is to rely on a fact, and to explain what it is about a fact which makes it suitable for being relied on. Judged by this yardstick Strawson's theory is unsatisfactory.

In the sense of 'rely' which I have in mind, persons may rely on facts in thinking or doing something. But in precisely the same sense they may also rely on what they mistakenly conceive to be a fact (or on an irrelevant fact, or one inconsistent with their other beliefs). It seems, therefore, that reliance will turn out to be an intensional relation; and if it be granted that causal relations are extensional, we shall have to allow that there is a kind of reliance for which no causal account will do.

The possibility of causal relations between facts and opinions cannot be ruled out at this stage. But we cannot conclude in advance of evidence that facts irrelevant to, or even inconsistent with, an opinion might not cause it. In the case of a false opinion, for instance, it seems that if any fact is to cause it, it cannot be its truth ground, so that causal relations between facts and opinions, and reliance relations between facts and opinions, must fall apart.

Example: A certain person feels inferior to another person who is more endowed with natural gifts, and this feeling of inferiority is said to be the cause of a belief that the other man is his enemy. This belief is false. Now the sense of inferiority may cause the false belief, but it does not follow that the person relies on it for his belief, let alone that he is entitled to rely on it.

Reliance needs to be explained in terms of support. True, we sometimes rely for our opinions on what does not support them, but then we are in error. Support gives point to reliance. Reliance without support is defective or mistaken. Whether a fact is worthy of being relied on for an opinion can be decided only when the fact is stated. Thus we cannot normally replace expressions of the type 'the fact that p' with expressions like 'the only fact which Jones mentioned', even though the only fact which Jones mentioned is the fact that p. Rational support and causal support must be distinguished. Here we are concerned with the rational kind. Determining whether a given fact does or does not support a theory is a matter for rational reflection. To answer correctly, one must understand the theory and operate with an express statement of the fact under which its relevance and support are to be appraised. Thus if Jones' being interviewed by a policeman would support our belief that Jones is in trouble, and he was in fact so interviewed, it will not do, from our point of view, to characterize the event as Jones being interviewed by a man, even though, of course, he was interviewed by a man. Thus characterized, the occurrence does not support the belief which stands in need of support.

In the case of physical support the reverse holds. It does not matter whether we refer to the man of whom we assert that he supports Jones (or Jones' weight) as a policeman or as an Englishman, provided that he is both.

Thus, although

I.   (a) Jones' being interviewed by a policeman
supports (b) the belief that Jones is in trouble,
and though (c) the policeman is a man,
    yet (d) Jones' being interviewed by a man does *not* support (b) the belief that Jones is in trouble.

Yet II.

    If (*a*) a policeman
supports (*b*) Jones (or Jones' body) in the water
   and if (*c*) the policeman is a man
      then (*d*) a man *does* support (*b*) Jones (or) Jones' body in the water.

I must add that my remarks about the openness of reference in causal statements must not be taken as support for the doctrine that, without commitment to type or category, it is possible to individuate an object (or event) as that which causes a certain effect. For instance, that which supports Jones' weight in the water cannot turn out to be a dream or a number.

At this point I should like to digress for a short discussion of intensionality. Intensionality of various kinds will get repeated mention in this paper, and it will be easiest if at least one of the distinctions on which I propose to rely is prefaced to the main argument. The distinction is between what I propose to call existence-intensionality and substitution-intensionality respectively.

A relation aRb, where b is an object, will be said to be *existentially intensional* if the truth value of the proposition aRb is invariant with respect to the existence or non-existence of b. For instance: 'He relied on the inheritance which he expected.' The truth of this proposition is not affected if it turns out that he inherited nothing. By way of contrast, 'He killed his maternal aunt' is *existentially extensional* because it is incompatible with the non-existence of a maternal aunt.

For *substitution-intensionality* we need to presuppose a set of non-synonymous expressions b, b', b'', etc., where $b = b' = b'' = \ldots$, etc. Now the relation aRb is substitution-intensional if some proposition obtained by substituting b' or any other member of the set for b, in the proposition aRb, has the opposite truth value of the proposition aRb. Thus in substitution-intensionality the truth value of aRb varies with respect to the substitution for b of b' or any other member of a set of co-referring expressions of which b is a member. Examples of substitution-intensionality are to be found in the writings of Quine.[1] Given that E-intensionality and S-intensionality are defined as I have defined them here, I

---

[1] W. V. O. Quine, *Word and Object*, New York, 1960, pp. 144 ff.

can see no reason why they should not be regarded as logically independent characteristics.

S-intensionality is bedevilled by the fact that many relations have both S-extensional and S-intensional variants. For instance, the relation '. . . relies on . . .' may be construed as extensional, but it has the S-intensional variant '. . . relies on . . . as such'. Let us assume that Jones' motorcar is the vehicle in which he will kill himself. In a hurry to get to London he relies on his motorcar, and therefore on the vehicle in which he will kill himself. But he does not rely on it *as* the vehicle in which he will kill himself. In order for him to do so, he would have to be both prescient and suicidal.

Also, Jones intends to marry the charming Jennifer who—though he does not know it—is his sister. Therefore he intends to marry his sister. But not as such. In order for him to intend to marry her as such, he would have to reconcile himself to incest, and he would have to know that she is his sister.

We must add that where S-intensional relations have an extensional variant which operates in third person grammar, this variant does not generally carry over into first person present tense grammar. Jones' intention to marry the charming Jennifer who—though he does not know it—is his sister, may live peacefully side by side with his determination on no account to marry his sister.

If Jones is ignorant of the fact that Jennifer is his sister, and *does* intend to marry only Jennifer, and if he nevertheless avows that he intends to marry his sister, he lies, even though his words express a true proposition *per accidens*. The interpretation under which what he says is true, requires us to take intending as an S-extensional relation. The interpretation under which what he says is false requires us to take intending as an S-intensional relation. Avowals differ from other statements primarily in that they exclude S-extensional interpretation.

Further refinements may be added, roughly to the effect that any intensional first person statement is misleading if it identifies the intensional object under a description which, though known to be apt, is irrelevant as a ground of the intensional relation. Thus if Jones intends to marry Jennifer and knows that she is his sister, but intends to marry her *qua* pretty girl rather than on account of her consanguinity, there are situations in which he misleads if he

says that he intends to marry his sister. For in certain contexts
this may be taken to mean that he intends to marry his sister, whoever she may turn out to be, which is false if he will marry none
but Jennifer.

Whether it gets mentioned in avowals or in third person
statements does not affect the E-status of the reliance relation. As
regards S-status, there is an extensional variant which is satisfactory for third person statements only, and an intensional one
('relying on . . . as such') which is satisfactory for third person
statements and avowals alike.

II

In this section, I shall attempt to fit together Strawson's account of
facts and my account of intellectual reliance.

We must begin with a distinction between two kinds of reliance
locution. They are

(*a*) Jones relies on the fact that the cat is on the mat.
(*b*) Jones relies on the cat's being on the mat.

These will be referred to as (*a*) the substantival and (*b*) the
gerundial locution respectively. It will be evident that (*a*) carries
speaker-commitment, and that (*b*) does not. It is self-contradictory
to say that: Jones relies on the fact that the cat is on the mat and
there is no such fact.

Therefore whoever asserts (*a*) must also be prepared to assert
that it is a fact that the cat is on the mat. As regards (*b*) things are
different. This proposition carries no commitment to the existence
of the object of reliance. The object here is the cat's being on the
mat, a gerundial object, as I propose to say. Without contradiction
the speaker may assert that Jones relies on the cat's being on the
mat, whether or not he is prepared to assert that any such gerundial
object exists, and incidentally also, whether or not he is prepared
to assert that the cat *is* on the mat. Thus it is clear that reliance
as in (*a*) is E-extensional, and reliance as in (*b*) is E-intensional.

Now let us attempt, in terms of Strawson's definition, to make
sense of a statement such as: Jones relies on the fact that-*p*. By
substituting definiens for definiendum we get: Jones relies on
what the true statement that-*p* states. This substitution must be
permissible despite the apparent intensionality of the verb 'to
rely on' since the identity of definiens and definiendum is one of

sense, rather than of reference. Now we may wish to eliminate speaker-commitment. We can do this by writing: Jones relies on its being a fact that-p which if $p =$ the cat is on the mat, is equivalent to: Jones relies on the cat's being on the mat. On this basis we can analyse: Jones relies on the fact that the cat is on the mat, as: Jones relies on the cat's being on the mat and the cat is on the mat. The second conjunct can then be detached as irrelevant to the relation between Jones and the object of Jones' reliance. The resultant locution will be discussed below.

We have argued that Strawson is committed to the intelligibility of: Jones relies on what the true statement that-p states. Is the adjunct 'true' detachable *salva veritate*? Is it detachable *salva congruitate*? We seem to have a *prima facie* reason for an affirmative answer to both questions, namely that the true statement that-p is *the same statement as* the statement that-p. To assert that this is so is equivalent to asserting that the adjunct 'true' does not fulfil a referential role in the above expression. If an adjunct is employed to individuate the referent of a substantive, as in, e.g. Arabia Felix, we cannot obtain a true statement by detaching it on one side of an identity and leaving it on the other. Thus it is false that Arabia = Arabia Felix. Arabia Felix is not the same country as Arabia.

On the other hand, if an adjunct operates non-referentially (as in American journalese, where it often serves as a device for gratuitously conveying information) it may be detached on one side of a true identity, and retained on the other. For example: The ageing de Gaulle = de Gaulle, and thus: The ageing de Gaulle is bald $\leftrightarrows$ de Gaulle is bald and de Gaulle is ageing. Of course it is possible to use 'de Gaulle' as equivalent to the predicative expression 'called de Gaulle' and to single out one person from amongst the people called de Gaulle, namely the ageing one. Thus interpreted, the formula: The ageing de Gaulle = de Gaulle, is not so much false as nonsense.

There seems to be a conclusive reason for saying that in the formula 'Jones relies on what the true statement that p states' the adjunct 'true' operates non-referentially. For if it operated referentially, then the adjunct would be *needed* to specify what is relied on: it follows that its absence would make the phrase 'what the statement that p states' non-specific. In that case it would have to be possible in principle for there to be several type-statements that p, of which presumably one would be individuable as *the true one*, and the others would have to be false or devoid of truth value. But, clearly, two type-statements of contrary truth value cannot both be univocally that *p*. If the statement type 'Napoleon died on St Helena' states what is true, there cannot be another statement type, 'Napoleon died on St Helena', which is false, supposing 'Napoleon died on St Helena' to be univocal.

Now from the fact that the adjunct 'true' does not operate referentially it may seem to follow (though I shall presently argue to the contrary) that it is detachable *salva veritate*. But detachment would be disastrous.

To say that 'Jones relies on what the statement that-*p* states as distinct from its being true' is certainly to commit a category mistake. It is as if a holiday maker bent on an outing relied on Sunday as distinct from Sunday's being fine. Of course one may argue that *in* relying on Sunday for his outing, the holiday maker relies on *its being* fine and one may thus treat the phrase 'relying on Sunday' as elliptical *i.e.* as implicitly doing the same job as 'Sunday's being fine'. But it is absurd to say that the holiday maker relies on Sunday *tout court as distinct from* Sunday's being fine (though he may rely on Sunday's being uncommitted). And likewise it is absurd to say that Jones relies on the statement that *p*, *as distinct from* its being true.

The question is whether in the formula: Jones relies on what the true statement that *p* states the adjunct 'true' is detachable, and we argued that there is a strong *prima facie* reason for answering yes. We also argued that detachment involves something like a category mistake. If the reason offered as *prima facie* were conclusive, the argument against Strawson would end here. He would have to countenance the detachment of the undetachable. But it may seem obvious to some of us that it is illicit to detach the adjunct. It will be granted that the true statement that *p* = the statement that *p*. This notwithstanding, it will be said that detachment presupposes the extensionality of the relation '. . . relies on . . .'. while it is plainly intensional. If so, the context is referentially opaque, and substitution over identity is impermissible.

But clearly, as it stands, this objection is inconclusive. To begin with, the distinction between E-intensionality and S-intensionality is ignored: for the objection to be valid the reliance relation will have to be shown to be S-intensional rather than E-intensional. Further, there are S-extensional reliance locutions. For instance, we said that, although Jones may not rely on the motorcar in which he will kill himself as such, nevertheless, he does (plainly) rely on it, and if this will serve as a model for intellectual reliance, then the objection from referential opacity will not hold water. I shall argue later that both the argument from referential opacity and its rebuttal have inadmissible presuppositions; I do not therefore rely on the rebuttal. But neither can the objection carry the day; thus the question remains open.

Our task is to analyse the formula: Jones relies on what the true statement that-p states. We decided that the detachment of the adjunct 'true' would render the formula nonsensical, and also, that if it is non-detachable, this does not arise from its referential role. If sense is to be made of the formula, therefore, we must find some other ground of non-detachability, and at this point I also should like to rely on the intensional character of the reliance-relation, though not in Quine's way. Let us vary an example of Quine's. The statement

'Tom believes that Cicero denounced Catiline, and Cicero is the same person as Tully', entails that 'Tom believes that Tully (under this or some other mode of reference) denounced Catiline'.

This is compatible with the statement: 'Tom does not know that Cicero is Tully'. Here it is perfectly feasible to say that the verb 'to believe' has S-extensional and S-intensional variants. The intensional variant will be something like 'believe, under such and such a mode of reference'.

But we cannot treat the formula under examination thus, *i.e.*: Jones relies on what the true statement that-p states and the true statement that-p is the same as the statement that-p. By analogy with the Quinean example, this ought to entail: Jones relies on what the statement that-p states, under this or some other mode of reference. But as I have argued above, the entailed statement must either be treated as a slipshod way of saying that Jones relies on the statement that-p's being true, or, be reduced to a category mistake. A statement not considered under the aspect of truth is not of the right sort for intellectual reliance.

Let us reduce our original formula to gerundial form and try to make sense of it thus: Jones relies on what the true statement that-p states, now becomes: Jones relies on the statement that-p's being true and (I the speaker assert that) it is true. Inasmuch as

F

it is thus reducible, I should like to say—disregarding speaker-commitment—that the adjunct 'true' is intensionally non-detachable.

Just as the holiday maker stakes his money on Sunday's being fine, and not on Sunday as such, nor on the fineness of some other day or thing, Jones in his intellectual reliance stakes his money on the truth of the statement that the cat is on the mat (or on its being true), and not on the statement as such, any more than on the truth of some other statement or thing.

Thus insofar as Jones relies on the statement that the cat is on the mat, he does so under the aspect of truth. If he takes a risk, it is that the statement may turn out to be false.

We may formulate this in a number of ways. For instance: Jones relies on the statement 'The cat is on the mat' *as* true, or: Jones relies on the statement 'The cat is on the mat' *in respect of* truth, or *qua* truth, or: Jones relies on the statement's 'The cat is on the mat' *being* true.

These formulae are constructed to ensure that, though 'true' performs a non-referential role, it is nevertheless non-detachable. The last formula takes a gerundial object and it may seem that but for speaker-commitment, it would be equivalent to: Jones relies on what the true statement that-p states. I should like to argue that in these formulae non-detachability arises from a kind of intensionality which is distinct both from E- and S-intensionality. I propose to call it Q-intensionality.

Q-intensionality, unlike S-intensionality, does not pre-suppose a set of non-synonymous co-referential expressions. Rather, given certain object-expressions consisting of adjunctively qualified nominals, it arises from the fact that contextually their sense requires us to read them as hyphenated or slurred. This shows itself in the truncation of what would otherwise have been sound entailments. For example

(1) Jones admires Agatha.
(2) Agatha is the girl in the pink mini-skirt.

(*a*) 1 and 2 imply 3.

(3) Jones admires the girl in the pink mini-skirt (n.b. 'To admire' operates S-extensionally here.)

(*b*) 3 implies the conjunction of 4 and 5.

(4) Jones admires a girl.

(5) Jones admires something (someone) in a pink mini-skirt.

Now 6 introduces a *Q-intensional context*.

(6) Jones admires Agatha as a dancer (*qua* dancer).

(*c*) 6 does not imply 1.

(*d*) 6 is equivalent to the conjunction of 2 and 7.

(7) Jones admires the girl in the pink mini-skirt as a dancer.

In 6 we can substitute over identity, but we cannot detach the adjunctive phrase 'as a dancer'. Thus the intensionality of 6 cannot consist in that the expression 'Agatha as a dancer' resists substitution over identity. That is precisely what we do legitimately in 7. Rather it consists in that we may not, *salva veritate*, detach the adjunct. In such a case I shall say that *the adjunct is Q-intensionally tied* to the noun which it qualifies, and that Agatha-as-a-dancer is the *Q-intensional object* of Jones' admiration.

We must note however that not all 'as a . . .' contexts are Q-intensional. E.g.

(8) Jones attended the conference as a delegate.

(*e*) 8 implies the conjunction of 9 and 10.

(9) Jones attended the conference.

(10) There is something which Jones did as a delegate.

The adjunctive phrase 'as a delegate' is therefore detachable.

In our example that 'as a dancer' is intentionally tied to 'Agatha', and the real object of Jones' liking is Agatha as a dancer, rather than either Agatha *tout court*, or Agatha, together with the fact that she dances. We must add that Jones' liking for Agatha (if any) is to be conceived of as *distinct* from his liking of her *as* a dancer. In practice of course, that one likes a person as a dancer may be in some way constitutive of liking her *tout court*. But it does not *follow* that if I like Agatha as a dancer, I like Agatha *tout court*, and if I do, I may like her *greatly* as a dancer, and as a person only a little.

Jones relies either properly or improperly. If he relies properly then (at least) that which he relies on supports his opinion.

But we have shown that gerundial statement reliance is unaffected by truth value. It is E-intensional.

Thus 'Jones relies on its being true that the cat is on the mat' is compatible with there being no such thing as its being true that the cat is on the mat: that is, it is compatible with its being false that the cat is on the mat. But if it is false that the cat is on the mat, then in relying on its being true, Jones misrelies. Then what he relies on will not support his opinion. Thus we get a paradox:

(1) Jones, *in relying on its being true that p*, given relevance, relies properly only if *p*.
(2) Jones, *in relying on its being true that p*, given relevance, relies improperly if ~*p*.
(3) Propriety of reliance depends, given relevance, on the object of reliance being fit to be relied on. Thus there must be some sense in which—given relevance—the object of reliance *determines the propriety of relying on it*.
(4) Therefore one and the same object of reliance—given relevance—may determine an opinion to be either proper or improper.

This seems absurd.

We clearly need to introduce some internal difference in objects of reliance if (granted relevance) we wish to say that one object is properly relied on and another is not, or that one object is fit to be relied on and another is unfit. Roughly, the conditions 'if *p*' in (1) and 'if ~*p*' in (2) need to be taken into the object of reliance. At first sight it may seem that we can achieve this by simply asserting *p* or ~*p*. If so, we will write: Jones relies on its being true that *p*, and *p* is true. But, clearly, this will not do, because in this formulation the second conjunct is outside the scope of Jones' reliance. I suggest that we must now write: Jones relies on the fact that *p*. Only thus can we include fitness for reliance in the characterization of the object itself. *A fact is something fit to be relied on.*

If I rely on the cat's being on the mat, I may misrely in one of two ways:

(1) because the cat is not on the mat.
(2) because the cat's being on the mat does not support my opinion.

If I misrely in the first of these two ways, then *every* other opinion which relies on the cat's being on the mat also misrelies. If I misrely in the second of these two ways, then there may be some other opinion for which I might adequately rely on the cat's being on the mat. If I misrely in the first of these two ways then what I rely on is *not fit to be relied on for any opinion.* Conversely, if I rely on what is fit to be relied on, a fact, for instance, then I cannot misrely in the first way. If I misrely in the second way, then I mistake the relevance of the object of reliance to the opinion for which I rely on it.

We have uncovered an apparent conflict between our desire to say that what Jones relies on must be *the same*, whether he relies on it properly or improperly, and our equally reasonable desire to say that the object of reliance determines its propriety. The first inclination drives us towards gerundial objects and an E-intensional interpretation of reliance. The second drives us towards substantival objects and an E-extensional interpretation of reliance. The trouble with gerundial (or E-intensional) reliance is that it is *unstable* or *proliferative*.

In this connection it does not matter whether we rely on the cat's being on the mat, or on its being true that the cat is on the mat, or on its being justifiable to assume that the cat is on the mat. Introducing the adjective 'true' into the gerundial formula alters nothing. Reliance on a gerundial object, obtained by no matter what operation on the formula of a statement, is compatible with the falsity of that statement. But if the statement is false, then reliance is defective, and thus—quite apart from relevance— gerundial objects are open, as regards our propriety in relying on them. If what we rely on for an opinion is something which— granted relevance—does not justify that opinion *per se*, but only justifies it on some added condition (in this case, that *p* is true) then we must say that *the fulfilment of this added condition is itself relied on.* Here we must resist the temptation of treating the added condition as an added object of reliance. The object of reliance now is *not* the conjunction of two logically independent conditions, but rather it is an object in which the added condition is Q-intensionally non-detachable from the condition originally stated. Treating the object of reliance thus, we arrive at: Jones relies on the fact that the statement that-*p* is true.

We may attempt to escape from this formula by distinguishing between two kinds of reliance, plain reliance and proper reliance respectively. Plain reliance will take a gerundial object, and proper reliance a substantival one.

But it would be a mistake to treat plain reliance and proper reliance as two distinct species of a common genus. Clearly, the idea in relying is to rely properly, and the notion that a man may purposely rely improperly is destructively paradoxical. Plain reliance may be adequately defined as that which has proper reliance as its perfection and justification as its *telos*; improper reliance is defective reliance. Impropriety in reliance is a privation of propriety. Thus we can arrive at the idea of a reliance failure through the idea of the non-fulfilment of the conditions of success, but we cannot similarly arrive at the idea of reliance success by adding something to what is involved in all reliance (successful and unsuccessful).

I conclude:

(i) that Strawson's facts are constitutionally gerundial;
(ii) that intellectual reliance on a gerundial object is unable to accommodate one of the dimensions of propriety; and
(iii) that gerundial reliance is conceptually secondary to substantival reliance (or reliance on facts).

One way of escaping from the gerundial analysis of fact-reliance remains open. It consists in retaining fact-locutions, though at a higher level. Thus, if we must analyse: Jones relies on the fact that p, as: Jones relies on p's being true, there is nothing to prevent us from eliminating the gerundial expression by re-introducing facts in connection with the truth value of propositions. Then we get: Jones relies on the fact that the statement that p is true. I now propose to examine the notion that plain facts are really facts about the truth value of propositions.

III

First, if we write 'Jones relies on the fact that the statement that-p is true' we engender an infinite regress. For this new kind of fact reliance, in which the fact concerns the truth of a statement instead of, let us say, the position of a tree, is no less open to gerundial analysis than ordinary fact reliance. We now get 'Jones relies on its being true that "The statement that-p is true".' By repetition of the operation a zig-zag regress can be constructed. Zig members of the regress will be substantival and E-extensional. Zag members will be gerundial and E-intensional. Objections may come from an aversion to abstract entities, but no such objection will be pressed here.

The regress which we have engendered is innocuous. To appreciate this we must understand that it does not shift the ground of reliance. To be sure, we will write 'Jones relies on the fact that the statement "The statement that p is true" is true'. But for this Jones need not rely on a third order fact. He may equally well rely on a first order fact, because all the members of the hierarchical set are equivalent. Thus it is not open to us to argue that the ultimate ground of reliance must be the last member of a hierarchy of higher order facts which has no last member. The ultimate ground of reliance is the set itself, and since all its members are logically equivalent, it is not misleading to say that the ultimate ground is the first member of the set.

Let us call facts about electrons and people worldly facts, and facts about statements propositional facts. Now Strawson may be interpreted as saying that worldly facts analyse into propositional facts, into facts about the truth value of statements, that is to say. I have admittedly argued that facts are *ex officio* suitable as objects of reliance, and propositional facts (if the concept proves coherent) are no exception. But clearly, if in relying on the fact that the statement that p is true, I do *no more than* rely on its being true that the statement that the statement that p is true, is true, I have no warrant to suppose that I rely on what is fit for being relied on. Clearly, there is no such thing as the fact that the statement that p is true, unless the statement itself is true, and that is as may be.

It seems to me that unless the statement that p is self-guaranteeing, I must look for the ground of reliance-worthiness outside the zig-zag regress. Roughly, the idea that I am entitled to rely on any member of the regress presupposes that I am entitled to rely on the first member, and clearly I cannot rely on the statement that p as true, unless I know, or at least have good reason to believe, that p is a true proposition. But on what may I rely for this belief? There is nothing in the regress on which I may rely, and on Strawson's amended view there is no fact that p outside the regress: therefore I must rely on some other proposition for my belief that the statement that p is true. In gerundial terms, I must rely on some statement-that-q's being true. Thus we engender another regress, and *this* regress is genuinely vicious.

Reliance is a justificatory relation. Suppose A stands in need of support, and B is offered as a support. It is clear that B is not worthy of reliance unless there is something else which supports it—let us call it C—which in its turn is not worthy of reliance unless . . . and so on, *ad infinitum*. Here it seems reasonable to say that A is not supported at all. A justificatory regress must have an end. To quote Bradley:[1]

'We are fastened to a chain, and we wish to know if we are really secure. What ought we to do? Is it much use to say, "This link we are tied to is certainly solid, and it is fast to the next: beyond this we can not see more than a certain moderate distance, but, so far as we know, it all holds together"? The practical man would first of all ask, "Where can I find the last link of my chain? When I know that is fast, and not hung in the air, it is time enough to inspect the connection". But the chain is such that every link begets, so soon as we come to it, a new one; and, ascending in our search, at each remove we are still no nearer the last link of all, on which everything depends.'

It is tempting to say that if we abandon the idea of reliance on a worldly fact and replace it with the idea of reliance on a propositional fact, we must *really* be relying on the *opinion* that the relevant statement is true. Many philosophers prefer opinions to propositional facts. Opinions can be treated as psychological occurrences which enter into causal relations, and thus they have an empirical air about them. If such philosophers hesitate to make opinions as such into objects of reliance, it is yet open to them to make the reliance-worthiness of an object into a matter of opinion, such that, in the absence of a favourable opinion concerning the object, it is not relied on. Thus a statement acquires status as an object of reliance simply by the opinion that it is true. It seems to follow that our opinions ultimately rely on the opinions which we have about the truth-value of statements, that is to say, on other opinions after all. Bradley's dilemma is fatal to a regress of opinions as well as to a regress of propositional facts.

Happily, we do not need to rely on another opinion in order for a given opinion to be well founded. True, I rely on the flicker of my vacuum gauge for my view that a valve spring is broken in my engine, but why should I not rely on it for my view (or knowledge) that the vacuum gauge flickers. In epistemically suitable conditions, for instance when I see that the vacuum-gauge flickers, I rely on the actual flicker of the vacuum-gauge for my opinion (or knowledge) that it flickers. I would not be using the verb 'to base' correctly, if I said that I based my know-

[1] F. H. Bradley, *The Principles of Logic*, London, 1883, p. 100.

ledge that the vacuum gauge flickers on my knowledge that the statement that the vacuum gauge flickers is true. The same goes for any other statement. I think that in relying on a fact I rely on something which actually happens in the material universe.

IV

We are now ready for the principal thesis of this paper. Facts are events conceived as proper objects of reliance for thought or deed. Events are here to be taken as widely as possible—they cover states of affairs and anything which can be said to be actual, or to eventuate or come about. Events may or may not occur—but if they do not occur, they are improperly relied on. A plurality of nonsynonymous expressions may individuate an occurrence. These expressions refer to the same occurrence but not to the same events. Events are the intensions of occurrences: occurrences are the extensions of events. Occurrences as such do not support thought or deed, they support them only *qua*—or under—some characterization or other. Existences and occurrences must be distinguished from the objects which are *said or taken* to exist or occur. Thus an event, for instance the execution of Goering, is a suitable object for reference, even though he prevented it by committing suicide. Goering's execution belongs to the type of events—it certainly cannot be a substance or a property or a class, etc. But it is not an actual occurrence because it never occurred and never will occur. I realize that the idea of reference to what does not exist is alien to the whole of modern extensional logic, and that Russell's theory of description was constructed in order to render it superfluous. But we shall see that reference to the non-existent is unavoidable in intensional contexts.

Let us have another look at the reliance relation. Proper reliance is E-extensional. It does not follow that it is also S-extensional. Suppose there to be neither a carriage step, nor a shadow below a carriage door, and suppose Jones in descending to rely on there being a step below the carriage door. Now extensionally the phrases 'The step below the carriage door' and 'The shadow below the carriage door' refer to exactly the same thing, namely nothing. Nevertheless we cannot infer that Jones relies on there being a shadow below the carriage door. True, he relies improperly (in one of the dimensions of impropriety), if what he relies on does not exist, whatever it is. But if what he relies on is that there is a carriage door, *he would rely properly* if a carriage door did exist: if on the other hand he relies on there being a shadow, *he relies improperly whether or not a shadow exists.*

The reason why different *non-existent* objects of reliance must *not* be treated as identical is that fitness for reliance depends on intension. In descending from a carriage, a man may suitably rely on there being a carriage step, but unsuitably on there being a shadow. Let us allow (counter to inclination) that one and the same thing might on a certain occasion be correctly described both as a step and as a shadow. Yet this identity would be irrelevant to the question of fitness for reliance. Plain reliance may be S-extensional, but reliance on what is fit to be relied on resists substitution over identity: it is S-intensional. We must add that a non-existent step and a non-existent shadow cannot be onto-logically identical, for questions of ontological identity arise only for variables within the scope of existential quantifiers. The question whether a non-existent step is ontologically identical with a non-existent shadow is therefore absurd.

The occurrence of an event is called a fact inasmuch as it is conceived as properly supporting some action or opinion or claim to knowledge. Events mistakenly believed to occur may be improperly relied on, but we cannot say that persons who misrely in this fashion rely on facts. Events are E-intensional objects of opinion reliance in general, but they are E-extensional objects of *proper* opinion reliance.

Occurrent events are subject to ontological criteria of identity: the same occurrence may be described or referred to in many different ways. But *qua* justification reliance depends on *how* an event is described. For instance, the view that Jones is in trouble is better supported by the fact that he is being interrogated by a policeman than by the fact that he is being interrogated by a man in a brown trilby hat, even though the man in the brown trilby hat is a policeman. In such cases it seems natural to say that two opinions rely on different facts, though, as it so happens, these facts coincide in one and the same occurrence. For instance, the fact that Jones marries the woman he loves—which supports the opinion that he makes an honest woman of her—is not the same fact as that he marries his sister, which does not support that opinion, even though the only woman he loves *is* his sister. The same occurrence is the basis of two different facts. We cannot say that these different facts simply *are* the same occurrence, relying on the 'is' of identity, because things which are identical with the same thing (here, with the occurrence itself) are identical with each other. We therefore need the idea of a ground or basis, and I should like to suggest that this is provided for us by the form-matter distinction.

For instance, we distinguish between mark and symbol, even though a symbol is embodied in a mark. The mark '+' embodies two distinct symbols, namely the cross or Christian symbol of the passion, and the plus or symbol of addition. The mark as such is conceived in geometrical terms—roughly, it consists of two strokes intersecting at right angles, while the symbols are conceived in terms of their roles or in terms of their significance. I propose to say that the symbols are embodied in the mark, rather than that they are identical with the mark, precisely because if they were identical with the mark, they would be identical with each other. If we dogmatize that whenever 'is' is not of predication or of composition, it must be the 'is' of identity, then what I have just said is absurd. But I believe that there is also the 'is' of embodiment, for instance in 'The symbol of the passion is a cross'. Unless I am mistaken, this is the fundamental idea in Aristotle's matter-form distinction, and relying on this distinction I should like to say that the occurrence of one and the same event may be the embodiment of different facts. Facts are to occurrences, then, as form to matter.

We must now briefly comment on error in the light of our account of facts. If I make a mistake about a matter of fact, this may be because I rely on the occurring of an event which does not occur. I rely on this E-intensionally: the non-occurrence does not therefore vitiate my reliance itself, but it does vitiate its propriety. We may add appropriate explanations of the genesis of error, though the theory of the nature of error is in no way dependent on the kind of explanation which we supply. For instance, we may, on occasion, attribute our readiness to rely on what is not there to a malfunctioning of the senses.

The language of facts is proper to intellectual reliance but it is not at home in accounts of natural processes. Occurrences have causes, yet we do not properly say that facts (as such) have causes. For instance, it is inexact to say 'The fact that the glass broke was caused by its being dropped.' Better: 'The breaking of the glass (the occurrence) was caused by the glass being dropped.'

Again, the process, rather than the fact, of digestion intervenes between mastication and excretion, but we rely on the fact that food is chewed when we produce a theory of digestion. A certain event occurred in the drawing room at half past three: this was the cause of damage, but we do not properly say that the damage was caused by the *fact* that, say, a bomb exploded.

V

Our theory of facts has been criticized on the grounds that it treats occurrences as *bare* or *ineffable* particulars. According to the theory, there is no such thing as describing or referring to occurrences without mention of facts, and this might strike some as an objection, perhaps on the grounds that facts (unlike occurrences) involve conceptual superstructure; so that our conception of what occurs independently of intellectual operations must be distorted.

Admittedly, there are insuperable difficulties in referring to occurrences in fact-neutral terms—for instance, spatio-temporally without further description, or purely as whatever caused such and such an effect, or as whatever was the effect of such and such a cause.

But it is not clear that occurrences referred to as events are thereby incorrectly characterized. If Jones beat his son and thereby punished him we have the facts: (1) that Jones beat his son (2) that Jones punished his son. That the occurrence in question can be characterized in many ways surely does not bear out the view that it cannot be characterized at all. The fact that the beating characterization supports the view that Jones is strong of arm, whereas the punishment characterization supports the quite different view that he is old fashioned in his ideas of education, does not show that the occurrence was not a beating and a punishing as well.

In referring to facts we refer to occurrences. The famous event which occurred at Pearl Harbor in December 1941 may be characterized as the bombing of a fleet, or as the first strategic move in a war: if our object is to *refer* to it, we can rely on either characterization and add the rider 'or however it is to be characterized'. The occurrence thus identified can then be placed in causal relationships: for instance, as the cause of some changes in the structure of the harbour wharves.

If the individuation of occurrences through facts is illicit, then the individuation of propositions through sentences must also be illicit. But propositions are characteristically individuated through sentences. For instance, the proposition 'The dog is dead' may be indifferently expressed in the sentences 'The dog is dead' and '*Le chien est mort*'. If we are concerned merely to *refer* to this proposition, then we may write: 'The proposition "The dog is dead" (or however it is to be expressed)'. Facts stand to occurrences as sentences stand to propositions.

We must conclude by reverting to the topic of intellectual reliance. On what do we rely? It seems that when we rely successfully we rely on facts, and that if facts are occurrences conceived in a certain way, we rely on occurrences conceived in a certain way. But it does not follow that we rely on occurrences *tout court*, because, for purposes of intellectual reliance, the qualifying phrase 'conceived in a certain way' is Q-intensionally attached to 'occurrences'.

Although when we rely successfully we rely on facts, it does not follow that we do *not* rely on gerundial objects. We do not, as it were, have the choice between two alternative objects of reliance, facts and gerundials. Therefore intellectual virtue does not consist in opting for facts and eschewing gerundials. Rather we may say that in proper reliance we rely on facts *in* that we rely on gerundials, the relation being internal.

Intellectual reliance does not have a definition *per se*. The correct method of proceeding seems to be to define *proper* reliance, and then to indicate possible defects. Reliance is that of which proper reliance is the perfection: the *telos* of relying is to be justified. While we regard reliance as a merely psychological relation we cannot hope to understand it. It is essentially subject to canons of propriety, and in attempting to shed these we only succeed in disintegrating the concept.

Even if the view is taken that in unsuccessful reliance we do not rely on facts (supposing the idea of E-intensional fact reliance to be contradictory), we certainly *aspire* to rely on facts. That is not because our motives are miraculously and uniformly pure, but because we are committed by the *telos* of relying. On this view, the objects of intellectual reliance in general (successful *and* unsuccessful, that is to say) cannot be simply 'facts' any more than they can be simply 'gerundials'. The first answer ignores the possibility of misreliance, the second ignores the internal relation between the two.

The view that there is a distinction of kind between plain reliance and proper reliance requires us to postulate objects differing in kind. Plain reliance gets gerundials then, while proper reliance gets facts. The telic view of reliance, on the other hand, may incline us to say that we always rely on facts, albeit E-intensionally. This is quite compatible with saying that successful (or proper) reliance is E-extensional.

Thus it appears that we can eliminate gerundials as objects of intellectual reliance after all. But we must not forget that expressions of the kind 'A relies on the fact that p' carry speaker commitment, because 'A relies on the fact that p, but there is no such fact' presents itself as self-contradictory. Rather, if we think that there is no such fact as the fact that p, then we should say 'A relies on there being such a fact as that p', or more simply 'A relies on . . .' where the blank is a place for a gerundial object, such as 'the cat's being on the mat'. True, we may construct an analogy with 'Jones relies on an inheritance' and deny the need for an E-extensional gerundial expression such as 'Jones relies on the materializing of his inheritance'. Perhaps we should say that the expression 'Jones relies on his inheritance', E-intensionally understood, does the same job. On the other hand, Jones himself may be reluctant to say 'I rely on my inheritance', if this commits him to the belief that he will inherit. He may, having doubts on that score, prefer to say 'I rely on inheriting' or 'I rely on my inheritance materializing', his reliance now being speculative. Similarly, he may be reluctant to assert that in his speculative opinion that q, he relies on the fact that p, preferring to say that he relies on its being a fact that p, or on . . . (blank being the place for a gerundial).

Nevertheless, it seems possible to detach speaker-commitment from some fact-locutions. We may retain speaker-commitment in locutions like 'Jones stated the fact that p' or 'Jones discovered the fact that p' and deny it for intensional locutions like 'Jones thought about the fact that p' or 'Jones relied on the fact that p'. If this is feasible there really seems to be nothing to prevent us from saying that intellectual reliance in general is E-intensional fact reliance, though it is not clear that much is gained by saying this, since we must add that the concept of reliance in general is derivative from the concept of proper reliance, which is E-extensional relative to facts.

The question whether reliance on gerundials as such—were it granted—would be E-extensional may also be asked. It leads straight to ontological speculation of a particularly difficult kind. If (lacking a taste for desert landscapes) one sees no difficulty in asserting the existence of gerundials, it is not clear that one is committed to thinking that a pure gerundial object, non-contradictorily referred to, can be said *not* to exist. The view may well be taken that the *esse* of 'existence' in such cases is the consistency of the referring expression. That is, if gerundials are pure intensions, then the only way in which a gerundial phrase can lack a referent may be by being self-contradictory.

Is intellectual reliance S-intensional? If we take the objects of intellectual reliance to be occurrences, it is clear that the answer is yes, because we do rely on an occurrence under one characterization rather than another. Thus if Jones relies on an occurrence under characterization *a*, we cannot conclude that he also relies on it under characterization *b*, supposing *a* and *b* to differ in sense. Whether Jones relies properly or improperly does not affect the matter.

As regards gerundials, it is difficult to see whether the prerequisites of S-intensionality are met. I argued above that S-status (intensional and extensional) requires a set of non-synonymous referring expressions with a common referent. If gerundial objects are, as I have suggested, pure intensions (for instance, events prescinding from the question of whether or not they occur) there does not seem to be any sense in the suggestion that expressions differing in sense might refer to the same gerundial object. However, there are qualifications to this simple solution, which, since an analogous problem arises with reliance on facts, I will not discuss separately.

What then if the objects of reliance are facts? If facts are occurrences thus and thus characterized, the preconditions of S-status of either kind again seem unfulfilled. To rely on B, that is, an occurrence-characterized-as-a-thrashing (the hyphenated expression being Q-intensionally tied) clearly is to rely on a different object from B-characterized-as-a-punishment, and so in this connection at least, the question of S-status does not arise.

Can we make sense of the idea that B-characterized-as-a-thrashing might itself be referred to by expressions differing in sense? If so, the question of S-status comes back into its own. It does seem possible that a fact on which a certain man relies for his opinion might be referred to by devices other than stating it, for instance as the last fact which Henry stated.

Now if the fact in question is that Smith thrashed his son, and if that very same fact can be referred to as the last fact which Henry stated, then there does appear to be a plurality of expressions, differing in sense, referring to the same fact. If so, the prerequisites for S-status are satisfied, and then it is clear that fact reliance is S-extensional, because the conjunction of 'Jones relies on the fact that Smith thrashed his son' with 'That Smith thrashed his son is the last fact which Henry stated' entails 'Jones relies on the last fact which Henry stated'. It does not follow, of course, that he relies on it as such.

But it must be borne in mind that the alternative modes of reference to a fact are derivative from a basic mode of reference, namely stating it. Once a fact has been singled out by being stated, we can bestow a name on it, or refer to it obliquely by a variety of devices, but the reverse procedure is not possible. If someone mentions a fact, as the last fact which Henry stated, we may still enquire which fact this is, and upon being told that it is the fact named Ezekiel, repeat the same question. But upon being told that Ezekiel is the fact that President Kennedy was assassinated, we cannot further enquire what fact *this* is. By being stated, it is revealed. In the regress of questions 'What fact is this?' the statement of it is rock bottom.

Thus it seems to me that primitive fact-reliance is neither S-intensional not S-extensional, though, with the introduction of derivative referring devices, a claim for S-extensionality can be made out.

5

MAX DEUTSCHER

A CAUSAL ACCOUNT OF INFERRING

I. THE PROPOSED ANALYSIS

My thesis is quite simple. Person A inferred that-q at t_x from p's being the case, or from the 'supposed' fact that-p, if and only if:

(1) He came to believe that-q at t_x

(2) He already believed that-p at t_x

(3a) His state of belief that-p was an operative condition of his coming to believe that-q at t_x

(4) At t_x he believes that, in the light of what he already believes, the fact (or supposed fact) that-p makes it *at least* not completely unreasonable to believe that-q. That belief is a condition of his coming to believe that-q.

Some explanation is necessary for (3a), and it will be given in Section IIIa. Also it needs to be strengthened by criterion (3b). This is done in Section IVb.

This analysis, if correct, immediately answers the question 'What is it to infer?' To infer from a fact is to come to believe as a result of having a true belief. To infer from a supposed fact is to come to believe as a result of having a belief, whether true or false, which was not properly based. To infer from something or other, is to come to believe as a result of having an unspecific sort of belief. Reality cannot be vague, but our beliefs about reality can. Inferring from things in the remote past, or from things at a great distance, is coming to believe as a result of a belief that something has happened in the remote past, or at a great distance. To infer from premises is to gain a belief in virtue of one's belief in the premises.

If someone speaking of an inference wishes to remain silent on the question whether the person who inferred had a true initial belief, then he will say that the inference was from a 'supposed'

G

fact. A precisely similar point holds for the final belief, although there is also the alternative form: 'From . . . he inferred that-q.' To say that a person inferred that-q is, in normal circumstances, to remain silent on the question whether the acquired belief that q, is true. To make it clear that the person's initial and final beliefs are false, we say 'He inferred from what he wrongly guessed, mistakenly believed, etc., that . . .'. It will be quite apparent that the proposed account of inference can take care of inferring from supposed facts, etc., as easily as inferring from facts, and I shall say no more about the points of usage involved. For brevity, I shall talk mostly of inferring from and to facts, but they may be 'supposed' or 'non-existent' facts. This commits me merely to the existence of false beliefs and not to subsistent entities which do not exist.

We may also speak of inference to and from the 'existence of things', 'states of affairs', 'things being so', 'a thing's having properties', 'the occurrence of events', and 'the presence of objects'. I tend to use 'fact' to the exclusion of these other terms, but this is only for convenience, and also I wish to leave open the question 'What makes beliefs true?'

II(a). BELIEF THAT-p, AND INFERENCE FROM THE FACT THAT-p

The first question concerning the analysis is this: Must a person believe that-p, if he infers from the fact that-p? It may be thought to be beyond dispute. However, many philosophers and logicians are more interested in whether one statement is *inferable* from another than they are in what it is to infer. In consequence they tend to overlook the relevance of belief to inferring. Once our attention is focussed on inferring, and is diverted from the conditions of inferability, little objection can be raised against answering 'Yes' to the question just raised. Nevertheless it is worth reflecting on the following case.

It is plain that in our reading a detective novel, there may occur the formal analogue to inferring. The reader notices various clues, puts two and two together, and exclaims to himself, 'By Jove, the bishop strangled the actress!' This process is like inferring except for the factor of belief. Belief is involved; the reader comes to believe that the evidence justifies a certain conclusion. However, *that* is not what we are tempted to say he infers

I think that we should resist the inclination to say the reader infers that the bishop strangled the actress. After all, an uncritical acceptance of the reader's remarks would lead us equally to the conclusion that he believed the various propositions expressing the evidence, and *believed* that the bishop strangled the actress. In the same vein as he says 'I then inferred that the bishop strangled the actress,' he will also say 'Well, you see, the bishop couldn't have been at London by ten, as alleged, and so this led me to think that Blake was lying, and so what could one believe but that . . .?' When we are involved in fiction, the *logic* though not the *intention* of discourse as concerning reality is applicable in whole and not merely in part. In fact, our inclination to talk of inference when dealing with fictional matters can be seen to support the thesis that belief is involved in inferring. It is in the same sense that we 'believe' (even though we might not be told) that Blake must have been lying, that we 'infer' from Blake's having lied, etc.

These same remarks apply to the question raised in the following section.

II(*b*).   BELIEF THAT-*q* AND INFERENCE THAT-*q*

When a person infers that-*q* is it always true that he comes to believe that-*q*? It is clear, I think, that he must either believe or come to believe that-*q* at the time he infers. A person who does not believe in certain premises may show a conclusion to be derivable, but he cannot be said actually to infer it.

A person may believe something and then come to recognize additional evidence. Does he, in that case, infer what he already believes? I concede that the *analogue* of inferring can occur, as described in the case of reading a detective novel, but I suggest that such a person does not infer again what he accepts anyway. He does infer *something*; that what he believed is even better supported than he had thought.

Although the thesis of this paper is opposed to that of D. G. Brown (in 'The Nature of Inference', *Philosophical Review*, vol. LXIV, 1955), his approach reminds us that a person may be said to hold a belief as an inference, though at that time he is not inferring anything. It would be easy to over-react against Brown's extreme thesis that there is no such thing as an event or process of inferring, and to insist that a person holds '*q*' as an inference if and only if at some previous time he inferred that-*q*, and as a result still holds to the same opinion. This would involve us in two serious errors.

Firstly, a person may hold something as an inference from certain facts even though at no time did any event occur which could be called his inferring from those facts. A person might hold something for no particular reason, or for some reason other than the fact that-*p*. He might come to learn that-*p*, and accept that '*p*' adequately supports '*q*'. From then on he may hold '*q*' as an inference from what he has now learned. Something may be upheld by something else, though it was not brought about by it. One may have evidence for thinking that without the new information, the man may have lost his belief that-*q*.

The second error is this. A person who originally inferred that-*q* from the fact that-*p* and as a result continued to hold that-*q*, might continue to hold it but not as an inference from the fact that-*p*. Initially, new arguments were heard, and the new opinion was embraced. For some time the new opinion is held in such a manner that it would be given up in the light of counter-evidence. But as time goes on, what we might call doxastic conservatism sets in. The person continues to hold the opinion not for the old reasons or for new ones. He continues to believe merely because he already believes. Such a person might even half-heartedly recall the original reasons on which he formed his opinion. Yet we might judge from the way in which he treats criticism that he no longer holds his opinion *on the basis of* these or any other reasons. The strength of untroubled belief remains constant while debate swings this way and that.

So far I have tried to show that inferring involves a movement from belief to belief. It does not follow that we ought to speak always of inferring from *believing that-p*. I may infer from the fact that a man's hand is unsteady that he is drunk, perhaps. But what I may infer from believing that his hand is unsteady is quite a different matter. I might infer that I had noticed him slop a drink some time earlier, or that I tend to be sensitive to the way in which people begin to lose control of themselves. Similarly I infer *that he is drunk*, and not *that I believe he is drunk*. It is rather unusual to infer that you have certain beliefs. If you do know that you believe something, it is usually without inference. Thus, although inference is a matter of movement from belief to belief, we must distinguish sharply between the two questions: (1) From what, and to what, are we said to infer? (2) What are the initial and final psychological states of the person who infers?

Inference statements are to be analysed as a whole. Instead of explaining the nature of the entity which a man infers from, we say 'To infer from the fact that-p is to move from a true belief that-p'.

III. ARGUMENTS FOR THE CAUSAL CRITERION FOR INFERRING
(a). THE LACK OF AN ALTERNATIVE CRITERION

When we come to believe something, we do not infer it from everything else which we have come to believe. If it is inferred from some things which we believe, it is a good inference, from others it may be weak, or senseless. It would be flattering to humanity to hold the following criterion: *We infer from the facts we possess which make most reasonable the belief in question.* However, someone might learn certain things, and thus have a perfect right to infer that-q, and yet infer that-q from something else. He might not see that the facts he knows actually bear on the case, or he may think that something else supports the case better.

Also a person may be perfectly capable of seeing how certain parts of his knowledge bear on something he is wondering about, and yet it may not *strike* him that he knows what he needs in order to solve his problem. Finally a person may know that-p, know and realize that 'p' supports 'q' to a degree which he normally takes to be adequate as a basis for belief, and yet he simply may not proceed to the view that-q. This mental paralysis may be inexplicable to himself or to others. He may confess that he is irrational in it. Yet he may have to avow, in all honesty, that he does not hold that-q. It may well be typical in such cases that he should suspect the existence of some countervailing reason at the back of his mind. Yet it is not necessary to our understanding of the case that we insist either that he must have such a suspicion, or that he does have countervailing reasons.

Philosophers are not usually aware of the need for a criterion to specify the connection which must hold between the initial belief and the inferred belief. It is useful to think of the matter in the following way. Take the whole set of beliefs (including knowledge) which a man has held immediately prior to the time at which he infers that-q. To infer is to employ a certain proper subset of these beliefs. What is the criterion of membership of that subset? (For ease of expression I shall speak as if beliefs were inferred, and as if beliefs were the things from which we infer.) Plainly it will not do to say that the beliefs employed are to be picked out as those whose propositional content entails the content of the belief inferred. It may sometimes be the case that what we infer from entails what we infer, but this is neither a necessary nor a sufficient condition of those beliefs being the ones from which we infer. It is not a necessary condition for inferring, since people infer what is not entailed by anything which they believe. Also, entailment is not a sufficient condition for inferring, since a person may believe something which entails what he infers, and yet he may actually infer from something else. He may not realize the extent of his epistemic or doxastic riches.

The arguments deployed against the view that entailment is the criterion for the connection between the beliefs involved in inferring, are general enough to establish the following point. No weaker logical relation such as 'being reasonably based', 'implication', 'confirmation', or 'inductive support' is either a necessary or a sufficient condition of the connection which holds between beliefs in cases of inferring.

One powerful, although not demonstrative, argument for the causal criterion for inferring, is the failure of any other criterion which has been suggested. Such an argument rests on the presupposition that there must be some type of connection between the belief inferred from, and the belief inferred. It might be suggested that this presupposition is a distorted reflection of the real truth that the person who infers must merely *believe* that the initial belief makes the final belief at least reasonable or probable. Let us speak of the belief from which a man infers as an initial, or i-belief; of the belief which he infers as the concluded, or c-belief; and of the belief that the i-belief justifies him in holding the c-belief as the justification or j-belief.

Now we have seen that a person may believe both that-p and that 'p' adequately supports 'q', and yet not believe that-q. Hence it must be possible that when he does come to believe that-q, he does not infer from 'p', but is convinced on some other basis. Therefore we need a more substantial account of what it is for someone to hold one belief on the basis of something else which he believes.

To say that the causal criterion is generally necessary in the definition of inferring is to make a strong claim. It is to claim, amongst other things, that there is no special sub-class of cases in which a sufficient account of inferring could be given without implicit or explicit appeal to a causal connection between the i-belief and c-belief. It might be thought plain that if, at a certain time, a man is aware that he believes that-p, and is aware or at least consciously takes it that 'p' entails 'q', then he cannot but believe that-q. Surely, the critic might urge, the existence of these two consciously-held beliefs must be a logically sufficient condition of inferring. He might concede that this does not show that a causal criterion is not needed for cases in which a weaker i-belief was consciously held, or where the j-belief was not consciously held, or when no j-belief was held. (On such a view, no set of necessary conditions could be given, sufficient to define inferring. The concept of inferring would be a cluster concept.) But the position just outlined will not stand. The fundamental reason is that some real move must be involved in inferring.

Let us first suppose that it is logically possible for a person at the one time to think that-p, and to think that 'p' entails 'q', and yet not to believe that-q. In that case it is logically possible for him to believe that-q on some basis other than the belief that-p. Next, let us suppose that it is not logically possible for a person at the one time to think both that-p and that 'p' entails 'q', and yet not to think that-q. To infer he must acquire a belief on the basis of some other matter he accepts. At a certain time he may already think that-p and that 'p' entails 'q'. On the supposition which we are considering, it follows that he already thinks that-q, and hence cannot, at that time, infer it. On this supposition, if he *arrives* at the belief both that-p and that 'p' entails 'q', he will indeed arrive at the belief that-q. Yet even in this case, there can be no question of his inferring that-q from the supposed fact that-p. If his holding the belief that-p and that 'p' entails 'q', entails his holding the belief that-q, there can be no *sequence* of thought from his beliefs that-p and that 'p' entails 'q' to his holding that-q. If there is no sequence of thoughts or beliefs then there can be no inference. For if the person already has come to believe that-q when he came to believe that-p and that 'p' entailed 'q', then for the general reason that he cannot infer what he has already accepted, he cannot infer that-q.

We have now seen that in no case in which a man may be said to infer can it be true that his holding both the i-belief and the

j-belief entails his holding the c-belief. Hence our central problem arises again. What sort of connection is being said to hold between the i-belief and the c-belief when a person is said to infer? What can it be, other than to say that it is *because* he holds the i-belief that he holds the c-belief; that his holding the i-belief *makes* him hold the c-belief; that his holding the c-belief is *on account of*, or *due to* his holding the i-belief?

One final blow[1] can be dealt the thesis that, in inferring, the j-belief can adequately link the i-belief and c-belief. A person might be asked from what he inferred that-q. He may reply that it was from p's being the case, which supports very strongly the view that-q. Then he may pause, and say: 'But perhaps I am rationalizing. I was already strongly pre-disposed to think that-q, by that irrational fear I told you about a while ago.' The person is not, or need not, be wondering whether he does have the i-belief and the j-belief. Surely he is wondering whether his holding those beliefs did make him believe that-q. He is wondering whether his belief that-q really *is* due to those beliefs which would make him a paragon of logical virtue rather than a victim of his own emotions.

III(b).   THE ARGUMENT BY SUBTRACTION

A powerful argument for the necessity of a criterion C for the application of a concept F is this:

'Describe a case which satisfies all necessary conditions for the application of the concept F, except the candidate condition C, which is being argued to be necessary. If an unprejudiced description of the case makes plain that the case is not an instance of F, then it has been shown that C is a necessary condition of the proper application of the concept F.'

I call an argument of this form an argument by subtraction.

Let us attempt to construct an argument of the form just described. In fact, only a modified version of the form of argument is applicable, but it is useful to see it as a certain departure from the simple form described. Suppose that a person believes that-p, and believes that 'p' constitutes good support for believing that-q, but has not formed the belief that-q. (On hearing a good argument, it is rare for us to change our views immediately, even when we have no

---

[1] I owe this point to Professor D. M. Armstrong.

suspicion of unfair play or an unnoticed weakness in the argument. It simply takes some time for us to adjust our minds to holding a new view.) While the person is in this state of suspension of belief, he, in company with a dozen other people, is kidnapped by an unethical neuro-surgeon who wishes to test with live patients the hypothesis that a certain structure of neural connections is a sufficient condition for a person with a certain general educational background to hold the belief that-q. The other people have a similar background to that of our friend, but none of them believes that-q, nor has any reason to do so. Having been operated on without their knowledge, all now wake up from their anaesthesia, and each of them, in consequence of the operation, believes firmly that-q. Our friend believes that-q with the same degree of confidence as the others.

As for the others besides our friend, it would be absurd to say that they inferred that-q. As for him, although he passes any normal positive test for having inferred that-q, we must have the gravest doubts about whether, any more than the rest of the group, he has inferred that-q. We might ask him whether he believes that-p. He might then remember that he does, and that he has been convinced that 'p' supports 'q'. He might say, 'I suppose that the argument has been working on my mind, for I now firmly believe that-q.' Since the same operation was performed on him, it is most probable that neither the belief that-p nor the belief that 'p' supports 'q' played any part in his coming to believe that-q. Although he has come to hold that-q, it is probable nevertheless that he has not inferred it. It seems that if he has not, the reason can only be that his beliefs that-p and that 'p' supports 'q' played no part in his coming to believe that-q.

The foregoing would be a decisive argument by subtraction, were it plain that the man did *not* infer that-q. All I can say is that most probably he did not. The galling aspect of the matter is that the argument by subtraction cannot be a knock-down one for the very reason that a causal criterion is essential for inferring. This may seem a strange remark. The reason for it is this. A causal condition need not be a generally necessary condition for an effect which it helps to produce on a given occasion. That is well known. There are more ways of killing a cat than choking it with butter, to give the moral a different point. It is not so clearly realized that an operative part of the set of conditions which together bring about an effect may not be necessary, on a particular occasion, for the effect produced. (I mean by 'condition' not a specification, but a particular event or state of affairs which satisfies a specification.) It is not difficult to describe a mechanism in which, although one condition operated, yet if it had not, then another condition would have obtained at the same time so that the same effect would have been produced.[1] Since this is so, the fact that the neuro-surgeon created our friend's belief does not *prove* that it was not formed also on the basis of our friend's own beliefs.

If it is only because of the nature of causality that the argument by subtraction cannot be a clear and conclusive argument for the necessity of the causal criterion, then that detracts little from the argument. To put it dialectically, an opponent of the causal criterion will himself have to consider a causal view of inferring in order to explain that the necessity for the causal criterion has not been established. Therefore his criterion may properly be atacked *ad hominem*. Since a particular causal condition need not be necessary for its particular effect, one cannot say that a condition is not causal, merely on the ground that the effect would have occurred in any case. On the basis of the case described, I *can* say that whether or not he had heard the reasons for it, our friend would have believed that-q. It cannot strictly be deduced that there was no inference from the reasons he heard before the operation. Equally, it cannot be deduced that the argument could begin firmly from the premise that those beliefs had no effect on his coming to believe that-q. However, the argument by subtraction would then fail completely, since a necessary condition other than the causal one would have been omitted. It is easy to see that if a person is to infer from p's being the case, he must at that time believe that-p.

Despite these difficulties, the essence of the argument by subtraction can still be preserved. There is doubt about whether the person has inferred that-q from p's being the case (or from anything at all). Yet he seems to have passed any normally accepted test for inferring. Unless a causal criterion for inferring is necessary, what can we be in doubt about? We wonder whether his believing that-p had any effect on his coming to believe that-q. Let us suppose that it did not: all that was operative was the surgeon's apparatus. In that case, there is no causal connection between the person's previous beliefs, and his belief that-q. Surely if *only* the

---

[1] A more detailed consideration of this matter may be found in 'Remembering', C. B. Martin and M. Deutscher, *Philosophical Review*, Vol. LXXV, 1966, pp. 178–80.

surgeon's work had *any* part to play in producing our friend's belief that-q, then he did not infer that-q! No matter how clear-cut an argument by subtraction may be, there comes a point at which each person must decide in terms of his own understanding of the concept being tested, whether the omitted condition is necessary. Surely, to suppose that only the surgeon's interference had any effect on our friend's coming to believe that-q, is to suppose that he did not infer that-q.

Let us look at the matter from another point of view. When we wonder whether the man *did* infer that-q, what can be in question? We know that he held an i-belief and a j-belief and that he has come to hold the corresponding c-belief. I can think of nothing which is in doubt, other than the answer to the question 'Were his i-beliefs and his j-beliefs at least part of the source of his c-belief?' The question about the source can only be 'Did his belief that-p, etc., make any difference to his coming to hold that-q?'[1]

I conclude from the preceding arguments that it is not logically possible for a person to infer that-q, from p's being the case, unless his believing that-p is at least part of the cause of his believing that-q.

Like most criteria which interest philosophers, this one is followed in practice rather than enunciated by the users of it. But it comes close to the surface in the following common type of case. Someone is asked what he inferred from. He makes a few statements concerning things which he was told, and something he has seen. We say 'Is that all you inferred from? Are you sure that you were influenced only by those considerations?'

In claiming that we need a causal criterion for inference, I have not said that we ordinarily have any knowledge of the processes which mediate between one belief and another. All we ordinarily mean is that the first belief causes the second, *in some way or another*. At some time a physiologist may discover the particular nature of the way in which the connection is achieved. It is hard to see in what other way more could be known about the connection.

The conjecture presupposes that beliefs may either be states of

---

[1] We have noted that something may be part of the cause of another, though that effect would have occurred without that part of the cause. Yet while it may have made no difference whether a particular condition did occur, the condition makes a difference if it does occur. Paradoxically, it makes a difference, though there would have been no difference had it not occurred. The sound of paradox disappears when we recollect that had it not occurred, something else would have made the same difference.

the brain, or at the least, that they may determine and be produced by such states of the brain. Of course it is no part of the *concept* of inference, that inferring should be a change in the central nervous system. Nevertheless, it is interesting to notice that given the proposed analysis of the concept, together with some highly probable neuro-physiological facts, the most reasonable conjecture is that inferring involves some sort of change in the central nervous system. If a more radical conjecture is correct, and beliefs may be *identified* as states of the central nervous system, then inferring is a certain change in the central nervous system.

IV(*a*). REMEMBERING AND INFERRING

Must a person be able to remember that-*p*, at the time when he infers from the fact that-*p*? As the concept of inference stands in ordinary language, I doubt that this question has a definite answer. The usual sort of situation when we infer is this: we have acquired a good deal of information, and then we speak as if new and striking information alone justifies holding a new belief. (Notice the analogy with our way of speaking about causes.) Then we talk of inferring from the striking new facts. The other background material is not recalled, and most of it cannot be. But it may be both causally operative, and also essential to justify the belief that-*q*. For instance, I might infer that someone is a good philosopher from the fact that a friend of mine speaks well of him. But I would not have come to believe this, if I had not known from considerable experience of my friend, that he was a competent judge of philosophers. I would not have been justified in my inference without this general experience. When we say that we have learned 'from experience', and cannot say anything more, then we are expressing the belief that what has happened in the past justifies our present belief, although we may be unable to say what has justified it.

Should we say that, in such cases, I *infer* from my particular past experiences? Plainly, there is no difficulty in saying that I infer from the fact that I have had considerable experience of my friend's judgment, since I do consciously believe that. All that is in question is whether I should say that I (unconsciously) also infer from the *particular experiences* of my friend's judgment.

To settle the issue, it is sufficient to insist that I cannot infer from what I do not at the time believe. If I can no longer recall the particular experiences of my friend's judgments then the content of my *present* belief is, presumably, only that I have had experience of my friend's good judgment, or heard about it from someone else whose judgment I have reason to trust, or the like. And so the fact which I infer from (amongst other things) is that I have had some experience of my friend's good judgments. In these cases, what is of more than linguistic importance is to recognize that past experience may justify, as well as produce, present beliefs and habits even though that past experience cannot be recalled.

IV(*b*). A RESTRICTION ON THE CAUSAL CRITERION

Moore[1] suggested a causal account of inference, and a certain counter-case against it. The restriction proposed in this section covers his difficulty. A person's belief that-*p* can be causally operative for the acquisition of his belief that-*q*, but in a manner completely irrelevant to the question of inference. As a result of believing that-*p*, a person A might tell a friend, B, that-*p*. B might then infer that-*q*, and as a result tell A that-*q*. Thus A might, as a result of his having believed that-*p*, come to believe that-*q*. He may well happen to think that the fact that-*p* makes it likely that-*q*, but it still does not follow that he infers from the fact that-*p*. One possibility is that his belief that-*p* inclined him to infer that-*q*, and his friend's saying so clinched the matter. I wish to consider the other possibility, viz. that the person does not infer at all from the fact that-*p*, but simply believes what his friend says. The difficulty is that A's belief that-*p* is an operative condition of his coming to believe that-*q*, and yet he simply believes that-*q* because he is told it, and does not infer that-*q* from the fact that-*p*.

I cannot evade this difficulty simply by ruling that no such telling by someone else must be an operative condition of a person's coming to believe that-*q*. Such a requirement would be too strong, as the following case shows.

Our person, A, is rather inclined but not yet prepared to infer that-*q*, from the fact that-*p*. Previously A told his friend that-*p*. His friend infers that-*q*, and tells A that-*q*. A is then prepared to believe that-*q*, and thus infers it *both* from the fact that-*p*, and from his friend telling him that-*q*. This problem would arise in any case in which a person's earlier belief resulted in an observation which intervened in the causal chain between that earlier belief

---

[1] Moore's suggestion is published in the *Commonplace Book of G. E. Moore*, edited by Casimir Lewy, London, 1962, p. 7.

and the subsequent belief in the inferred fact. (For brevity, I shall from now on mention only the case of an intervening observation.) The rule which will solve the difficulty is this:

> *Criterion 3b. If some observation X is an intervening factor between the belief that-p, and the belief that-q, then the belief that-p must be operative in producing the belief that-q, in the circumstance that X obtains, and not merely operative for producing the circumstance X.*

The belief that-p must not be operative only *for* the intervening observation. What must be made clear is the difference between:

B_1 (belief that-p) being operative *for* O (the observation) which in turn helps to bring about B_2 (belief that-q)

and

B_1 being operative *in* the circumstance O which helps to bring about B_2.

This may appear forbidding, but a simple example should make clear what I mean.

Case A

A brick is thrown according to the pre-arranged signal of a low-pitched whistle. It is partly because of the whistle that the brick is thrown. The brick then breaks a window. Thus the low-pitched whistle is, by transitivity, an operative condition *for* the window's being broken. But it is not operative in bringing it about that the window is broken *in* the circumstance that a brick was thrown at it.

This distinction can be hard to see. Compare the case just described with the following one in which the whistle is operative both for, and in, the circumstance that a ball is thrown.

Case B

A tennis ball is thrown according to the pre-arranged signal of a high-pitched whistle. It is partly because of the whistle that the ball is thrown. The ball may not be thrown hard enough to break the window by itself. The additional effect of the sound waves from the whistle may also be needed. Thus the high-pitched whistle is operative both *for* and *in* the circumstance that the ball is thrown.

The following diagrams picture the difference between the cases:

CASE A   Whistle ⟶ Brick thrown ⟶ Window broken
CASE B   Whistle ⟶ Ball thrown ⟶ Window broken
                    ⟶

The rule deals with the previous difficulty about the man who believes what he is told rather than inferring it. The man's belief that-p was a factor involved in bringing about hearing his friend maintain that-q, and this perception was a factor involved in his coming to believe that-q. The new rule correctly excludes this as a case of inferring since the man's belief that-p was not a factor involved in bringing about his belief that-q, *in* the circumstance of his hearing from his friend that-q. At that stage it was causally irrelevant whether he had ever believed that-p.

IV(*c*).   INFERENCE, AND BELIEF THAT 'p' MAKES 'q' IN SOME DEGREE PROBABLE

(1) *Is the Criterion Necessary?*

Some want to say that a move must be to some extent reasonable if it is to be called inference. This is a mistake. Inferences may be reasonable. Also they can be rash, unwise, or senseless. A man may astutely infer from the way someone speaks that he is lying, or he may insanely infer from the wilting of the flowers that the sun will not rise the next day. One may easily be hypnotized by the implication of the first person present tense. If a person makes any assertion in an unqualified direct manner, then he implies that he is in a position to do so. It would be absurd to infer from this that *part* of every assertion is the implied claim that the speaker is reasonable. When a person asserts that the cat is on the mat, *that* is what he asserts, and there is an end to it. When a person says that he infers, it is his saying so which implies that he thinks he is not unreasonable in inferring. This gives us no reason to suppose that what he says is false if he is unreasonable in his inference.

Must the person believe that, in the light of what he already knows, the fact that-p makes it at least likely that-q? ('At least' is inserted, since one might believe that the fact that-p makes it *certain* that-q.)

This belief, as will be made clear in the next section, is equivalent to the belief that what makes it reasonable to believe that-p, includes what makes it reasonable to believe that-q. It is what I called a j-belief.

It is cavalier to say that we have a case of inference whenever one belief is causally operative (in the way circumscribed in the previous section) in producing another. If we thought that the causal criterion specified a *sufficient* condition for inferring then we should have to say that the following was a case of inferring. A man rightly thinks that he is rude to anyone in authority over him whom he does not respect. He also rightly thinks that he will not be promoted in his office if he is rude to the boss. As a result of these beliefs and a desire to get on, he comes to think that the boss is not such a contemptible man after all. After a time, he might suddenly realize that he has changed his opinion of the boss, and might be shrewd enough to guess what has happened to him. Although he realizes that two of his beliefs have made him hold a third, he does not thereby think he has made the following inference: 'I will not get on if I am rude to the boss; I will be rude to anyone in authority whom I despise; hence the boss is not contemptible.' A man would have to be very stupid to infer in such a way. The man in the office, however, need not be stupid. He shows a certain weakness of character rather than of intelligence. In fact a person requires firmness of character and personal insight to combat such subtle tendencies to modify and conform in his opinions. From this it might seem that it is a necessary condition for inferring that the person should have a j-belief. Yet this would not be correct. We have seen that, if the requisite j-belief is held in addition to the satisfaction of the causal criteria, then inferring has occurred. Nevertheless the following case shows that holding a belief is not a generally necessary condition for inferring.

A person may know full well that he has come to believe that most Belgians are rogues because he was twice cheated by Belgians. He may say: 'I cannot dispute that I am unreasonable to infer in that way. I am not trying to justify myself when I say that I inferred that-q, from what I took to be the fact that-p. It is just that I cannot but admit that I did in fact infer in this way. I cannot imagine that, even at the time, I really thought that it was reasonable to infer from my limited experience that most Belgians are rogues.'[1]

---

[1] D. G. Brown (*op. cit.*, pp. 351–69) claims that when I say that I infer from 'p' to 'q', I present 'p' as a sufficient reason for 'q'. This is surely false. At the very least one must qualify it to 'I present "p" as making up a sufficient reason when taken in conjunction with other things I know, or reasonably believe'. Even so, the claim will mislead unless set against the point that I can confess to having inferred in a way which I did not at the time and do not now regard as reasonable.

This last case might suggest that it would be sufficient for inferring that the person concerned should be aware that his holding one belief makes him hold another. What might be necessary in addition to the causal condition is that either the man holds a *j*-belief and partly on that account comes to hold that-*q*, or else that he is aware that he is believing that-*p* is making him believe that-*q*. (Thus we would deal also with the case of the man in the office.)

Unfortunately we would still be in error. Suppose that you found that when you heard the birds twittering, you could not help thinking that the third world war was about to begin. You know that there is nothing about the twittering, or the circumstances in which the twittering occurs, or any fact which you know or believe but cannot recall at the moment, which would make it at all rational to suppose that the third world war is imminent, but this does not control the way you think. Would you not disclaim responsibility for the way you are thinking? It was no more irrational of you to move from the twittering of the birds to the outbreak of the third world war than it is dishonest of a kleptomaniac to take other people's property. If a person has made an inference, then it is possible to say of him that he was reasonable or unreasonable, or even that it was totally irrational of him to have made such a move. In my view, since you would be a subject of pity and commiseration rather than of criticism and logical education, it would be incorrect and unfair to say that you had inferred.

It is possible to describe a move as one which a person is reasonable or unreasonable in making, only upon the following condition: the person's own view about the legitimacy of the move from '*p*' to '*q*' exercises some degree of control over his transition from his believing that-*p* to his believing that-*q*. Nevertheless, something may support someone's belief, whether or not the person himself can judge the degree of support for his belief. This point can be brought out by considering the case of intelligent animals. A dog's judgment about how to deal with sheep may be subtle and manifest. But it seems strained and unreal to suggest that the dog has beliefs about the degree of experiential support for its practical judgment. So far as I can see, it is simply for that reason that we do not wish to speak of the dog as reasonable or unreasonable, although it may be cunning or stupid. Equally, we do not want to say that it infers that the sheep ought to be handled circumspectly, though certainly it knows how to handle the sheep, and has learned this from experience.

H

At the moment, we are in a pretty pickle. One case (the man in the office) suggests that a person who infers should think that his move is reasonable. Another case (the man deceived by Belgians) shows that a person who infers need not think that his move is reasonable, since he may never have thought the move reasonable and still have to admit that he did infer that Belgians are rogues. Yet another case shows that if a man infers, then his own view that a move is completely senseless must be able to exercise some control over what he is inclined to think.

The concept of inferring may be a ragbag, indiscriminately stuffed with unrelated pieces. Yet we ought not concede too readily that there is no set of necessary and sufficient conditions.

These three cases may be dealt with in one consistent and non-disjunctive account. We merely need to require that the person who infers that-q must at least think that his move is not completely unreasonable, and that this view should exercise control over his holding the belief that-q. The man in the office does not satisfy this condition; the man taken down by Belgians does satisfy it; the man in the grip of senseless thoughts fails the test. In each case we have the correct result.

I can think of one remaining hurdle. Is not a child said to infer things before anyone would dream of asserting that it had opinions about the rationality of its beliefs? Might not a child infer that when its mother offers a teaspoon of food with an unusually bright smile, the spoon holds something nasty? Once we have conceded this, we can recognize also that where a person's move *is* well based and sensible, as is the child's, we are prepared to waive the condition that the one who infers should have an opinion about the rationality of his move. The more logical a person's process of belief, the less it matters, to the question whether he infers, that he should consider his move logical. The more senseless a process of thought, the more we insist that, if it is to be described as an inference, then at least the person himself must think that his moves are not completely silly. What do we have here? A real case of a disjunctive condition, or myopia and dull wits?

It is important to note that we can still, of course, distinguish the case of the intelligent dog from the knowing child. The latter is capable of learning to evaluate its own processes of thought. (I do not mean to join that crowd of rash philosophers who claim *a priori*, that no animal could evaluate its activities.)

(2) *How is the criterion to be satisfied?*

What is it, at the time that one comes to believe that-q, to believe that in the light of what one believes, the fact that-p makes it to some degree likely that-q? The belief cannot be analysed even partially in terms of what the person would say were he asked or if he considered the matter. For if he were asked, or were he to consider the matter, he might change his mind and come to think that he was not justified. If he had not been asked, then perhaps he would have continued to believe that he was justified. A rule that anyone who infers should be generally prepared to make similar moves, would be at once too weak and too strong. It is too weak because a person might regularly be caused by a certain type of belief to hold a belief of another given type, and yet never infer. The man in the office might modify his belief not infrequently in the way described in this case. The rule would be too strong, since a person might for only a brief period be prepared to make an inference.

If we allow that this man's j-belief need be no more than unconscious, it would be hard to say how it differed from a mere propensity to come to believe that-q on coming to believe that-p. In that case we would not have succeeded in strengthening the first three criteria.

There is no doubt that a man does infer if he satisfies the first three criteria and also, at t_x, consciously takes it that the fact that-p in some way, in the light of his other beliefs, makes it reasonable to conclude that-q, and on that account comes to believe that-q. Also it is enough if his j-belief is preconscious, in that if he is asked whether he had the j-belief at t_x, he can fairly readily recollect that at some previous time he had consciously held it, and has no reason to believe that he has since changed his mind. To go further than listing such sufficient conditions, is to attempt to analyse fully what it is to hold a belief that one thing supports another. This must be set aside as another project.

I conclude this section with the remark that in some cases the i-belief and the j-belief are fused. When a man astutely infers from the look on someone's face that he is dishonest, his i-belief is, of course, not merely 'that there is something about his face'. There is 'something' about anyone's face. His i-belief might be relevantly characterized only as the belief that there is something of deep dishonesty in the friendly smiles and open frank eyes. Perhaps there is something too steady about the gaze: the man is doing what he thinks an honest person does, and keeping it up a little too long. In consequence of this characterization of the *i*-belief, there is no separate characterization of the *j*-belief. The *j*-belief can have only the unilluminating form: 'If the man has the look of dishonesty, then in the light of my other beliefs (in this case, that nothing I have already learned indicates that he really is honest) it is at least to some degree reasonable to believe that the man is dishonest.'

V. INFERENCE AND JUSTIFICATION

Earlier, when I argued that to infer that-*q* from the fact that-*p* is to come to believe that-*q* as a result of believing that-*p*, I denied that we should 'strictly' be said to infer from our believing that-*p*, to our believing that-*q*. To infer from one's believing that-*p* is quite another matter, and not the same inference expressed more strictly. This might be accepted as a brute fact, but I am puzzled by it. Why does the analysis not show that really we infer from our believing things, even if we do not ordinarily speak in that way? Furthermore, come to think of it, if I explain that we may speak of inferring not only from what we observe, but also from things as 'remote' as the existence of mammoths in the Ice Age, by saying that we move from our *belief* about them, how can this tie in with the justification for the belief which I gain by inference? Surely my justification is neither the past existence of mammoths, nor something so personal as my own beliefs about them. If I infer from *p*'s being the case, is not *p*'s being the case my ground or justification for coming to believe what I do? In what way should one understand this? The existence of mammoths cannot be a justification without further ado. Yet the alternative cannot be that I am justified because I hold beliefs. We must distinguish between 'What do we infer from?' and 'What grounds have we for coming to believe?' The answers to these questions are not necessarily the same. Although we infer from the past existence of mammoths, it is not their past existence, but rather our present basis for thinking that they existed, which provides us with a basis for inferring the reason why men used to live in caves.

Someone will object, 'Having a basis X for a certain belief cannot always boil down to believing that X exists on some basis Y. This would involve a regress in any account of justification for belief.' This objection is perfectly sound. What it shows is that not all cases of having well-based beliefs are cases of having inferred beliefs.[1] In ordinary speech, to believe as a result of seeing something, that it exists, is not to infer. Neither in terms of the present analysis is it to infer. When we see something, we believe, but because of what we observe. Take another example. If you have a headache, normally you know without inference that you have a headache. When we infer, we think one thing because of something else we *think*. When we know we have a headache, we think so because of what we *feel*. Hence, when we deny that knowledge by observation and knowledge of experience and sensations are cases of inference, we have no need to rely on the dubious claim that an eyewitness report or a person's judgments about his own sensations are incorrigible or infallible.

In conclusion, I wish to employ these remarks about inference and ground in order to support and clarify this claim: to infer from the fact that-*p* is not to infer from one's believing that-*p*. I have argued that if we infer that-*q* (only) from the fact that-*p*, then our basis for believing that-*q* is included in our basis for believing that-*p*. Thus, if we infer only from the fact that mammoths roamed during the Ice Age that men in the Ice Age lived in caves for safety, then our basis for thinking that men lived in caves for safety is included in our reasons for thinking that mammoths roamed during the Ice Age. For those of us who have not done the palaeontology ourselves, this basis would be our reading certain accounts in books, and our basis for believing what we read. If we said that in inferring from the fact that-*p* we were really inferring from our believing that-*p*, it would follow that our basis for believing that-*q* was to be found in our basis for believing *that we believed* that-*p*. In the 'Ice Age' case we would have to say that our reason for believing that men lived in caves was to be found in our reason for believing *that we believed* that mammoths were roaming during the Ice Age. This is ridiculous. The reason which we have for thinking that mammoths roamed is at least some reason for thinking that men lived in caves for safety. But the reason which we have for believing that we believe that mammoths roamed is no reason at all for thinking that men lived in caves for safety.

Normally, one's state of belief that-*q* is itself the basis on which

[1] See W. D. Joske, 'Inferring and Perceiving', *Philosophical Review*, Vol. LXXII, 1963, particularly pp. 442–3.

one thinks that one believes that-q. This is not to deny that cases can be found in which someone infers from his own behaviour that he has a certain belief. I have tried to make it clear why we cannot infer from believing that-p what we can infer from p's being the case.

Consider what you might infer from your believing that-p. If, for instance, you have the habit of refusing to believe until evidence is produced, then, finding yourself with a belief, you may be entitled to infer that you were at some time given reason to believe it. But what your holding of a certain belief entitles you to infer, is very different from what you may infer if you are entitled to hold that belief.

6

D. M. ARMSTRONG

COLOUR-REALISM AND THE ARGUMENT FROM MICROSCOPES

In this philosophical theory of perception, a Realist is one who holds with Berkeley's Hylas that 'to exist is one thing, to be perceived another'. A Colour Realist is therefore one who holds that the colour of the surface of an object, or the colour of an object as a whole, exists independently of its being perceived.

A Realist may be either a Direct or a Representative Realist. A Direct Realist holds that, in at least some cases, perception gives us a direct, that is, *non-inferential*, awareness of the nature of physical phenomena. A Representative Realist denies that perception can ever give us such non-inferential awareness. Clearly, it would be possible to be either a Direct or a Representative Realist about colour. In this paper, however, I will only be concerned with a *Direct* Realist account of colour.

What I shall contend in particular, is that an argument that is given its classical statement in Berkeley's *First Dialogue*, an argument that may be baptized the 'Argument from Microscopes', and which Berkeley and many others have thought refutes Direct Realism about colour, in fact does not do so. I have, of course, an interest in rebutting the Argument from Microscopes. I believe that Direct Realism about colour is correct. But here I will only be concerned with rebutting the Argument from Microscopes. Other, and powerful, arguments against a Direct Colour Realism will go unanswered. Still less will I be concerned to defend Direct Realism generally, although I also believe the general doctrine to be true.

One final preliminary. A Direct Colour Realism may be held in two forms, which may be called the Anti-Reductivist and the Reductivist form respectively. An Anti-Reductivist holds that the colour of a surface, for instance, is an irreducible quality perfectly distinct from, although no doubt correlated with, the light-waves emitted from that surface. A Reductivist, however, holds that the colour of the surface is nothing but the light-waves emitted from that surface, or something of that sort. I myself accept not only a Direct Realist view of colour, but also a Reductivist account of the nature of colour. (I have argued for this view of colour, and the other secondary qualities, in *A Materialist Theory of the Mind*, London, 1967, Chapter 12.) But the rebuttal of the Argument from Microscopes here attempted is entirely independent of whether an Anti-Reductivist or a Reductivist view is taken of the nature of colour.

The point is important because in this paper I shall speak of 'correlating' colour of surface with the light-waves emitted from that surface. Now it is tempting to say that we can only correlate what are distinct things, and so that to talk of correlation is to be committed to an Anti-Reductivist view.

But this is a mistake. We can talk of 'correlating' while leaving it open whether the things correlated are distinct or not. The following example was given by Keith Campbell in discussion. We might correlate the characteristics of the criminal as deduced from clues at the scene of the crime with the characteristics known to be possessed by a certain suspect. Such correlation may leave it an open question whether the criminal and the suspect are, or are not, one and the same person. In the same way, talk of 'correlating' light-waves emitted from surfaces with colours of surfaces can leave it an open question whether light-waves and colour are, or are not, identical.

It can hardly be denied, even by the Direct Realist about colour, that some colour appearances are *mere* appearances. The distant hills look blue, but their surface is not really blue in colour. The problem arises for the Realist, therefore, how we can distinguish real colour of surfaces or objects from merely apparent colour.

In the *First Dialogue* Hylas begins by saying that the merely apparent colours are those which:

'appearing only at a distance, vanish upon a nearer approach' (*Works*, ed. Luce and Jessop, Vol. 2, p. 184).

A contemporary philosopher might say instead that real colours are those presented to normal observers in standard conditions. The observer's power of sight must be normal, light must be adequate, and the observer must be able to inspect the object quite closely. Under such conditions, the colours that appear are the real colours.

It is at this point that Berkeley brings in the objection from microscopes. Microscopes are instruments of revelation. They make us aware of many of the small-scale features of objects that we would not be aware of otherwise. But in the case of colours:

'. . . a microscope often discovers colours in an object different from those perceived by the unassisted sight.'

A drop of blood looks red all over to the naked eye. But, under the microscope, only a small amount of the area appears to be red: it is mostly colourless. The same thing, at the same time, and in the same part, cannot be differently coloured, or simultaneously be coloured and colourless. So the colour appearance presented to the naked eye and the colour appearance presented under the microscope cannot both be the real colour.

But now we are faced with the difficulty that there seems to be no reason to prefer one viewing condition to the other. It is logically possible that the lenses in our eyes should have had the magnifying power of the lenses in microscopes. In these circumstances, Hylas would have said that the microscopic colours were the real colours. It therefore seems totally arbitrary to select any particular magnification as the revealer of reality. So how do we determine real colour?

I shall first consider two answers to this question that I think are unsatisfactory, and then propose my own solution of the problem.

THE 'PHENOMENALIST' SOLUTION

Some philosophers react to the Argument from Microscopes by saying that what it proves is that all we *mean* by the real as opposed to the apparent colour of a surface or object is 'the colour appearance presented to a normal observer under standard conditions'. A normal observer is an ordinary observer with ordinary sensory equipment, including ordinary eyes. Standard conditions involve ordinary light, ordinary distances, ordinary physical conditions generally. If we look at an object under a microscope, then conditions of observation cannot be said to be standard. So the colour presented, if different from that presented in the standard cases, is a mere appearance. Philosophers who take this line freely admit, indeed insist, that *if* men had microscopic eyes, then the colour appearance presented to normal observers in standard conditions would be different, and so the real colour would be different. But men have not got such eyes, and so a drop of blood really is red, although it *looks* a different colour under the microscope.

This solution of the problem does offer an account of the distinction between real and apparent colour. But it does so at the cost of abandoning a Direct Realism about colour. For it gives an account of real colour as being nothing but a sub-species of apparent colour: apparent colour presented to normal observers under standard conditions. If the Argument from Microscopes is simply presented as an argument against the possibility of distinguishing real from apparent colour, then it seems to be met by drawing this distinction between standard and non-standard conditions of observation. But we are considering the Argument from Microscopes *as an argument against a Direct Realist account of colour.* The claim that we are trying to combat is that, in view of the evidence provided by microscopes, it is impossible to draw the distinction between real and apparent colour without abandoning the view that the (real) colours of things exist independently of their perceivers and can be (sometimes) directly perceived. So the 'Phenomenalist' solution is not available to us. It may be that the Argument from Microscopes forces us to abandon Direct Realism about colour. But let us see first whether there are any alternatives.

THE 'MINIMUM VISIBILE' SOLUTION

I pass on to consider a second solution. It is sometimes pointed out that when we look at an object under a microscope then, in general, the amount of the surface area perceived is so small that it is less than the least area that can be discerned by the naked eye. But, where this is the case, do the observations made by the microscope really conflict with the observations made by the naked eye? Is there any difficulty in supposing that very tiny areas may differ in colour from the overall colour of the surface?

Another observation made with microscopes may be adduced as a parallel. A line may look perfectly straight to the naked eye, but portions of the line, when viewed under the microscope, may not look straight at all. Is there any conflict of appearances here? It would seem not. The naked eye, let us say, is capable of discriminations of straightness to the nearest hundredth of an inch. Now the line may not merely look, but actually be, straight to that degree of approximation. The microscope, let us say, is capable of discriminations of straightness to the nearest ten-thousandth of an inch. Now the line viewed under the microscope may not merely look, but actually be, crooked to this stricter degree of approximation. So these observations with naked eye and microscope are perfectly compatible. It is true that there is an element of illusion in the case. The portion viewed under the microscope may look as big as the whole line viewed with the naked eye. But if this illusion is allowed for, both perceptions can be accepted as otherwise veridical. This, it may be suggested, is a model for colours perceived under a microscope.

In fact, however, it seems that the parallel cannot be maintained. Imagine that a microscope is deployed bit by bit over the whole of an area easily visible to the naked eye. A certain colour picture of the area could be built up—it could be literally pictured on some much larger area—which will, in general, be incompatible with the colour appearances presented to the naked eye. Thus, a drop of blood looks red all over to the naked eye, but a colour picture of the same drop obtained by deploying a microscope over the whole surface of the drop would not contain very much red.

This incompatibility between the deliverances of the naked eye and the microscope becomes still clearer when we contemplate the (logical) possibility of perceiving the whole drop of blood in one view, but with eyes that have the resolving power of microscopes. The colour pattern presented would be incompatible with the colour pattern presented to an ordinary eye. But in the case of the line there would be no conflict between ordinary eye and microscopic eye. The microscopic eye would simply see more detail. We might compare the latter to the case of a man who can see that the hen is speckled, but cannot make out how many speckles it has, but who then comes closer and can distinguish and number the speckles.

So it seems that, although this solution is not incompatible with a Direct Realist account of colour, it fails to solve the microscope problem for independent reasons.

THE 'SCIENTIFIC' SOLUTION

I pass on to what I take to be the proper answer of a Direct Realist about colour to the Argument from Microscopes. The principle of the answer is this: it is a question to be decided on *scientific* grounds what are the real colours of surfaces and objects. No mere thinking, no mere analysis of the concept of colour, can settle the matter. There is no question of finding a criterion which will logically determine the question. The best we can hope to do is to find an answer that is scientifically plausible.

And so, since it is colour that we are discussing, we are brought to the conclusion that the real colour of a surface is determined by the nature of the light-waves emitted from that surface. If a surface looks red, and is emitting light-waves of a sort or sorts characteristic of red surfaces, it is red. If it looks red, but is not emitting such a sort or sorts of light-waves, it only looks red. There is nothing logically sacrosanct about this answer, it is simply the best scientific guess we can make on the basis of available knowledge. (All this, remember, is abstracting from the further question —which also, I maintain, is to be decided on grounds of scientific plausibility—whether the colour is or is not *identical* with the light-waves.)

But does the appeal to scientifically established correlates really do much to answer the Argument from Microscopes? It is natural to counter what has been said so far in the following way. It is clear that any scientific hypothesis about the correlation of colour and light-waves must ultimately be tested by observation. We must *see* that a certain object has a certain colour, and then establish that the object does emit light-waves of a sort predicted by the hypothesis. But this means that we must *begin* with some idea of which are the real, as opposed to the merely apparent, colours. Once we have a plausible theory it will be possible to turn back and, in the interests of coherence, eliminate some of the cases which were originally taken to be veridical colour perceptions. But we cannot saw away the whole branch that we sit upon. It must therefore be accepted that, *by and large*, the cases taken to be veridical perceptions during the investigation will reappear as veridical in the final theory.

But now, the argument continues, what cases do we begin by taking to be veridical? Surely it must be the colour appearances presented to normal observers under standard conditions? But, if so, it is these cases that, *by and large*, will reappear in the final theory as cases of veridical perception. In that case, however, the appearances exhibited under a microscope, being incompatible in content with our ordinary perceptions, must, *by and large*, be illusory.

Once this conclusion is granted, the question can be renewed why normal vision should be thus honoured. Have not the colours that appear under the microscope at least as much right to be accounted the real colours of objects? It seems that the appeal to light-waves has simply gone a long way round to enforce the view that the real colours are those that appear to normal observers under standard conditions. Yet the Argument from Microscopes seems to show that this account is quite arbitrary.

I shall now try to show, however, that the 'scientific' solution to the problem posed by the Argument from Microscopes need not simply end up by endorsing ordinary perception. The Direct Realist about colour may, if detailed scientific considerations seem to warrant it, conclude that the microscope, not the naked eye, is the best guide to the real colour of objects.

The first point to be made is that the colour of a surface must clearly be correlated with the light-waves that are actually being emitted *at the surface*. For surely the colour of a surface is an intrinsic, as opposed to a relational, property of the surface? The real colour of the surface must therefore be a function of what goes on at the surface. It is only indirectly a function of the stimulation that actually enters the eye.

Let us now consider the case of the hills that look blue in the distance although they are not in fact blue. I discussed this illusion recently with a psychologist who works in the field of perception, and he denied that it was an illusion at all. I think his denial was mistaken because the hills *look* to have a colour that they do not in fact have, and failure of correspondence of perception to reality is a sufficient condition for perceptual illusion. But we can sympathize with his denial, because it is true that the *perceiver* is in no way causally responsible for the illusory character of the perception. The illusion is not due to the way the perceiver's eye or brain function. For the illusion is brought about by the presence of air between the perceiver and the surface of the object. The air prevents all except those patterns of light-waves that are associated with blue surfaces from reaching the eye. As we might put it, the eye does its best with the light-wave that it is given. Illusion arises because what it is given is not a true sample of the light-waves actually emitted at the surface.

There is a connected point about this case, a point of the greatest importance. Despite the illusion about the colour of the hills involved, we can use the case to build up or test hypotheses about the correlation of light-waves with the (real) colours of surfaces. For suppose we now consider, not the light-waves emitted at the surface of the hills, but the light-waves that actually enter the eye. We can properly correlate these survivors with blueness *of surface*. For if the sort or sorts of light-waves that actually entered the eye had been a representative sample of the light-waves actually emitted at the surface of the hill, then we would have been justified in saying that that surface was really blue. To repeat the point briefly: The wave-lengths that enter the eye are the 'blue' wave-lengths. So if these wave-lengths only are emitted at a certain surface, we are justified in saying that the surface is blue.

Now to use the discussion of this case to bolster the 'scientific' solution to the problems raised by the Argument from Microscopes. My suggestion is that the case of the distant hills stands to normal perception under standard conditions much as this normal perception stands to perception aided by microscopes. For what does a microscope do? It brings to the eye a much larger sample of the light-rays emitted from a particular portion of a surface than reach the naked eye from that portion of the surface. Relative to that portion of the surface, much more 'information' (in the engineering sense) enters the eye. Now the correlations between colour and wave-length that are built up in standard conditions of colour perception, can in fact only be correlations between colour and the waves that actually enter, and so influence, the eye. But if the waves that actually affect the eye are a bad or misleading sample of the waves emitted at the surface, then it would be possible to conclude that the real colour of the surface is not the colour that appears to normal perceivers in standard conditions. Yet, at the same time, the correlations between colour and wave-length built up in standard conditions could still be used as a guide to the real colours of surfaces, provided the correlations were based on the wave-lengths that actually managed to arrive at, and so to affect, the eye.

And so, *if detailed considerations of physical theory should warrant it*, it would seem perfectly possible for the Direct Realist to maintain that it is the microscope, and not the naked eye, that is our best guide to the colour of a surface. The microscope certainly brings us a bigger sample of the light-waves from a certain area. The way is therefore open to argue that it is a less misleading sample. Whether detailed considerations of physical theory do *in fact* enforce this conclusion, is hardly for the philosopher to say.

Nor does the contemplation of endlessly more powerful microscopes create any theoretical difficulty. For there is a theoretical limit to the process: the perfect instrument that captured, without distorting, *all* the light-waves emitted from a certain surface.

In this way, I suggest, the Direct Realist about colour can come to terms with the Argument from Microscopes. The line of argument involves allowing that there is nothing logically sacrosanct about the ordinary paradigms of colour. A drop of freshly drawn blood looks red all over to normal perceivers in standard conditions, and is a very suitable object to teach a child 'what redness is'. We can admit these facts, and yet still say it makes sense to deny the drop is really red all over. I do not think that there is anything counter-intuitive in this, although it does run counter to the prejudices of some modern philosophers (currently, perhaps, a decreasing band). Consider the following case. An object looks to be pink all over, but when examined closely is found to be a multitude of tiny red and white dots. Is it not logically possible that *every* 'pink' surface should turn out, on examination, to be a similar red and white mosaic? And, if so, would we not be justified in saying that, although many surfaces looked pink in colour, there was no surface that actually *was* pink in colour? (For the sake of convenience we might still *talk* about 'pink surfaces' as opposed to 'pink-looking surfaces' in ordinary life.) This example should embolden us to declare that the microscope *may* show us that our ordinary paradigms of surfaces of a certain colour do not in fact have that colour.

I append the following quotations as evidence that *scientists*, at least, are ready to speculate about the real colour of objects on the basis of theoretical considerations, even though such colour cannot be directly perceived:

'At a conference in 1953 Platzman was asked: "Do I understand that you think that irradiated ammonia ought to turn blue if it is pure?" He answered with remarkable foresight: "More than that I think irradiated water turns blue and we just don't see it."

'Since the initial observation of the absorption spectrum of the hydrated electron, numerous studies have been made on sodium radiation-produced solvated electrons in water and many other solvents. The lifetimes are shorter than the "twinkling of an eye", so that only instruments can "see" the colour, but the spectrum leaves no doubt that the characteristic blue colour of solvated electrons is present for a short time after irradiation.'[1]

There are two further objections to the line of reasoning adopted in this section that deserve brief consideration.

(1) It may be questioned whether, in answering the Argument from Microscopes, I have not abandoned *Direct* Realism about colour. For if we can only know the real colour of a surface after we know what light-waves it emits, we can hardly talk of a non-inferential awareness of the colour of the surface.

My answer to this objection is that to defend Direct Realism about colour is not to defend Naive Realism about colour. I have argued elsewhere (in *Perception and the Physical World*, London, 1961, Part Five) that it is perfectly legitimate for the Direct Realist to maintain that sensory illusion is a much more widespread affair than common sense allows. The scientific evidence suggests that this may be the case for most of our colour perceptions. But if, by luck, a particular colour perception is veridical, then, in default of further arguments against Direct Realism, why should we not say that our awareness is direct or non-inferential? (Non-inferential awareness is not, of course, incorrigible awareness nor is it necessarily *knowledge*.) At this point the question may be only one of terminology, but it seems to me that it is legitimate to call the view I am defending a Direct Realist theory of colour.

(2) I have assumed that, by and large, the same surfaces will appear to be of the same colour to different observers whenever the light actually entering their eye has the same composition. For otherwise there would be no possibility of correlating colour and light-waves. But this assumption may be questioned. The same cause may produce different effects upon different things, and may not the same light-waves produce different colour appearances when acting upon different eyes and nervous systems?

In fact, of course, such variations in the colour appearances are not merely possible, they actually occur. (For a summary of the evidence see Keith Campbell's paper 'Colours' in this volume, Sections 5 and 6.) A Direct Realist about colour, such as myself, will therefore be obliged to give reasons for treating some sub-class of the varying appearances as the real colours of the objects

---

[1] 'The Solvated Electron', James L. Dye, *The Scientific American*, Vol. 216, 1967, p. 80 (No. 2).

perceived. And it may turn out that it is not possible to find such a non-arbitrary criterion for determining real colour.

But the point to be made here is that all this has nothing to do with the *Argument from Microscopes*. If there is no clear way of correlating certain wave-lengths with colours, then there is certainly no hope for any Realist theory of colours, Direct or Representative, Reductivist or Anti-Reductivist. But then the Argument from Microscopes is completely redundant. Here, however, I am only attempting to answer the Argument from Microscopes. If we are to achieve clarity in this difficult field it seems to me to be very important to distinguish clearly, and evaluate independently, the *different* arguments that are used against the objectivity of colour.

TWO WAYS OF TALKING ABOUT COLOUR

There is, however, one troublesome little objection to the procedure of correlating the colour of a surface or an object with the sort or sorts of light-waves emitted by that surface or object which it does seem proper to consider here. Consider the following case. A piece of red cloth is put under a mercury-vapour lamp. It looks chocolate-brown. The light-waves being emitted from the cloth, or at any rate those that actually reach the eye, are presumably those associated with the colour of chocolate-brown. But we say that the cloth is red, not chocolate-brown. This suggests that, when correlating colour with light-waves, as well as reference to the light-waves emitted from a surface, reference to the conditions of the illumination is also required.

I think that this difficulty can be cleared up if the Direct Realist about colour asserts that there are two distinct senses in which surfaces and objects are (objectively) coloured.

The point can be illustrated by distinguishing two senses in which physical objects such as squash balls may be (objectively) spherical. In one sense of the word 'spherical' squash balls are, and remain, spherical. Following a terminology suggested by Keith Campbell, we may call this the 'standing' sense of the word. Manufacturers make squash balls spherical in this sense of the word, and if the balls ever cease to be spherical they are of no further use as squash balls. But in another sense of the word 'spherical', the 'transient' sense of the word, squash balls are, from time to time, not spherical in shape at all, for instance at the

I

moment of being hit by a squash racquet or of rebounding off a wall. And although this second sense in which a squash ball is (only sometimes) spherical is not one that finds much employment in ordinary language, it can be used as a primitive notion to give a definition of what it is to be spherical in the standing sense. A thing is spherical in the standing sense if, and only if, it is of such a nature that it is transiently spherical in normal conditions, that is, when no especial forces are acting upon it. Being spherical in the standing sense, and (normally) spherical in the transient sense, are objective characteristics of squash balls, characteristics that are perfectly independent of perceivers.

I suggest that there is room to distinguish two parallel senses of colour words like 'red'.

In one sense of the word 'red', the 'standing' sense, red dresses are, and remain, red until the colour fades or the dress is dyed another colour. Like the standing sense of 'spherical', this is a relatively permanent characteristic of the object, and is the sense of 'red' usually employed in practical life. But there is another sense of 'red', the 'transient' sense, in which red dresses are, from time to time, not red at all, for instance at the moment that they are under a mercury-vapour lamp. Red dresses are transiently red only under normal lighting conditions, for instance in ordinary daylight. Under mercury-vapour lamps red dresses are transiently chocolate-brown. This second sense of red, in which what we ordinarily call a red dress is not always red, finds less employment than the first sense. It is, however, of interest to those whose special concern is with visible things, for instance painters. It can also be used as a primitive notion to give a definition of standing redness. A thing is red in the standing sense if, and only if, it is of such a nature that it is transiently red in normal lighting conditions. Being red in the standing and in the transient senses, the Direct Realist will assert, are both objective characteristics of surfaces or objects, characteristics that are perfectly independent of perceivers. (Of course, if our earlier argument has been correct, objects that the ordinary perceiver in standard conditions takes to be red, either in the standing or the transient sense, may in fact not have those properties, and the evidence of microscopes, etc., may be relevant in showing that ordinary perception is so mistaken.)

It must be confessed here that when a red object is under a mercury-vapour lamp we are inclined to say that the object *looks* brown, rather than say it *is* (transiently) brown. But I think that this is simply a mistake embodied in ordinary language. Perhaps the mistake arises because of our tendency, embodied here in the use of the word 'looks', to assimilate the impermanent to the unreal.

Now that the distinction has been drawn between two senses in which a surface or object can be red, it can be suggested that it is *transient* redness, the less usual sense, and not standing redness, that ought to be correlated with the light-waves actually emitted at the surface. By contrast, objects or surfaces that are red in the standing sense are simply ones that emit these wave-lengths *in ordinary light*: in daylight.

This distinction between two senses of colour is not easily parallelled in the case of the other 'secondary' qualities. Sounds, for instance, would seem to be correlated with sound-waves, and there is no need for the distinguishing of standing and transient senses in which sounds attach to bodies. But sounds are not attributed to bodies in the way that colours are attributed to them or their surfaces. Heat, cold and taste are attributed to the bodies themselves, but there still seems no special call to distinguish permanent from transient modes of attachment.

I will conclude by noting that the distinction of senses in which colour may be (objectively) attributed to objects clears up the problem raised by Locke about the colour of porphyry in the dark (*Essay*, Bk. II, Ch. 8, Sec. 19). Locke says that it is plain that porphyry has *no* colour in the dark, and draws the conclusion that Direct Realism is false with respect to colour. For if colour is really in the object, he argues, the property would not alter in this way with every variation of light.

Consider a piece of red and white porphyry which is in the dark. Using our introduced terminology, we can say that the standing colour of the stone remains red and white, but that its transient colour is black. This is the sense in which it truly has no colour in the dark. But none of this is any objection to a Direct Realist view of colour. In the dark, the porphyry remains the sort of thing that, brought into light again, emits the 'red' and 'white' wave-lengths. In the dark it emits no wave-lengths, and lack of emission of light-waves from surfaces is correlated with the colour black. The standing red and white, and the transient blackness are, for any consideration that Locke has advanced, objective properties of the porphyry. We simply have a distinction between relatively stable and relatively evanescent properties of the stone. All cats really are grey in the dark: transiently grey.

7

KEITH CAMPBELL

COLOURS

1. THE CLASH OF COMMON EXPERIENCE AND PHYSICS OVER COLOUR

In common experience, colours are properties of what is seen. What is seen is, normally, a public, physical, existent, usually a body. In the detailed account scientists are now elaborating of those physical existents, colour properties have no place.

There are three quick and easy ways of dealing with this notorious triad of propositions. We can deny the second proposition and embrace either an idealist or a neutral sense-data account of the immediate objects of perception. We can disarm the third proposition by adopting some non-realist view of all the theoretical entities of physics. More moderately, we can maintain that the physicists' treatment of their subject matter is incomplete, and that associated with the features of physical existents which figure in physical theory are additional objective, but non-physical, colour properties.

Taking any of these courses will overcome our present difficulty. But each seems to me so objectionable, for reasons remote from the topic of colour, that rather than denying any member of the triad, the more arduous course of defending a direct denial of the triad's third member should at least be attempted. In this paper I consider attempts to find a place for colour properties in the physicists' account of nature.

2. THE AXIOMS OF UNITY: A FORMAL CONDITION ON ANY ACCEPTABLE ACCOUNT OF COLOUR

The adjectives of colour—red, green, grey, puce, turquoise, etc.— are terms too simple to give expression to family resemblances. Things are not alike in hue in virtue of a series of overlapping and criss-crossing similarities among them. To be alike in hue, things need have but a single likeness. So when the same colour term is rightly used of various things, that term ascribes to all those things a single constant feature.

Further, the colour terms are one-place predicates. Even if it should turn out that, like 'father' or 'employee', they apply only to objects standing in certain relations, they are not themselves relational terms. They apply to objects taken singly.

Still further, there is at least *some* sense in which it is correct to ascribe colours to most physical objects. These considerations generate a set of principles (which I here dub *The Axioms of Unity*) of which two examples are:

> Red objects have something in common not shared by blue or purple or dark brown ones;
>
> Khaki objects have something in common not shared by cerise or magenta ones.

The schema of these Axioms is:

> For any colour Cn, physical objects of that colour have something in common not shared by physical objects of colours $C_1 \ldots Cn - 1, Cn + 1 \ldots$.

To seek a place for, say, turquoise in the physicists' account of nature is to seek a physical quality, no matter how complex and derivative, with which turquoise might be identified. The Axioms of Unity place this necessary condition on any such identification: there must be one physical quality common and peculiar to objects which are turquoise.[1]

3. TRANSITORY AND STANDING COLOURS

It is a familiar feature of colour vision that the apparent colour of a reflecting surface varies with the illumination falling on it. Suppose a surface looks blue in daylight but magenta under an artificial illumination A. We can, and do, speak about this in three

[1] Bruce Aune, in *Knowledge, Mind and Nature*, New York, 1967, Ch. VII, argues that the commonsensical concept of colour is incompatible with contemporary physical theory realistically interpreted. He concludes, in effect, that this is so much the worse for common sense, and with this conclusion I generally agree. But we ought not to purchase scientific realism at the expense of concluding ourselves all mad; the Axioms of Unity represent the minimum (and perhaps also the maximum) of what in commonsense belief about colour can and must be preserved.

different ways. We can say that under change of illumination from daylight to A, the surface's colour has changed from blue to magenta; thus we make colour a transitory feature of surfaces.

Or we can choose a standard illumination and insist that the surface has retained throughout the change the colour it has under that standard illumination. If sunlight is our standard we say the surface is really blue throughout, and only appears to be magenta under the non-standard illumination. If A is our standard, the surface is and remains magenta. For many choices of standard illumination, of course, our surface would really be neither blue nor magenta, but some third colour.

A third way of describing the situation is to reform our colour terms to incorporate an explicit reference to illumination. We would then say the surface has remained both blue-in-sunlight and magenta-in-A throughout. This is an egalitarian course to take, for following it we do not discriminate among illuminations. None is selected as standard.

If we take the second way and nominate some illumination as standard, or if we adopt the third course and include specifications of illumination in our colour terms, we make colour a permanent property of surfaces—permanent under changes of illumination, that is. The choice we have between speaking of transitory or standing colours is like our choice between saying of magpies that they have the transitory property of *swooping* only in the nesting season, or that they have the standing property of *swooping in the nesting season* all year round. The choice we make will alter our turn of phrase in the doctrine of colour, but of course the realities of the matter will be unaffected, and whatever can be said in one way can be said in another.

Of the two alternatives, however, the concept of transitory colour is epistemically fundamental. We can define *standing blue* (= transitory blue when in standard illumination) and *blue-in-A* (= transitory blue when in A) in terms of transitory blue. Definitions in the other direction (e.g. transitory blue = now indistinguishable in colour from something blue-in-A in A) establish no real dependence. A transitory colour is a colour a surface now seems to have. The notion of distinguishability of colour is that of now seeming to have unlike colours. Judgments of either are equally immediate.

In any event, *transitory* colours are my main concern. Because standing colours can be accounted for in terms of transitory ones, this simplifies the treatment without making it less complete.

4. TRANSITORY COLOURS AS RELATIVE

The transitory colour of a surface can change with only the smallest of side-effects in the surface itself. It does not, of course, follow from this that transitory colour is not an objective feature of the natural world. Relative positions of things change without any but the slightest changes in those things themselves, yet we do not for that reason suppose relative position any the less objective.

And here is a closer analogy, showing that transitory colour can be a *relative* matter (relative to incident illumination) and yet an objective quality for all that. A city on the side of a volcano has always drawn its water supply by gravity from a crater lake of constant level. The inhabitants classify their water pipes by capacity: 10, 50, or 100 gallons-per-minute pipes. Because of their situation, they do not realize that the volume of water a pipe delivers is a function of pressure and diameter jointly. After an earthquake they move down onto the plain, and are surprised to find that their pipes now deliver 20,100 and 200 gallons per minute. They have discovered that the capacity of a pipe can change without change of the pipe itself. The sound philosophers among them will not conclude that there is anything subjective or merely apparent about pipe capacities. There was ignorance in their former belief that capacity was an independent or intrinsic property of pipes. They will fall into error if they postulate occult mechanisms inducing changes in transported pipes to account for the changed capacity. They will err if they conclude that 'capacity' names a relation between a pipe and some other object or objects. If they decide that *capacity* is an objective quality which a pipe has in a given circumstance of pressure, they will have reached our pinnacle of sagacity.

In the same way, the transitory colour which changes with changes in illumination may be an objective quality of surfaces in a given circumstance of illumination.

5. DOCTRINES OF COLOUR AS AN OBJECTIVE QUALITY

The idea that colours are intrinsic, physical qualities of surfaces, distinct from all other qualities of such surfaces, and all combinations of the other qualities, need not long detain us. Such a *non-reductive realism* about colours would be acceptable only if there were, associated with all and only red, blue, orange, green things, respective distinctive patterns of effect upon other physical objects. For only on that condition does a quality count as physical. Further, a quality counts as a distinct and irreducible physical quality only if the relevant pattern of effect is different from any which flow from other properties of the coloured things.

The failure of colours to satisfy this second condition is both total and notorious. If there were such peculiar patterns of effect associated with various colours, physics would need colour terms as primitives in some branch of explanation. It now has no such thing, and there is not the slightest reason to suppose some as yet unexplained body of phenomena in inanimate nature will be, one day, successfully treated by appeal to the colours of objects. There is no prospect of our having any reason to accept the view that colours are irreducible intrinsic physical qualities of surfaces.

Accordingly, proponents of objective doctrines of colour who wish to find a place for colours in the physicists' account of nature must hope to find some complex and derivative physical property common and peculiar to all those objects which are, say, turquoise.

They must urge that associated with turquoise things there is indeed a distinctive pattern of effect upon other physical objects, although not a pattern different from any flowing from combinations of other qualities in the coloured item. They must urge further, that the colour of a turquoise surface can be identified with its common physical peculiarity, thus offering a *reductive* physical realism for colour. What conditions are sufficient for the identification of one property with another is still a controverted question. Our concern here is with a less controversial necessary condition: For P to be identified with Q, being Q must be common and peculiar to whatever things are P. It must be the case that all and only P things are Q. If to be turquoise is just to possess some complex and derivative set of physical qualities, all and only turquoise things must have the complex and derivative set in question.

Men have known for ages that if there is any such set, it is subtle and unobtrusive. To guess how a red thing differs from its non-red fellows, we need to know not only that it is red, but also whether it is an apple, a poker, a chicken-pock, or whatever. Colour being an optical phenomenon, the natural hunting ground for the complex and subtle set of physical properties with which colours might be identified is the field of illumination and the effects of bodies on it. But even in the most promising hunting ground, the search for a common physical peculiarity of turquoise, or scarlet, objects fails.

Let us leave aside emitters of light. The necessary condition for a physical identification of colour fails even for objects seen by borrowed light, so emitters merely introduce unnecessary complications.

In the first place, although selective reflection is the most common, there are many other ways by which physical entities modify incident light and so come to be coloured. The sky is blue at noon and red at sunset on account not of reflection but of selective atmospheric scattering of sunlight. The sea's colour is a product chiefly of non-selective reflection. The colours of colloids (yellow through red) are a function of particle size, not of selective reflection. Some dyes are one colour in thin coatings and a different colour when a thicker coating makes the same selective action (internal reflection with absorption) cumulative.

In short, there are many different qualities of objects which enable two objects to so act on a given incident light as to match in colour. At most, the net effect of these actions—the result that incident light undergoes a certain transformation—is common to objects of like colour. It is just not true that all objects blue under a given illumination have a distinctive, intrinsic, light-modifying feature in common.

Nor will it do to say: the property blue is the property of having a special reflectance, or a different special selective scatterance, or a third special capacity for internal reflection and absorbing of light, or . . . If we insist that colours are intrinsic qualities of physical objects, it turns out that they are not single qualities at all, but *classes* of qualities, and open classes at that. And this result violates the Axioms of Unity enunciated above. Those Axioms affirm that all objects of the same colour share some *common* peculiarity. They are not to be interpreted as tautologies satisfied by an indefinite disjunction of properties which we are resolved to call a single property common to objects of like colour. The objection to such a Disjunctive Realism about colour is this: we identify *red* with $(F \vee G \vee H \vee \ldots)$. We now raise the question: 'Should J be added to the disjunction?' If the answer is arbitrary, *red* is not a quality at all, and the red things are a merely *ad hoc* collection. If the answer is determined by a more profound physical likeness W which J things share with F, G, and H things, then it is with W that *red* must be identified, and the Realism is no longer Disjunctive. If, as actually happens, J is included only if J things *look red*, the doctrine of colour as an intrinsic physical property has been abandoned.

6. DOCTRINES OF COLOURS AS PHYSICAL POWERS

Although the manners in which different yellow objects modify incident illumination are various, the result of the modifications may yet be in each case the same: the composition of light coming from the surfaces may be common and peculiar to cases where the surfaces are yellow. This naturally suggests a doctrine of colours as powers of objects to modify incident light.

Consider the view that for object O to be of transitory colour Cn is for O to have the power so to modify the incident light that the light O reflects has a composition characteristic for Cn objects.[1] When a different mode of action counts as a different power, this view faces the difficulty noticed above; there is then no such thing as *the* power to modify the illumination Cn-wise, just as there is no such disease as *the* ailment of the heart failure, nor any state of a business which is *the* virtue of commercial efficiency. To take a power doctrine in this sense thus makes each colour an open class of powers, in violation of the Axioms of Unity.

Emasculating the doctrine to avoid this result, we can interpret it so that a power is an unspecified causal property. Any two objects then have the same power provided only that they have the same net effect in the same circumstances, no matter how this effect be brought about. Understood in this way, the colours of objects are likened to paralysing snake bite, drug addiction, or company profit, all of which are familiar net-effects-of-never-mind-which-of-an-indefinite-family-of-processes.

On this type of power view, the superficiality of the distinction between transitory and standing colours is readily displayed. For the transitory colour Cn we say: Under illumination $L1$, object O

---

[1] 'Modify' should be read accommodatingly here. An object which reflects non-selectively (so that it is white in white light, green in green light, etc.) is included in the formula as a limiting case—here O *modifies* incident light in the sense that it operates upon it so as to produce reflected light with a certain composition. O does not operate on the incident light so as to produce a change in it.

exercises the power to modify incident light *Cn*-wise. For the standing colour *Cn* we say: object *O* has (whether or not it is exercising it) the power to modify illumination *L1 Cn*-wise.

One further consequence of power views of colour is worth noting: if *O* retains its powers when they are not being exercised, then of course *O* is many *standing* colours simultaneously, for *O* has (whether or not it is exercising it) the power not only to modify *L1 Cn*-wise but also the power to modify illumination *L2 Cn* + 1-wise, etc. This seems to run counter to our tenacious conviction of the incompatibility of colours. However, the situation is not seriously alarming. A surface can exercise but one of these powers at any one time, for there can be only one illumination at any one time. The transitory colours are thus incompatible one with another. This gives to the colours of a surface as much mutual exclusiveness as we have any right to require. After all, the transitory colours are the only ones we ever see.

On the doctrine now being considered, the transitory colour of a body is identified with an exercised disposition of that body to modify the composition of light. The transitory colour is an unspecified causal property of the body. Alternatively, colours might be identified with the effect of the power's exercise upon the incident light; the 'puce surface' we see by reflected light would then be strictly speaking not a puce surface but a surface seen by puce reflected light. Colours, on this second view, attach primarily to light and only secondarily to any surface by whose agency light comes to have its colour property.

These two doctrines, that colour is a power to modify incident light into a special form, and that colour is the effect of such a power's operation, stand or fall together on the question: 'Is there any common peculiarity of the light by which turquoise, olive or magenta objects are respectively seen?'

7. THE COMPOSITION OF LIGHT WHEREBY COLOURED OBJECTS ARE SEEN

Let us avoid needless complication by considering only coloured bodies seen by reflected light and coloured by virtue of selective reflection at and near their surfaces.

The properties of a reflecting surface crucial in determining what colour it will appear are those which determine the proportions of any incident light, considered wavelength by wavelength, which the surface will reflect (rather than absorb or transmit).[1] These proportions can be summarily represented in a graph where the percentage of incident light of a given wavelength reflected is plotted against this wavelength. The result, called a *relative reflectance curve*, shows how strongly the surface reflects light of various wavelengths.

But of course the relative reflectance curve does not by itself determine the character of the light leaving the surface, which is what matters as far as colour is concerned. The incident light has its total energy distributed in some proportion among the wavelengths which compose it: the energy distribution of light leaving the surface is fixed jointly by the proportion of the incident light's energy at each wavelength and the reflectance of the surface at that wavelength.

Because the composition of light leaving the surface is jointly fixed in this way, it is scarcely surprising that a body's transitory colour will in general change under change of illumination. And it is inevitable that a body turquoise under illumination $L1$ will have a different relative reflectance curve from that of a body turquoise under $L2$. However, this has no bearing on our present question, which is: 'Is the relative reflectance curve common and peculiar to all bodies turquoise under $L1$?'

The answer is: it is not. Where other conditions are constant, surfaces seen by reflected lights of indefinitely many different resultant energy distributions match in colour. That is, surfaces with indefinitely many different relative reflectance curves can be turquoise in a given illumination.[2] In this the colour of a surface contrasts sharply with the capacity of a pipe in a given circumstance of pressure. It is not the case that pipes of indefinitely many different diameters have the same capacity for a given pressure.

Although no physical feature of the situation so far considered has been distinctive of all and only the occasions on which a body is turquoise in a given illimination, the philosopher defending a view of colours as reducible physical powers need not despair

---

[1] For this and other information about colours the curious reader is referred to Evans, R. M., *An Introduction to Color*, New York, 1948.

[2] There is an analogous result for light-emitters: indefinitely many sets of three monochromatic (single wavelength) sources can, by additive mixing in varying proportions with white, produce a match for any given colour, for example, turquoise.

quite yet. If colour vision is to be intelligible at all, so one might reason, then when other conditions are constant all these various compositions of light which make two objects match in colour must be united by some formula governing their wavelength-by-wavelength energy distribution. Light from matching surfaces must satisfy some formula which is not satisfied by light from a surface which does not match. It matters not that this formula is unknown. It matters not that it seems to be insignificant for physics. There must be such a formula.[1] And by its means, so this new proposal runs, we can specify a complex physical property distinctive of blue objects, a property which can be identified with their blueness.

The property is: exercising a power (e.g. relative reflectance) such that light leaving its surface satisfies the unknown formula for blue.

For the alternative view which makes colours attach primarily to light, the property is: satisfying the unknown formula for blue.

The question: 'Can colours be given a place in the physicists' account of nature?' now takes the form: 'Are all and only blue objects seen by light characterized by some composition-and-intensity formula?' And the answer is: no.

To establish this, we must note some of the notoriously wide range of further conditions that bear upon which colour is seen when light of a certain composition falls upon the eye.

8. OTHER CONDITIONS DETERMINING WHAT COLOUR IS SEEN

The most pervasive of these further conditions is adaptation. Investigations of colour matching have led to the discovery that for people with normal colour vision we need no fewer than three coloured lights, together with white, to be able to make a match for every colour they can see. This and other results obtained by direct investigation of the eye encourage the hypothesis that there are—in the normal eye—pigments sensitive over three different ranges of visible wavelength, rod receptors and three types of cone receptor, and four different patterns of connection between

---

[1] Although the formula contains *total light intensity* as a parameter, too (for it is not only the distribution of energy among wavelengths, but total energy in light leaving a surface which determines its transitory colour), the argument is not affected by this detail.

receptors. Not all of this apparatus has yet been identified, but there is good reason to postulate its presence.[1]

Under substantial stimulation these receptor-systems become fatigued and respond less to an equal stimulus than when they are fresh. The important consequence of this is that the systems can become differentially fatigued. For example, exposure to a light of predominantly long wavelength (red) will fatigue the appropriate long-wavelength-sensitive system more than the others. The more stimulated parts of the total system become relatively less sensitive. This fatigued condition lasts an appreciable time. So that when the eye looks at something new, the long wavelength components of the new stimulus will have *less* effect than they would on a fresh eye. The colour seen in the new situation will be shifted towards the complementary of the previously experienced one (viz. blue-green). The complementary after-image produced by a white ground when part of the retina has been fatigued by a pure colour, is a dramatic illustration of this constantly occurring effect. The colours of the new stimulus to a fresh eye, to an eye differentially fatigued in one way, and to an eye fatigued in another way, will all be different. This phenomenon is called *adaptation* because its net effect is to assimilate the transitory colours of the same object under different illuminations.

Other factors, in altering, alter the colour a surface looks to be although the composition of the light coming from it remains constant. Some of these are the composition of light from proximate surfaces, the size of the surface itself, whether or not the thing seen is recognized, and the closeness of resolution possible for that surface (the minimum area distinctly perceptible). This last is exemplified in the colour changes a bucket of sand, a football crowd, or a *pointilliste* painting, can undergo on closer approach, and in the colour surprises we get with a microscope.

In consequence, light whose composition satisfies some formula *Fn* can, under divers conditions, make the surface from which it comes appear any one of a large range of colours. And between those colours there is nothing to choose. We cannot say a surface which has the power to modify the light now falling upon it so that it satisfies formula *Fn* is of colour *Cn*. For we might equally claim it to be any of the colours $Cn + 1$, $Cn + 2 \ldots$, which it

---

[1] A way into the details of this material is De Valois, R. L. and Abramov, I.: 'Colour Vision' in *Annual Review of Psychology* 1966, pp. 337–62.

equally appears to be, under the same illumination, on another occasion.

The position is similar for the alternative doctrine on which light is chosen as the true bearer of colour. Light satisfying formula Fn cannot be said to be Cn rather than $Cn + 1$ or $Cn + 2$. In short, our hypothetical formula Fn proves not to be correlated with any one colour. It is not the case that all and only sky-blue objects are seen by light satisfying some formula Fn. The necessary condition for a reductive identification of colours with physical circumstances remains unsatisfied.

To repeat and emphasize this last point: under constant illumination, surfaces reflecting light satisfying formula $F1$, will sometimes match surfaces reflecting light satisfying formula $F2$. And two surfaces which reflect light satisfying formula $F1$ will sometimes match and sometimes not. Consequently, the attempt to find in the hypothetical formula a physical property common and peculiar to all surfaces that are, say, transitory sky-blue, does not succeed.

9. A LINE OF DEFENCE TO SAVE OBJECTIVE DOCTRINES OF COLOUR

There is variability in colour appearance of unchanging objects in unchanging lights. From this we have inferred that colours are not properties or powers of objects or of lights considered in isolation from the perceiving of them. We must now consider an attempt to avoid this conclusion.

The attempt consists in distinguishing among colours the real from the merely apparent. The variability in colour appearance of formula Fn-fitting light will be of no importance if one of these appearances can be singled out as the real one, and all others dismissed as mere appearance. Although no physical property is to be found common and peculiar to all objects which look tangerine to someone under *some* set of circumstances, there may well be such a physical property for objects which really are tangerine, given an adroit choice of reality criterion.

After all, these factors of recent sensory history of percipient; size, orientation, and environment of perceived surface; and recognition of object, give rise to variations in the seen-shape, seen-size, felt-roughness, and felt-temperature of unchanging physical existents.[1] We do not on this account despair of treating shape, size, roughness, or temperature, as objective features of physical bodies. Instead we distinguish real from apparent shape, size, etc., and concentrate upon the former. We make this distinction non-arbitrarily in terms of the characteristic mode of interaction of (really) square, rectangular, six-feet-longish, etc. bodies *with other bodies*, thereby specifying a property possessed by the body quite irrespective of what looks like what to whom. In particular, in determining the real shape, size, temperature, or roughness, we need make no appeal to some privileged set of observation conditions, under which the apparent feature is also the real one. The shape determined by mode of interaction with other bodies has two clear titles to the superiority implied in calling it the real shape: it belongs to the object quite irrespective of the way the object affects any perceiver, and it plays a central role in our explanations of how the object comes to have the various apparent shapes which, under various conditions, it can seem to have.

But now compare the case of colour. Colours have no characteristic modes of interaction. Indeed, it would be amazing if they had. Objects with very different relative reflectances can look the same transitory colour under the same conditions. But relative reflectance is the only property belonging to the object *simpliciter* which enters into the matter. Consequently no 'real colour' can be specified by its mode of interaction. *A fortiori*, no such 'real colour' can enter into explanations of an object's colour appearances.

So some other way of fixing which colour is the *real* one must be found. The usual strategy is to nominate a standard set of observation conditions and settle for the colour seen under those conditions. This strategy is unsatisfactory; the favoured conditions are all open to objection.

Because we have concerned ourselves with transitory colours, we can leave aside the arbitrary element involved in nominating a standard illumination for fixing the 'real' standing colour. But difficulties still abound. The *optimum viewing distance* is insufficiently determinate; what is the optimum viewing distance of a mountain or a piece of woven fabric? Further, it does not

[1] There are some significant *dis*analogies too between perception of colour and perception of these other qualities. Distance and haze, for example, make it harder to distinguish differences in both colour and shape. But with colours there is in addition an overall colour shift: distance blues and haze reddens. There is no corresponding overall shift for shape.

always fix the real colour unambiguously. In illumination of the same composition, and hence where transitory colour should be constant, variations in the intensity of light from a surface at optimum viewing distance can alter the colour seen. So we would have to specify an optimum viewing intensity also, and the slide into total arbitrariness has begun. The *most usual distance* is clearly ontologically frivolous; mass migration of humans to the moon would change the real colours of things left behind on earth. *The circumstances permitting maximum colour discrimination* suffer from non-existence. There is no unique set of circumstances in which all discriminations possible under any circumstance can be made. We need think only of the use of polarized light in studies of surfaces to appreciate this. And why insist that a surface is really uniformly coloured (as it is under ordinary light) rather than parti-coloured (as it is under polarized light) just because more shades of colour in *other* surfaces can be detected using ordinary light?

David Armstrong, that most tenacious of objectivists, is full of ingenious suggestions for more satisfactory standard viewing conditions. He proposes (in his paper on the argument from microscopes elsewhere in this volume) to consider as standard the circumstance in which the most detail in the composition of light leaving the surface can be used by the retina. The real colour is identified with the total photonic pattern at the surface. All colours actually seen arise from the more or less degenerate sample of that pattern available to the eye in any actual observation. The less degenerate the sample, the more nearly the colour seen approaches the real colour.

This deals satisfactorily with distance, haze, coloured glasses, the microscope, and interference from light leaving adjacent surfaces. But it can not cope with the phenomenon of adaptation. The difficulty is not just that because of the inevitable degenera-tion of the photonic pattern in any observation we can never know what the real colour is. The difficulty is rather that there is no clear sense in which the real colour *is* red rather than purple or brown or some other colour no one ever sees. The question 'Which pattern is to be identified with which colour?' has an unambiguous answer only if some adaptive condition in the perceiver is chosen as standard. But to insist that the circumstances leading to one adaptive state enable us to see colour aright, while all others turn vision awry, is to be partial beyond reason. It involves determining the real colour of a surface (which is supposed

K

to be an objective, physical, property) on grounds totally remote from the physical circumstances of the surface (e.g. that it looks magenta to normal eyes after exposure to room sunlight, although not otherwise).

The essence of the objection is this: the real colour cannot be determined by appealing to standard conditions of observation unless these conditions include a specification of the observer's adaptive state. But then the real colour cannot be accorded any ontological pre-eminence over its rivals. For nothing *in rebus* distinguishes the 'real' red from the 'merely apparent' purple or *vice versa*.

The situation can be succinctly expressed this way: colours run foul of a valid form of Bennett's *phenol argument*.[1] The major premiss of the argument is: if surface S can change from magenta to blue without physical change, then neither magenta nor blue is a physical property of S. So far as we know, a general change in the relative sensitivities of sub-systems in the unfatigued human eye is perfectly possible. Such a change would result in a race of men whose colour perceptions were very different from our own. Let us say that surfaces which in standard observation conditions C look magenta to us look blue to these new men. Both the magenta now seen and the blue then seen are 'real' qualities of the surfaces. Precisely because we lack a criterion of real colour independent of observers, we cannot say that one or both of the seen colours is merely apparent. Whence surface S can change from magenta to blue without physical change, and therefore neither magenta nor blue is a physical property of S.

10.   COLOURS AS SUBJECTIVE

We cannot reasonably discriminate real from merely apparent colours. Many of the possible colour appearances of a surface reflecting light satisfying formula $F1$ must be accorded equal status, and no one specific colour is associated with light satisfying that formula. The peculiarity common to each shade of colour, without which the Axioms of Unity will not be satisfied, therefore lies in the way coloured things look.

If we hold fast to the view that colour belongs primarily to

[1] Bennett, Jonathan, 'Substance, Reality, and Primary Qualities' in *American Philosophical Quarterly*, Vol. 2, No. 1 (1965).

physical existents, we are led to embrace the doctrine of Locke: to be tangerine is to have the power to give rise to impressions of tangerine in a normal percipient. Transitory tangerine, on such a doctrine, is the colour power of the surface in the present illumination. Standing tangerine is the power to give rise to impressions of tangerine when under a suitable illuminant. Many standing colours co-exist in any surface.

If that which gives rise to impressions of tangerine *is* tangerine, colours are as they seem. The colour words name the looks of things, for if a body gives rise to impressions of magenta then it looks magenta and it is magenta. And conversely, *only* that which does or could give rise to impressions of tangerine is tangerine. So there is a sense in which the *esse* of colours is *percipi*.

There is no ontologically significant distinction between real and apparent colours. We do operate such a distinction, for example in the paint trade, but it is a pragmatic convenience with a pragmatically justified but not otherwise significant set of standard conditions of observation.

Subjective doctrines of colour all maintain that in the case of, for example, crimson surfaces, their only common peculiarity is the *impressions of crimson* to which they give rise. Having an impression of crimson is, however, something which happens to an observer. It does not happen where the crimson surface is, and the impression, if it is anywhere at all, is not in the same place as the surface. It is therefore important to emphasize the precise character of the subjectivism concerning colours towards which empirical investigations inexorably lead. Colours are subjective in this sense: what it is to be red can be specified only by reference to perceivers pretty much like men. To be red is to have the power to give rise to impressions of red. The only feature distinguishing all and only red things is that they elicit in beings like ourselves a common sensory awareness. The only way in which red things *are* alike is that they *look* alike.

It does *not* follow from this that colours are subjective in the stronger sense that the true bearers of colour are not physical objects but sense-impressions. The only common feature of red things is their like effect upon perceivers; we need not conclude from this that the truly red items are those effects. Many physically different things look red to us, we can not tell the difference between them. But it is they which are red, not their lookings.

The specific subjective view of colour here urged is, then, that colours are properties of physical entities, but not observer-independent properties of those entities. Such a view can meet an objection which originates with Berkeley: the objection that perception of shape and of colour go hand in hand.

The objection runs: one cannot see a shape without seeing a colour. It is by way of seeing colours that we see shapes. If we did not see the colours we would not be able to see the shapes. Yet colour is being made a subjective impression ('here') while shape remains an objective property ('over there'). How then can the one serve as the way by which we perceive the other?

In rebuttal, we repeat that colours are not qualities of the subjective impression. They do not belong to some item other than the item with shape. So they are not for that reason unsuitable as qualities through which shapes can be perceived.

Further, the power to produce in us impressions of, say, red, is distributed over a surface which looks red and stops when the surface stops. In perceiving the location and extent of the area which is red (i.e. looks red), we can not fail to perceive by eye the size and shape of the perceived surface. So far from being a mystery, the visual perception of shape through colour is no more than an exercised ability to produce a special effect in us. This ability of a surface but not its environment to produce a special effect in us is indeed one of the features that marks the shape for what it is (a square, circle, or whatever).

Although this meets the Berkeleyan objection, it is worthwhile to go into the matter in a little more detail. There are two aspects to the perception of colour: *difference of colour* (reds can be distinguished from blues, and both of them from magentas), and *quality of colour* (that elusive, indescribable, character of yellows which makes them not only different from browns, but different from them in their own special way, a way that violets, equally different from browns, do not have). *Quality of colour* has been our theme so far. The Axioms of Unity pertain to quality of colour. It is by those axioms that we disqualify any reduction of colours to complex, observer-independent, physical properties.

Berkeley's objection, however, arises from a half-truth about *colour difference*. Perception of a colour difference merely, and not also colour quality, is sufficient for visual perception of shape. To see the shape of the furniture, we need not see the green quality of the furniture's colour; it is enough to perceive that it differs in colour from the background. It is true that in normal men both perceptions go together. We see that two adjacent surfaces differ in colour by perceiving that one is, say, blue and the other green. We perceive that two surfaces differ in colour by perceiving thereby the colour-difference. But this need not be so, and so we believe, is not for many animals and even for some men. To perceive shape by eye, we need only perceive that a surface and its adjacent environment differently modify the incident illumination. Difference of colour is sufficient for this, although not necessary. Where two simultaneously viewed surfaces differ in colour, there will in general be a difference in the wavelength-by-wavelength composition of the light reflected from them. Our way of being aware of their exercised power to modify, in different ways, a common incident light is by seeing not only that two surfaces differ in colour but seeing also the colours and the colour-difference. So there is a real sense in which perception of colour is a needless luxury even in the *visual* perception of shape; the Berkeleyan objection pitches too high the dependence of perception of shape on the perception of colour.

Finally, those different ways of modifying light which we see as colour differences are differences *in rebus;* they are complex, physical, objective qualities to which perception of colour difference is a rather crude but very reliable guide. There is therefore no paradox in our epistemic reliance upon colour-difference.

In calling perception of colour difference a crude but reliable guide I am referring only to the asymmetrical situation in which difference of colour establishes difference of reflected light while sameness of colour establishes no sameness of reflected light. This asymmetry should cause no misgivings, for the absence of perception of any difference in the composition of two lights which happen to satisfy the same formula Fn is not the same as the perception of the absence of difference. There is no difficulty in the idea that detecting a difference should be more reliable than failing to do so.

II. COLOUR QUALIA

I spoke above of quality of colour as that elusive, indescribable, character of yellows which makes them not only different from browns, but different from them in their own special way, a way peculiar to the yellows alone. Let us call these distinctive features of each discriminable hue *qualia*.

The question now to be faced is 'Does the existence of *qualia* show, in the light of the physical diversity of coloured objects, that strictly speaking, colour is a quality of impressions? Does the existence of *qualia* show colours to be subjective not only in the sense that they can be specified only by reference to impressions in observers, but also in the sense that they attach to subjective items, viz. impressions?'

Consider this argument: the *quale* of yellow, the yellowness of yellow, is our way of being aware of some aspect of the perceptual situations: *seeing something as yellow*. The *quale* is the same in all cases of seeing something as yellow, and hence is our way of being aware of the same aspect in all those cases. But as has already been established, the *only* common aspect of all cases of seeing something as yellow lies in the effect upon the perceiver, the bringing about in him of impressions of yellow. The *quale* of yellow is therefore our way of being aware of the effect wrought in us by the yellow-looking surface, presumably connected with some common response of the retinal and central nervous systems. The *quale* of yellow is so intimate a part of the colour as experienced that it must be a way of being aware of the item which is, in strictness of language, coloured. It is therefore the subjective item, the impression, which is, strictly speaking, coloured.

The success of this argument would not only revive the Berkeleyan objection just discussed, it would also leave us wondering why colours seem to be on surfaces of objects and not in the eyes or further inside the head. So it is fortunate that the argument fails.

It fails at the first mediate conclusion. The *quale* is indeed the same in all cases, but it does not follow from this that it is our way of being aware of the same aspect of the yellow item in all cases. If surfaces S_1 and S_2 with relative reflectance R_1 and R_2 both look yellow if we are in adaptive state A_1, and S_3 with relative reflectance R_3 looks yellow if we are in adaptive state A_2, then *ex hypothesi* we cannot tell the difference between them. They look alike. The yellowness of S_1 can be how R_1 looks to us in A_1, and the yellowness of S_2 can be how R_2 looks to us in A_1. The yellowness of S_3 can be how R_3 looks to us in A_2. To say we cannot tell the difference between S_1, S_2 and S_3 is just to say our way of being aware of their different features is the same. If it were not so, we *could* see a difference between them. So although a *quale* is a way of being aware of an aspect of the situation, and although all yellows have a common *quale*, not all *qualia* are ways of being aware of the *same* aspect of the situation. What we are aware of, in experiencing the yellowness of different yellow things, need not be the same from case to case.

It is no use complaining that it cannot be R_1 that the observer is aware of in seeing S_1 as yellow because yellow surfaces do not appear to be R_1. The world is full of surprises. *A priori*, we can have no opinion about how a property will seem to him who is affected by it. To a man in adaptive state A_1, yellow *is* how R_1 surfaces seem. It is not the case that the surface does not appear to be R_1; in looking yellow it *does* appear to be R_1. That is how an R_1 thing should look to a man in A_1. To complain that a normally sighted but scientifically ignorant man would not spontaneously declare S_1 to have the relative reflectance it does have is to complain that human eyes are not wave-frequency or wave-length analysers. Although this last is true, it does not show that in seeing the surface as yellow, a man in A_1 is not being aware of R_1 in the surface.

With the remainder of the argument we can cordially agree. If the *quale* of yellow is on some occasion our way of being aware of R_1, then in strictness of language it is S_1 which is the coloured item.

12. THE PHYSICAL REDUCTION OF IMPRESSIONS

This paper began with a triad of propositions which are *prima facie* inconsistent:

> Colours are properties of what is seen.
> What is seen is a physical object.
> Colours are not physical, observer-independent, properties.

Determined efforts to show the third of these is false have failed. To be turquoise is to give rise in observers to impressions of turquoise: that is the only unity turquoise items enjoy. The three propositions are thus brought into reconciliation not through denial of the third but through modification of the first.

Colours are not, in the simple sense, properties of what is seen; they are powers to bring about effects in observers. They are only seen when transitory, that is, when exercised, that is, when bringing about such an effect in observers as to look the colour they do.

Although the doctrine advanced avoids making colours objective but beyond the scope of physics, or making colours properties of subjective items, or denying the empirical facts, it does generate a new triad to embarrass us:

Having a colour impression is an effect in an observer.
An observer is a physical object.
Having a colour impression is not a physical effect.

As before, we can avoid any clash by assigning to impressions of colour—of crimson, olive, or grey—a separate existence beyond the scope of physics. But as before, it is worthwhile to explore the alternatives to such a desperate bifurcation of the world.

Recent attempts to furnish an analysis of

(a) S sees O as red (S has impressions of red on looking at O)

in terms of unimpeachable physical purity seem to me to have failed.

Hayek[1] maintains that a colour quality, say red, is constituted by the totality of relationships in which it stands to other sensory experiences. He proposes, in short, to reduce impressions of colour to the awareness of colour difference and to awareness of other differences among sense objects. Then if *being aware of a difference* could be accounted for in terms solely of differential effects on an organism *via* the senses, Hayek's proposal would achieve a physical reduction of colour quality impressions. His view is clear, uncompromising, and incredible. Hayek's only argument for it is that any residue in the colour quality impression, when the impression is considered in abstraction from all its relations, would be indescribable. Accordingly, the residue could not constitute a scientific problem. This is scarcely enough in dealing with a phenomenological reality whose salient feature has traditionally been its indescribability.

Hayek would have to propose that

(a) S sees O as red

be glossed on the lines

(b) S distinguishes O from items which are green, blue, sweet, sour, shrill, soothing . . .

where *distinguishing* is an actual or potential piece of classing behaviour. And he would have to claim that somehow the whole

[1] Hayek, F. A., *The Sensory Order*, London, 1952, pp. 30 ff.

set of such distinguishing-statements is not viciously circular. We can see that his view is not only incredible but false by considering Smart's[1] treatment of (a) above, which is similar, and unsuccessful.

Smart concedes that

(a) S sees O as red

cannot be analysed as

(i) S has trouble distinguishing O among carnation petals (or other paradigm) but not among lettuce leaves (or other paradigm).

This analysis is vulnerable to C. B. Martin's objection[2] that systematic colour changes in things could make (a) false yet (i) true. It is also vulnerable to M. C. Bradley's objection[3] that if S saw everything in shades of grey (a) would be false yet (i) could be true.

So the analysis of (a) must be supplemented by

(ii) S is having impressions of red.

But now if (a)'s analysis is to be in solely physical terms, (ii) cannot be left as it is. It in turn gives way to

(iii) Something is going on in S like what has hitherto gone on in him when he looks at red surfaces.

As Bradley points out in his review,[4] this is circular in that it introduces red surfaces into part of the analysis of (a). For on Smart's account O *is* red surface only if S sees O as red. Now if (iii) is altered to avoid this, so that it becomes

(iv) Something is going on in S like what has hitherto gone on in him when he looks at ripe tomatoes (or other paradigm),

then the whole analysis of (a) as (i) and (iv) is once more vulnerable to the original objections of Martin and Bradley, that under colour shift or vision in shades of grey (i) and (iv) could both be true, yet (a) be false. I believe similar objections will hold against any attempt to analyse seeing colours in terms of the causes or effects of that seeing.

The moral is that the colour vocabulary has a life of its own.

---

[1] J. J. C. Smart, *Philosophy and Scientific Realism*, London, 1963, Chapters IV and V.
[2] Discussed by Smart on pp. 81–2.   [3] *Op. cit.*, p. 83.
[4] *Australasian Journal of Philosophy*, Vol. 42, no. 2, 1964, pp. 262–83.

It can be introduced in full by ostension only. All 'analyses' of (a) are either trivial or circular.

But that will not settle any ontological question about impressions of crimson, olive, or grey. Consider this parallel case: suppose no definition of 'having an Australian accent' in terms of the qualities of sound wave patterns of speech is forthcoming, so that we can introduce this term by direct acquaintance only. Any analysis along the lines

(c) S has an Australian accent if, and only if,

(d) S has a sort of speech easy to pick out in London but not in Sydney

will fail. For corresponding to Martin's objection above we can suppose massive overnight migrations of Sydneysiders and Londoners. Or, in the spirit of Bradley, we can suppose everybody in Sydney, and S, starts to click his tongue after every word. In the first case (c) can be true yet (d) be false. In the second case (c) can be false yet (d) true.

No one, however, supposes that there is anything ontologically mysterious, supervenient, non-physical or otherwise untoward about Australian accents. Introducing a concept by direct acquaintance with its instances is the most ontologically noncommittal way there is. The fact that 'impression of crimson' and hence 'crimson' are terms involving reference to how things seem can not determine the ontological status of impressions.

So despite the failure of attempts to analyse 'S sees O as red' in unequivocally physical terms, or indeed in any terms, it may nevertheless be the case that for S to have colour impressions is for nothing but a physical state or process to occur in S. Although an explicitly physical analysis of 'S is having impressions of crimson' is not a necessary condition for the identification of having a crimson impression with entering some bodily state, a condition of common peculiarity must be satisfied.

Attempts to identify colours with complex observer-independent physical qualities of their bearers failed because there is no such common peculiarity distinctive of crimson, turquoise, or grey things. Attempts to identify having impressions of crimson with complex physical conditions of him who enjoys them will fail if there is no common peculiarity in the bodily condition of S on that occasion.

However, it is an entirely reasonable conjecture that this necessary condition can be satisfied. The information flow in the optic nerve pertains immediately to the condition of the eyes, and the entirely reasonable conjecture is that one aspect of this flow is common and peculiar to the occasions on which we have impressions of turquoise. The aspect in question is that consequent upon the relative outputs, at the relevant region of the retinas, of the postulated four different sensory subsystems. Such a conjecture is reasonable not only on particular grounds but on the general ground that human perception is not a magical process. The distinctive composition of this four-fold output is a candidate for that bodily condition of S with which having impressions of crimson might be identified.

A retinal, rather than cortical, candidate is proposed to enable us to retain as useful notions *colour-hallucination* (as in dreams), when the cortical condition does not have visual causal antecedents, and *colour-illusion* (if it turns out, for example, that the colours seen when the disc with a black and white spiral design on it is rapidly rotated arise not from a discrimination failure at the retina but from a processing failure in the cortex). In this way the notions of hallucination and illusion in colour vision are not dependent on an objectivist doctrine of colour.

13. DIFFICULTIES FACING A PHYSICAL REDUCTION OF IMPRESSIONS

There are many difficulties facing the proposal to identify having colour impressions with having a nervous system in a suitable state. I will here consider two.

First: the best hypothesis about the role of the nervous system in perception is that it is an information-transmitting, information-processing and information-storing device. When we are considering perception, the significant way in which neural states differ from one another is the information which they encode. Now an impression of one colour is different from an impression of another, and if both are neural states they must be different such states. By our best hypothesis, therefore, they must encode different information. But the very possibility of Martin's colour reversal and Bradley's total colour blindness show that the *same* information about the external world can be obtained by way of *different* colour-quality experiences. In other words, the colour-quality impressions may differ yet the information they encode may be the same. It follows, so the objection runs, that differences of colour-quality impression, not being informational differences, are not differences of neural state. Impressions of colour therefore require the existence of a non-physical mind, non-informational modifications of which correspond to seeing different colours.

This objection has already been met, by anticipation, in considering the nature of information encoded in brain states. The information flow in the optic nerve pertains, immediately, to the condition of the eyes. Only mediately is it information concerning the state of the environment. The experience of *colour difference* is associated with difference in this condition from one retinal region to another; by this difference we apprehend a real difference in things seen. Where *colour quality* is concerned, it is the actual condition of various retinal regions that counts. That a given region has a certain distinctive four-fold output is the information the brain receives when we have colour-quality impressions.

So there is after all distinctive information involved in having colour-quality impressions even if there is no distinctive information concerning the external world. In having different colour-quality impressions we do after all enter different information-encoding states. This first objection to identifying S's impressions of colour with physical states of S therefore fails. The fact that the immediate retinal information involved proves to be no guide to an intrinsic property of what is seen does not alleviate the failure.

The second difficulty in the view that having colour-impressions is enjoying distinctive retinal outputs is that this is not what it seems to be. To be turquoise is to so affect the perceiver as to look turquoise. The relevant affection proves to be a distinctive retinal response. But there is no element in the experience of seeing O as turquoise which seems to be a distinctive retinal response. The reply to this is that we are not aware of the *impression* at all. The event of O's looking red to us is not one of which we have either sensory or introspective cognisance. The impression of turquoise does not appear to us in any way. No wonder it does not seem to be a retinal response.

If occurrences of impressions of colour can not be identified with the cortical modifications which encode information of relative retinal response, the reasons must be other than the two just discussed.

14. SUMMARY

To summarize the course of my argument:

The Axioms of Unity place a minimum logical condition on any reconciliation of our colourful experience of the world with a colourless physics which has pretensions to ontological adequacy. This condition is that there be something common and peculiar to all things having the same colour.

Under this condition experimental investigations disqualify all doctrines which identify colour quality with a complex, observer-independent, physical property or power of objects.

The errors of the common-sense metaphysic of colours are that colours are simple and intrinsic qualities of objects, but the view that they do qualify physical objects is not an error. The mistake the operation of our eyes makes inevitable is a mis-assimilation of like objects, not a mis-location of colours.

In consequence, any satisfactory account of colour involves essential reference both to objects and to the affections of perceivers. 'O is turquoise' is true just in case 'O has the power to produce impressions of turquoise in some perceiver'.

'S has impressions of turquoise' has no significant analysis, but yet such impressions can be contingently identified with a physical state of S.

Thus when S sees O as turquoise (when O gives S impressions of turquoise):

(i) O exists and S sees it.

(ii) O differs in colour from its ground, and S is aware of this.

(iii) There is a specific area of S's retinae, in virtue of the stimulation of which, by light emanating from O, S sees O.

(iv) The ratios of the outputs of the four postulated receptor systems in the retinal regions mentioned in (iii) are distinctive.

(v) Perceptual malfunction aside, whenever the ratios mentioned in (iv) have this distinctive value, O looks turquoise.

(vi) There is no common feature in the objects O, O_1, O_2 . . ., in virtue of which they elicit the response mentioned in (iv), but an open class of features.

(vii) Whichever of this open class O possesses is the feature of O which S sees in seeing that O is turquoise.

8

C. B. MARTIN

PEOPLE

I

In this first section I shall make explicit the dualistic model that is implicit in Strawson's notion of a person.

Strawson introduces his notion of a person by saying: 'What I mean by the concept of a person is the concept of a type of entity such that *both* predicates ascribing states of consciousness *and* predicates ascribing corporeal characteristics, a physical situation, etc. are equally applicable to a single individual of the single type.' (pp. 101–2) In order to bring out what is involved in the characterization of this type of individual, Strawson makes 'a rough division, into two, of the kinds of predicates properly applied to individuals of this type. The first kind of predicate consists of those which are also properly applied to material bodies to which we would not dream of applying predicates ascribing states of consciousness. I will call this first kind M-predicates; and they include things like "weighs 10 stone", "is in the drawing-room" and so on. The second kind consists of all the other predicates we apply to persons. These I shall call P-predicates. P-predicates, of course, will be very various. They will include things like "is smiling", "is going for a walk", as well as things like "is in pain", "thinking hard", "believes in God" and so on.' (p. 104)

Strawson brings some sort of order to the variety of P-predicates by saying, 'For though not all P-predicates are what we should call "predicates ascribing states of consciousness" (e.g. "going for a walk" is not), they may be said to have this in common, that they imply the possession of consciousness on the part of that to which they are ascribed.' (p. 105) I shall call the sort of P-predicates that ascribe states of consciousness C-predicates and the others Q-predicates.

The class of Q-predicates is marked by two necessary conditions

Note: Quotations in this paper are taken from P. F. Strawson, *Individuals*, London, 1959.

which are presumably jointly sufficient. The first is the negative
necessary condition that such predicates do not indicate 'at all
precisely any very definite sensation or experience'. The second is
the positive necessary condition that such predicates 'imply the
possession of consciousness on the part of that to which they are
ascribed'.

Unfortunately, there is a passage on the same page (p. 105) that
obscures the distinction between Q-predicates and M-predicates.
I have in mind the following passage.

'I implied also that the Cartesian error is just a special case of the
more general error, present in a different form in theories of the
no-ownership type, of thinking of the designations, or apparent
designations, of persons as *not* denoting precisely the same thing
or entity for all kinds of predicate ascribed to the entity designated.
That is, if we are to avoid the general form of this error, we must
not think of "I" or "Smith" as suffering from type-ambiguity.
Indeed, if we want to locate type-ambiguity somewhere, we would
do better to locate it in certain predicates like "is in the drawing-
room", "was hit by a stone" etc., and say they mean one thing when
applied to material objects and another when applied to persons.'
(p. 105)

On the previous page, Strawson has said that 'is in the drawing-
room', etc., are *M*-predicates. If we 'say they mean one thing
when applied to material objects and another thing when applied
to persons', what is the 'other thing' they mean when applied to
persons? Surely, nothing short of their 'implying the possession of
consciousness on the part of that to which they are ascribed'. But
then they would be indistinguishable, on Strawson's own terms,
from Q-predicates. If he is serious, then it is not easy to see how
he is consistent. If he is not serious, then he must mean that 'if we
want to locate type-ambiguity somewhere' we will make a mistake,
and that 'we would do better' to make the mistake of locating the
type-ambiguity in certain predicate terms rather than in certain
subject terms. But it is not clear how one 'would do better' to make
one mistake rather than the other.

Strawson says, 'What I mean by the concept of a person is the
concept of a type of entity such that *both* predicates ascribing
states of consciousness *and* predicates ascribing corporeal characteristics, a physical situation, etc., are equally applicable to a single

individual of that single type.' (pp. 101-2) He also says, 'Perhaps I should repeat that once we have identified a particular *person*, there is nothing to stop us, and nothing does stop us, from making identifying references to a particular of a different type, namely the consciousness of that person. It is in this way that the concept of a particular consciousness can exist, as the concept of a non-basic, non-primary type of particular. And only in this way.' (p. 133) If what Strawson says in these two passages is taken quite literally, then what he says is false. Predicates ascribing conscious states and predicates ascribing corporeal characteristics are not 'equally applicable'. After identifying a person, there *may* be something to stop us from making identifying reference to that particular that is the consciousness of the person, for the person may not *be* in a conscious state at the time, though he cannot fail to *be* in a bodily state at the time.

It may be objected that Strawson does not mean that for the concept 'person' to apply to an entity at a particular time any predicates ascribing states of consciousness are truly affirmable of that entity at that time, but really means only that it makes *sense* to affirm such predicates of the entity at the time. My reply is:

(*a*) Strawson has not *said* this.

(*b*) If such an interpretation is given to Strawson's words then it is not consistent with other things he says. For this condition of sense-making could apply to an entity that does *not* possess consciousness. An infant is born comatose. Scientists are interested to find out how long it can be kept alive. It lives for twenty-three years in a comatose condition.

(*c*) Furthermore, 'making sense' is hardly enough for 'making identifying reference' as Strawson would be the first to insist.

It is not necessary that a particular person at a particular time should *be* in any conscious state whatever. We can say of an existing person that *no* C-predicates ascribing conscious states are truly affirmable of that person at that time. It is, however, necessary that a particular person at a particular time should *be* in some corporeal state. We *cannot* say of an existing person that *no* M-predicates ascribing corporeal states are truly affirmable of that person at that time.

To think of an existent particular, an object of identifying reference, that is in *no* actual state whatever, is to think a thought that is not clear to me and, I would guess, not clear to Strawson either.

(It was for this reason that Descartes said that the soul must always be conscious, that is, in some actual conscious state just as a body must be in some actual extensional state.) It follows then, that the consciousness of a person who at a particular time is not in any *actual* conscious state does *not* at *that* time exist as a particular or as an object of identifying reference. Therefore, there *is* 'something to stop us' from making identifying reference to a particular consciousness of a person who is not conscious at the time of 'reference'. In such a case, the only existent particular or object of identifying reference would be the body and no more than the body. This follows from the fact that a person who is not at the time in any actual conscious state is in no *actual* state other than a corporeal state. The person and the body of the person are, for *that* time, the one and the same identical object of the identifying reference.

The truth of this is obscured but not affected by the fact that we would still ascribe to the unconscious person predicates such as 'is knocked out', 'is kind', 'believes in God', etc., which we would not ascribe *simply* to a body. An analogy may help to make this clear.

Parallel to what Strawson says of the concept of a person, I shall say, 'What I mean by the concept of a garden is the concept of a type of entity such that *both* predicates ascribing states of vegetation *and* predicates ascribing states of soil, are equally applicable to a single individual of that single type.' And just as Strawson says that a person possesses a body and a person possesses consciousness, I shall say that a garden possesses soil and a garden possesses vegetation. In place of P-predicates ascribed to persons, I shall introduce G-predicates ascribed to gardens. Just as some P-predicates, what I have called C-predicates, ascribe a fairly specific kind of conscious state (e.g. 'has a severe pain') and others do not, similarly some G-predicates ascribe a fairly specific kind of vegetative state (e.g., 'has some beautiful roses') and others do not. In working out the analogy with Q-predicates that do not ascribe any very specific conscious state, I shall consider G-predicates of the latter sort.

Consider, then, these parallels:

(*a*) Q-predicates that imply that the individual is *not* conscious. Examples of such Q-predicates are 'has been knocked out', 'is in a coma'.

G-predicates that imply that the individual is *not* in any

L

actual vegetative state. Examples of such G-predicates are 'is barren', 'is ready for planting'.

(b) Q-predicates that have *no* implications as to whether the individual is conscious or not. Examples of such Q-predicates are what Strawson calls 'those which carry assessments of character or capability', e.g., 'is kind', 'is intelligent'. 'Believes in God' would be another sort of example. G-predicates that have *no* implications as to whether the individual is in any actual vegetative state or not. Examples of such G-predicates are 'is profitable' and 'is well irrigated'.

(c) Q-predicates that imply that the individual *is* conscious with *no* indications as to the kind of consciousness. Examples of such Q-predicates are 'has come out of the coma', 'is awake'.

G-predicates that imply that the individual *is* in some actual vegetative state with *no* indication as to the kind of vegetation. An example of such a G-predicate is 'is flourishing'.

(d) Q-predicates that imply that the individual *is* conscious with only a *rough* indication as to the kind of consciousness. Examples of such Q-predicates are 'observing a flower', and, Strawson's own examples, 'going for a walk', 'coiling a rope', 'playing ball', 'writing a letter'.

G-predicates that imply that the individual *is* in some actual vegetative state with only a *rough* indication as to the kind of vegetation. Examples of such G-predicates are 'is in full bloom', 'is ready for reaping'.

It is not necessary that a particular garden at a particular time should *have* vegetation, should *be* in any vegetative state whatever. We can say of an existing garden that *no* predicates ascribing vegetative states are truly affirmable of that garden at that time. It *is* necessary that a particular garden at a particular time should *have* soil,[1] should *be* in some soil state. We *cannot* say of an existing garden that *no* predicates ascribing soil states are truly affirmable of that garden at that time.

The vegetation of a garden that has no vegetation at the time (that is, when the garden is not in any actual vegetative state) does not at *that* time exist as a particular or as an object of identifying reference. In such a case, the existent particular or object of identifying reference would be the soil and no more than the soil. This

---

[1] 'Soil' here can mean something as wide as 'stuff in which plants can grow.'

follows from the fact that a garden that is not in any actual vegetative state at the time is in no *actual* state other than a soil state. The garden and the soil of the garden are for that time the one and the same identical object of identifying reference.

The truth of this is obscured but not affected by the fact that we would still ascribe to the garden lacking vegetation, predicates that we would not ascribe *simply* to an area of soil.

Strawson speaks of the individual consciousness or ego of a person as a particular. It follows from the foregoing discussion that it is a discontinuous or intermittent particular in a way that the body is not. Similarly, one might speak of the vegetation (through the years) as a particular. But it will be a discontinuous or intermittent particular in a way that the soil is not.

Strawson speaks of the 'private experiences' of a person as 'particulars'. When a person is in no conscious state, it possesses no such particulars. At *such* a time, how are the person and the body of a person to be distinguished as the actual objects of identifying reference? Similarly, one might speak of the plants of a garden as particulars. When a garden is in no vegetative state, it possesses no such particulars. At such a time, how are the garden and the soil of a garden to be distinguished as the actual objects of identifying reference?

So it seems that for the concept 'person' to apply to something that thing must *always* have a body and must *sometimes* have private experiences. For the concept 'garden' to apply to something that thing must always have soil and must *sometimes* have plants.

Working with these concepts we say that the *person* has after-images and we do not say that the body has after-images; we say the *garden* has roses and we do not say the soil has roses. To refer to something as a person is to refer to what has, in its present as well as its past and future history, a body *and* to what has, in its present *or* past *or* future history, private experiences. To refer to something as a garden is to refer to what has, in its present as well as its past and future history, an area of soil *and* to what has, or is expected to have in its present *or* past *or* future history, plants. This explains the fact that when we refer to a person who is at the time in no conscious state, the body *is* the only existent object of reference, yet we do not refer to the person simply as a body. And it explains the fact that when we refer to a garden that is at the time in no vegetative state, the area of soil *is* the only existent object of reference, yet we do not refer to the garden simply *as* an area of soil.

A garden is composed or constituted of its soil (which it must always have) and its plants (which it must at least sometimes have) and no more and no less. A Strawsonian person is composed or constituted of its body (which it must always have) and its experiences (which it must at least sometimes have) and no more and no less.

It is obvious that the garden analogy is not a complete one. The vegetation does *not* depend for its identifiability and reidentifiability upon the garden that possesses it. It can cease to be possessed by a garden (that is, the vegetation can be harvested) and *still* be identifiable and reidentifiable. The consciousness *does* depend for its identifiability and reidentifiability upon the person that possesses it. It can cease to be possessed by a person (that is, the consciousness can be disembodied) and thus ceases to be identifiable and reidentifiable.

Strawson says that '. . . the strictly disembodied individual is strictly solitary, and it must remain for him indeed an utterly empty, though not meaningless, speculation, as to whether there are any other members of his class.' (pp. 115–16) I take this to mean that the criteria of identifiability and reidentifiability lapse concerning such an individual.

The disanalogies that I have mentioned do not affect the force of the garden analogy in highlighting the implicit dualistic model in Strawson's account.

I shall now consider the consequences of some of the things that Strawson has said and allowed to be said of people.

II

In this section problems peculiar to Strawsonian people will be presented, and the suggestion of 'tripleism' in Strawson's account will be examined.

As Strawson has said, it is 'a conceptual truth . . . that persons have material bodies.' (p. 58) But it is 'a contingent matter', he says, 'that for each person there is one body which occupies a certain *causal* position in relation to that person's perceptual experience.' (p. 92) (He imagines a complex case in which a person's perceptual experience is caused by the states of three bodies. There is not space to consider whether or not this case can be coherently

stated. I can only point out the implications of Strawson's acceptance of it.) He allows also that experience causally dependent
upon the state of one particular body, 'might have been causally
dependent upon the state of some other body.' (p. 96) He says that
the contingent facts concerning the causal dependence of a
person's experiences upon one body rather than several, or rather
than some other body instead, 'provide a good reason why a
subject of experience should have a very special regard for just one
body, why he should think of it as unique and perhaps more
important than any other. They explain—if I may be permitted to
put it so—why I feel peculiarly attached to what in fact I call my
own body; they even might be said to explain why, granted that
I am going to speak of one body as *mine*, I should speak of this
body as mine' (p. 93).

Elsewhere he says that 'I am not denying that we might, in
unusual circumstances, be prepared to speak of two persons alternately sharing a body, or of persons changing bodies, etc.' (p. 133).

So the ownership or possession by a Strawsonian person of one
body rather than several and of one body rather than another is a
contingent matter and such ownership is transferable between
persons.

What about the ownership or possession by a Strawsonian
person of experience? He says,

'It does not seem to make sense to suggest, for example, that the
identical pain which was in fact one's own might have been another's. We do not have to seek far in order to understand the place
of this logically non-transferable kind of ownership in our general
scheme of thought. For if we think, once more, of the requirements
of identifying reference in speech to *particular* states of consciousness, or private experiences, we see that such particulars cannot be
thus identifyingly referred to except as the states or experiences *of*
some identified *person*. States, or experiences, one might say, *owe*
their identity as particulars to the identity of the person whose
states or experiences they are.' (p. 97)

So a Strawsonian person is that which can have more than one
body and can share or exchange a body with some other person.
And whatever body or bodies it has, it could have had other
people's instead.

But a particular person is that which cannot have more than one set of experiences or consciousness and cannot share or exchange a consciousness with some other person. And whatever consciousness, set of experiences it has, it could not have had other people's instead.

Let me mention some consequences of this way of thinking.

(1) Concerning two or more people alternately sharing the same body, Strawson would seem to have in mind those strange and rare cases of split personality. The psychiatrist, though he has need of only one couch, is treating two people. Having scant regard for the sanctity of personal life, the ghoulish success of his treatment involves the removal of a person, a basic particular, from the land of the living.

(2) Again, two people alternately sharing the same body are in a somewhat curious position. For while one person has the body, the other person ceases to exist, and exists again only when it is his turn. So they switch on and off in existence. The out-of-turn person is in one way worse than dead, because we cannot at *that* time call any body his. He cannot even be decently buried. In another way, he is better than dead, because when his turn comes around he will exist again.

(3) The sharing and changing of bodies are cited by Strawson to illustrate his claim that the criteria for the reidentification of people are multiple and that these criteria are *not* the same as the criteria for reidentifying material bodies.

Leaving aside the question of personal identity and reidentifiability, how can he, in the same paragraph, allow persons to share the same body alternately, and also say that 'Persons, having corporeal characteristics, perceptibly occupying space and time, can be distinguished and identified, as other items having a material place in the spatio-temporal framework can be distinguished and identified?' (p. 132) How *can* such persons be distinguished in this way when there is, *ex hypothesi*, only *one* body, one material item, to work with? Surely, 'Other items having a material place' are distinguished spatially as well as temporally. But these people are distinguished temporally and not spatially.

(4) What is *two* about the two Strawsonian persons who exchange bodies or alternately share one body? Is it not what Strawson says two persons *must* have but *cannot* share or exchange— namely their two sets of experiences or individual consciousnesses? What logically follows from the fact that there are two persons and

not just one, is the fact that there are two individual consciousnesses. These consciousnesses are not that in virtue of which the
two persons are identified and distinguished. But they are that in
virtue of which there are two persons, rather than one, to be
identified and distinguished. It would seem then that people *owe*
their identity as particulars to that about them which is not share-
able with or transferable to others, namely, their individual consciousnesses.

(5) Remember that Strawson has argued that the identification
and reidentification of particulars 'rests ultimately on the use of
demonstrative or ego-centric or token-reflexive expressions'
(pp. 117–18) because of the theoretical possibility 'of massive
reduplication in the universe.' (pp. 20–2 and 30) (This, of course,
is a very familiar point made and discussed by Reichenbach and
others. When I say that the point is a 'familiar' one, I do not wish
to suggest that I am being *critical* of Strawson here. Indeed as
against Quine, I think that this is a difficult and important problem.
Quine would put it with his 'don't cares'. So on Quine's three-
valued logic of 'true', 'false', and 'boring', the statements that
there is and is not such symmetrical duplication have the same value
—'boring'.)

Strawson allows, then, that two persons could have qualitatively
similar bodies and be in qualitatively similar physical situations,
etc. and he allows the 'series of states of consciousness of two
persons' to be qualitatively indistinguishable. (p. 125) Now, what
if they exchange bodies?

Strawson indicates that the admission of the body-changing
and body-sharing possibilities does not affect his claim that the
concept of a person is a primary concept, the concept of a primary
or basic particular. For, he says, 'none of these admissions counts
against the thesis that the primary concept is that of a type of
entity, a person such that a person necessarily has corporeal
attributes as well as other kinds of attributes.' (p. 133)

Surely, that concept is as much intact if two persons qualitatively
similar in their attributes exchange bodies. The transaction of
bodies *either* between qualitatively dissimilar people *or* between
qualitatively similar people is on a par on this score. In such a
transaction neither person would be deprived of what Strawson
says 'a person necessarily has' nor does anyone gain what a person
necessarily has *not*. However, the transaction would be, as it were,
very, very quiet.

Two main difficulties arise here for Strawson.

(*a*) Strawson assures us that '. . . the residual problem of personal identity, though still debatable, appears as one of relatively minor significance and relatively little difficulty. I shall not discuss this problem now. But perhaps I should say one thing. The criteria of personal identity are certainly mutiple. In saying that a personal body gives us a necessary point of application for these criteria, I am not saying that the criteria for reidentifying persons are the same as the criteria for reidentifying material bodies.' (p. 133) However, if qualitatively similar people are not prohibited from exchanging bodies, then the problem of formulating criteria for reidentification is an *insuperable* one.

(*b*) Perhaps more surprisingly a difficulty is generated for Strawson's general account of the identification and reidentification of material bodies.

Strawson is concerned to connect the problem of identification with the problem of reidentification. He says of elements in the spatio-temporal framework, 'It is the essence of the matter that we use the same framework on different occasions. We must not only identify some elements in a non-relative way, we must identify them as just the elements they are of a single continuously usable system of elements. For the occasions of reference themselves have different places in the single system of reference. We cannot attach one occasion to another unless, from occasion to occasion, we can reidentify elements common to different occasions.' (p. 32)

For Strawson, the solution of the theoretical problems of ensuring uniqueness of reference in the face of the possibility of massive reduplication

'. . . lay in the fact that, for a speaker making references, his own immediate environment supplied common points of reference in relation to which uniqueness of reference to any other item belonging to the single spatio-temporal framework in which he himself was located could be secured. To accept this solution was to accept the general theoretical position that the identification of particulars rests ultimately on the use of expressions with some demonstrative, or egocentric, or token-reflexive force. For the significance of the theoretically central position of the point of reference in the speaker's vicinity is that ambiguities of reference with regard to this point are ruled out by the use of demonstratives, in conjunction with suitable, though not elaborate, descriptions.

It is true that the theoretical problem to which this was the solution appeared as a highly artificial one. It is also true that the solution was nevertheless shown to hold the key to the structure of our actual thinking; that particular-identification was shown to rest in fact on the use of expressions which, directly, or indirectly, embody a demonstrative force; for such identification rests upon the use of a unified framework of knowledge of particulars in which we our-selves have a known place.' (pp. 117–18)

But, if qualitatively similar people, in qualitatively similar environ-ments, exchange bodies, then they unknowingly change place and 'frameworks' and can not, in the required sense, 'know their place'.

Strawson may insist at this point that the exchange of bodies is logically possible only if the people are qualitatively dissimilar (perhaps even to some marked degree). So instead of invoking, as did Leibniz, the principle of the identity of indiscernibles, Straw-son could invoke what I may call the principle of the discern-ibility of body-exchangeable identifiables. However, this has the appearance of an *ad hoc* move.

On the other hand, Strawson may give up saying that it is a contingent matter what particular body a person possesses and claim that it is logically necessary that a person possess one par-ticular body rather than some other. This would be a major change in his position. And it is difficult to see how this change could avoid the consequence of endorsing a model that it has been his aim to reject. Namely, the model of the conscious states of a particular person as states of a particular body.

It may be said that my exposition of the nature of Strawson-ian people is faulty, because it suggests that such people are composites of one basic particular body and one non-basic parti-cular consciousness. That is, it fails to take seriously Strawson's insistence that the person *itself* is a basic particular. Let me try to take that seriously now.

First, it is necessary to say something about the limbo status of the Strawsonian consciousness or ego. It is a 'logically secondary particular', that is, it depends for its identification and reidentifi-cation upon the identification and reidentification of the person who possesses it. It looks as if it is all right for it to exist in a non-identifiable, non-reidentifiable state as a disembodied individual, but perhaps not as a to-be-embodied individual.

What is clear is that the Strawsonian consciousness must be

counted as a real object of reference unlike those individuals that
Strawson calls 'non-particulars' such as numbers, qualities, relations, etc. And it is clear that such a consciousness or ego is a
particular of which mental predicates hold. This is important, so
I shall provide support for what will be obvious to any reader of
the text.

(a) Strawson says, 'Perhaps I should also repeat that once we
have identified a particular *person*, there is nothing to stop us, and
nothing does stop us, from making identifying references to a
particular of a different type, namely the consciousness of that
person. It is in this way that the concept of a particular consciousness can exist, as the concept of a non-basic, non-primary type of
particular. And only in this way.' (p. 133) Presumably, if the
referent, that is, the consciousness, is not stateless then its states are
conscious states.

(b) Strawson allows the possibility of the individual consciousness or ego continuing to exist as a disembodied individual.
(p. 103 and pp. 115–16) Unfortunately, Strawson is guilty of a
non-trivial terminological confusion in his account of this individual. He says, 'A person is not an embodied ego, but an ego
might be a disembodied person, retaining the logical benefit of
individuality from having been a person.' (p. 103) And he requires
of the disembodied individual '. . . that in order to retain his idea
of himself as an individual he must always think of himself as
dis-embodied, as a *former* person.' (p. 116)

But, of course, the consciousness or ego never *was* a person, for
a person is that which possesses both a body and a consciousness.
So the disembodied individual is not a former person, but is the
consciousness or ego of a former person. And if, in its non-
identifiable, non-reidentifiable state, it gets any 'logical benefit of
individuality' at all, it gets it not 'from having been a person' but
from having been the consciousness or ego of a person. So the
consciousness possessed by a person may continue to exist (having
thoughts, memories, some visual and auditory experiences, that is,
being in conscious states) when no longer possessed by that
person. The conscious states or experiences of the disembodied
individual are not states or experiences of a person or of what was
a person, but of what was possessed and is no longer possessed by
a person. Strawson's terminological confusion hides the seeming
inconsistency between his account of the disembodied individual
and his claim that 'States, or experiences, one might say, *owe* their

identity as particulars to the identity of the person whose states or experiences they are'. (p. 97) I shall not go into the many problems that Strawson makes for himself here. It is enough for my present purposes to have thoughts and experiences, to be in conscious states and so to have shown what should be obvious—that Strawson cannot deny the same to the consciousness of an actual person.

There is, I think, the verbal suggestion, not of dualism, but of tripleism. Strawson has said that '. . . that which one calls one's body is, at least, a body, a material thing' (p. 89), and '. . . things which are, or possess, material bodies must be the basic particulars.' (p. 39) 'Given, then, that our scheme of things includes the scheme of a common spatio-temporal world of particulars, it appears that a central place among particulars must be accorded to material bodies and to persons.' (p. 246) So the particular that is the body of a person does not possess, but *is*, a material body (and therefore is a basic particular), whereas the particular that is the person *is not* a material body but possesses a material body (and therefore is a basic particular). And then, of course, there is the particular that is the consciousness or ego of a person that does not possess but *is* a consciousness or ego, whereas the particular that is the person *is not* a consciousness or ego but *possesses* a consciousness or ego. Now, if one counts the particulars mentioned, I think the sum is three: two basic particulars—the material thing that is the body of the person, and the person—and one non-basic particular, the consciousness of the person.

A body or set of bodies is what is had or possessed by a person. A set of experiences, that is, a consciousness, is what is had or possessed by a person. And a person is what has or possesses these. A person is that which can be thought to have possessed or come to possess some other person's body but not some other person's set of experiences or consciousness. How, then, can that which could have possessed or come to possess a different body or different bodies from the one or several it does possess, be *itself* a particular observable spatio-temporal entity?

If the person-possessor is a third entity, not identical with some manner of combination of its possessions, then it can only be a feature-less sub-stratum that possesses the featured possessions.

But of course Strawson does not think of the person-possessor as a featureless substratum, for he insists that both physical and mental predicates do and must apply to a person. However, in avoiding the substratum model, he must also avoid what I shall call 'the duplication of effort'.

The body of a person is six feet tall and weighs 180 pounds. It seems a needless duplication of effort to say that the person possessing the body *also* is six feet tall and weighs 180 pounds. The consciousness of a person is in some conscious state. It seems a needless duplication of effort to say that the person possessing the consciousness is also in that mental state. Indeed, this duplication of effort seems not only needless, but incomprehensible. Surely, the physical and conscious-state predicates that apply to the person-possessor apply simply in virtue of the fact that they apply to the body and consciousness that it possesses. Otherwise, it would be an incomprehensible coincidence.

And now the way of avoiding the incomprehensibilities of the featureless substratum or the duplication of effort is, I think, evident. Strawson can accept the implications of his account of persons, and the model suggested by the garden analogy, that I made clear in the first section of this paper. In doing so, his account would become familiar. For we would be able to see its similarity to other accounts in the history of philosophy that Strawson and the rest of us have called 'dualistic'. If there is some other option, then it is up to Strawson or one of his defenders to make it clear.

9

M. C. BRADLEY

TWO ARGUMENTS AGAINST THE
IDENTITY THESIS

In what follows I discuss two separate arguments against the Identity Thesis, understood as Central State Materialism. The first derives from considerations of incorrigibility, and I argue that this, at least in the forms that I have been able to devise, is invalid. The second derives from considerations relating to the spatial location of somatic sensations, and the tentative upshot of my discussion on this point is that the argument is sound.

I

The Incorrigibility Thesis has frequently been seen as a potential source of objection to the Identity Thesis,[1] but I wish to show that there is no obvious argument from it against the Identity Thesis. So far as I know, the most explicit formulation of the supposed incompatibility between the two theses runs as follows:[2]

'If there is any contradiction involved in combining the Identity with the Incorrigibility Thesis, it will have to consist in the consequence of sensations being such that some one judger's judgment about them will have incompatible qualities. This does indeed appear to be what results from combining the theses. For it is being supposed that when a person reports a pain, then it is both the case that what is reported is a state of the brain, and also that the report is incorrigible.

'But how are we to think of anyone's report of a state of the brain being anything other than corrigible, whether the reporter is the owner of the brain, or not? Even if we can suppose that a sensa-

[1] See, e.g., Kurt Baier, 'Smart on Sensations', *Australasian Journal of Philosophy*, Vol. 40, 1962, pp. 57–68; J. J. C. Smart, *Philosophy and Scientific Realism*, London, 1963, pp. 99–101.

[2] M. C. Bradley, Critical Notice of *Philosophy and Scientific Realism*, *Australasian Journal of Philosophy*, Vol. 42, 1964, p. 274.

tion is the subject of incorrigible reports, it seems impossible to suppose that *any* physical state or process should be so. Further . . . it is not necessary that we suppose a disparity between our (incorrigible) judgments about our sensations and our (corrigible) judgments about our brain states actually occurring at some time, in order to be able to argue that the identification of sensation with brain states involves contradiction; for whether *or not* such a disparity ever emerges, we already have the contradiction of supposing that one and the same thing is the subject of judgments which are both corrigible and incorrigible.'

For present purposes I express this argument as follows. I take 'x is the subject of incorrigible judgments' to mean 'It is logically impossible that x is judged by a person to occur as part of his experience and x does not occur' (where the scope of 'It is logically impossible that' extends down to 'not occur').[1] 'Judges that' is to be taken as meaning 'explicitly formulates and assents to the proposition that'. This puts the thesis at its best (for if it does not hold of judgment, in this sense, it will certainly not hold of belief, in various weaker senses), and it is useful in a special argument below (see footnote on page 178). If, now, under the following law of identity,

$$(x)(y)((x = y) \supset (Fx \supset Fy))$$

we take x to be any mental state, and y to be the brain-state with which x is to be identified,[2] and 'Fx' as 'x is the subject of incorrigible judgments', and hence also as 'It is logically impossible that x is judged to occur and x does not occur', we can argue that

$(x = y) \supset$ [(It is logically impossible that x is judged to occur and x does not occur) $\supset$
(It is logically impossible that y is judged to occur and y does not occur)].

The antecedent of the right-hand side is true, according to the Incorrigibility Thesis, and the consequent of the right-hand side is

[1] The first conjunct is shortened below to 'x is judged to occur'. The difficulties engendered by the intensionality of 'judges', as distinct from those engendered by the intensionality of 'it is logically impossible that', are simply ignored at this point (though they become crucial below).

[2] The hypotheticals to be discussed must be thought of as containing names or definite descriptions for the variables 'x' and 'y' of the law. (For ease of reading the cases are nevertheless set down with 'x' and 'y'.) A difficulty that arises here is taken up below.

false according to everyone; hence the right-hand side is false, and hence '$(x = y)$' false. This holds for any choice of mental state as x, and for any choice of brain-state as y, though of course the latter choice is limited by considerations of correlation, and so on. I take this to be a fair recasting of the argument.

Now this argument is invalid. In showing this, I take the case of the evening star and the morning star, because of its familiarity, though there can reasonably be doubt whether 'the evening star' and 'the morning star' should not be capitalized and regarded as proper names. But obviously other suitable cases are readily available if this one is unacceptable. Now 'the morning star' means something like 'the last heavenly body observable before dawn in the eastern sky'. Taking the morning star as x, and the evening star as y, and 'Fx' as 'It is logically impossible that x is not observable before dawn in the eastern sky', we have

$(x = y) \supset$ [(It is logically impossible that x is not observable in the eastern sky) $\supset$ (It is logically impossible that y is not observable in the eastern sky)].

Evidently, it *is* logically impossible that the morning star is not under certain conditions observable in the eastern sky. But the consequent of the right-hand side is certainly false. Therefore '$(x = y)$' is false. But (as a matter of astronomy) '$(x = y)$' is true. Hence the hypothetical is false.

The source of the trouble is certainly not hard to see. For familiar modal reasons we do not derive a true hypothetical from our law,

$$(x)(y)((x = y) \supset (Fx \supset Fy))$$

if we offer interpretations of 'Fx' containing logical modalities. (The causal modalities are less perverse. If in the last example we drop both occurrences of 'It is logically impossible that', the upshot is undoubtedly true, despite the presence of 'observable'.)

It might be objected that the instances of '$(x)(y)((x = y) \supset (Fx \supset Fy))$' that have been tacitly taken, both in the original argument and in the refuting analogy, contain definite descriptions as grammatical subjects (e.g. 'the pain had by S at T', 'the morning star', etc.); and that since sentences with such subjects cannot appear as logical falsehoods on either of the theories of definite descriptions that hold the field, viz. Russell's and Strawson's, it follows that both the original argument and the refuting analogy are misconceived.

But the claim about Russell's theory would be false, and the claim about Strawson's not obviously true.

On Russell's theory the customary sense of

The king of France is not bald

is not expressed by

$$\sim[(\exists x)(Kx . (y)(Ky \supset (x = y)) . Bx)]$$

but is rather

$$(\exists x)(Kx . (y)(Ky \supset (x = y)) . \sim Bx)$$

Thus

The king of France is not a king of France

is *not* the negation of

$$(\exists x)(Kx . (y)(Ky \supset (x = y)) . Kx)$$

(which negation would certainly not be a logical falsehood) but is rather

$$(\exists x)(Kx . (y)(Ky \supset (x = y)) . \sim Kx)$$

which *is* a logical falsehood. Certainly, on Russell's theory,

The king of France is a king of France

being

$$(\exists x)(Kx . (y)(Ky \supset (x = y)) . Kx)$$

is *not* a logical *truth*. But neither the *refutandum* nor the refuting analogy says that it is.

Equally I can find no particular reason for thinking that the logical falsehoods postulated by the preceding argument are not available on Strawson's theory, though I do not consider the point further.

The conclusions reached so far are obvious enough, but it might be thought that since the trouble lies in permitting logical modalities to occur in the expressions replacing the predicate letters in the identity law, then success will come if one aims lower; if it is impossible that a sensation should be judged to occur, and yet not occur, then it is also the case that it is false that a sensation is judged to occur, and yet does not occur. The argument based on this latter proposition will clearly not suffer from the faults of its predecessor.

Taking '*Fx*' as 'It is not the case that *x* is judged to occur and *x* does not occur', we can now argue that

$$(x = y) \supset [\sim(x \text{ is judged to occur and } x \text{ does not occur})$$
$$\supset \sim(y \text{ is judged to occur and } y \text{ does not occur})].$$

For convenience, the whole hypothetical is called 'P'. The principal antecedent ('$(x = y)$') is called 'A', the principal consequent (everything within the square brackets) is called 'C', and the four constituent sentences of C are called '(1)', '(2)', '(3)', and '(4)' in the order of their appearance. Thus P asserts that

$$A \supset [\sim((1) \ \& \ (2)) \supset \sim((3) \ \& \ (4))]$$

Now it can be shown that the necessity of P, and thus the validity of the corresponding argument, imposes a certain condition on the 'judged' of (1) and (3). This can be shown by the following argument:

(a) On the assumptions that P is necessary, that A is true, that (1) is false and that (2) is true, then ((3) & (4)) is false.

(b) But then, on the same assumptions (in particular, that A is true and that (2) is true), (4) is true.

(c) So, in the case envisaged, (3) is false.

(d) So, in the case envisaged, if (1) is false, then (3) is false.

(e) So, if P is necessary, then 'judged' is referentially transparent.[1]

It may be objected that contention (e) fails to follow from what precedes it, since a relation shown to hold between (3) and (4),

---

[1] In Quine's sense, *Word and Object*, New York, 1960, p. 144. 'I call a mode of containment ϕ referentially transparent if, whenever an occurrence of a singular term t is purely referential in a term or sentence $\psi(t)$, it is purely referential also in the containing term or sentence $\phi (\psi(t))$.' The transparent idiom is no doubt an unusual one, but it exists. Quine, *op. cit.* pp. 148-9, claims to find a paradox in the idiom, but his argument is faulty. Briefly: Tom's logical acumen can hardly be supposed to operate on the sentences that he believes (transparently), *unless he is aware that he believes them* (transparently)—or else believes them opaquely. Thus, unless Tom believes (opaquely) that $\delta p = \delta$ (Cicero denounced Catiline) or, alternatively, is aware that he believes it (transparently), then he is not aware that he believes (transparently) that $\delta p = 1$, and hence the hypothesis of acumen fails to give 'Tom believes [transparently] that P.' If, however, Tom does believe (opaquely) that $\delta p = \delta$ (Cicero denounced Catiline), or alternatively is aware that he believes it (transparently), then Tom does believe (opaquely) that $\delta p = 1$, or, alternatively, is aware that he believes it (transparently). But if the cases of (transparent) belief that p, that are established, are just those cases where Tom believes (opaquely) that $\delta p = \delta$ (Cicero denounced Catiline), or is aware that he believes it (transparently), then they merely constitute the limited and unsurprising set of cases where Tom *already* believes (opaquely) or is aware that he believes (transparently) that p. Thus it does not follow from the fact that Tom has one transparent belief that he is transparently omniscient. A parallel argument saves the idiom from paradox in the case of Tom's false beliefs. Quine obscures the issue by writing as though his argument depended on 'declaring belief invariably transparent' (p. 149), but no such dependence is apparent.

M

and a consequent property of 'judged', by an arbitrary assignment of truth values to A, (1) and (2), cannot be regarded as establishing a property of 'judged' essential to the necessity of P, but only a property of 'judged' essential to the necessity of P *under that particular assignment of truth values*. But this seems a very strange position. What has been shown above is that if (3) can take on a truth-value independently of (1), i.e. if 'judged' is not transparent, then a certain assignment of truth values shows P false, and hence shows the corresponding argument invalid. If 'judged' is shown to be transparent *by* any one assignment of truth values, then it is shown to be so *for* all, as a condition of the necessity of P. (Not that this requires that (1) and (3) always have the same truth value. For if $x \neq y$, then any of the four permutations is available. To have F/T or T/F is not to say that 'judged' has ceased to be transparent, but only that the condition under which the transparency manifests itself, viz. where $x = y$, does not obtain.)

The preceding argument, then, establishes a condition of the necessity of P. Before saying how this condition militates against the use of P against the Identity Thesis, I want to indicate the precise way in which P might be thought to have the effect of refuting the Identity Thesis. In its previous use, the Incorrigibility Thesis was applied directly against the Identity Thesis, but no such direct use is possible here, since we certainly have no *a priori* guarantee that false judgments are in fact ever made by people about their own brain states. But, it might be argued, we could set up a laboratory devoted to the falsification of the Identity Thesis, and the *rationale* of the procedure would be given by P. The conditions are these:

(I) We arrange that S makes no judgments[1] at all about his current sensations. Thus (1) is made false, and $\sim((1)$ and $(2))$ is made true.

(II) A person of imposing academic appearance, declaring himself (perhaps truly) to be a Professor of Neurophysiology, misinforms the subject concerning the brain state, whatever it is, that is to be identified with a given sensation, declaring that the subject's brain is in that state when it is arranged that it is not. Subjects who do not succumb to this weight of authority are

---

[1] As defined above p. 174. All that is required is that the subject does not heedfully set himself to formulate to himself what his sensations are. This, so far from being a rare situation, is the usual one.

rejected. Thus accepted subjects satisfy both (3) and (4) with respect to that brain state, and thus $\sim$((3) and (4)) is made false. The inference then simply is that $x \neq y$.

The procedure is a bizarre one, but not lacking in force. It aims at showing that *any* given identification is incorrect, no matter what the evidence of correlation. But it is not being argued that any given set of identifications is incorrect, by the method of actually considering all sets; rather, a method is given for refuting any given identification by describing *readily* realizable conditions (viz. (I) and (II) above)[1] under which any such identification is falsified.

Now the method is ineffective, as can be shown by the following considerations:

(A) The user of the method argues that $\sim$((1) & (2)) is true, while $\sim$((3) & (4)) is false, i.e. that $(\sim(1) \text{ v } \sim(2))$ where $((3) \& (4))$.

(B) Call $(\sim(1) \text{ v } \sim(2))$ 'α' and $((3) \& (4))$ 'β'. Now in the present method it is proposed to show the truth of α by showing that $\sim(1)$. But then we make it impossible to show the truth of β. For that requires the concurrent *truth* of (3). But, since the 'judged' of (1) and of (3) has been shown to be transparent, the condition for this disparity in truth-value between (1) and (3) is that $x \neq y$. But the assumption of this condition is *petitio*.

The point involved can be brought out as follows. If $x = y$ then the transparency of 'judged', *a condition of the validity of the argument*, requires that (1) and (3) take the same truth value, *whatever the subject says or does*. All his protestations to the contrary notwithstanding, if $x = y$ then if (1) then (3), and if $\sim(1)$ then $\sim(3)$. That is the force of saying that 'judged' is transparent. Now in the experimental situation it is arranged that we have the subject's word for it that $\sim(1)$, and that we have the subject's word for it that (3). The inference to $(\sim(1) \& (3))$ is an inference that can only be made on the assumption that $x \neq y$. Thus the subject's claims about what he is and is not judging do *nothing* to establish that $(\sim(1) \& (3))$ unless we make the further assumption that $x \neq y$. (Here of course is the great difference between the transparent and the opaque senses of 'judged'.) But the assumption that does give the desired inference is clearly *petitio*. We would be proposing to argue against a thesis by adducing

---

[1] This point is amplified below.

evidence, part of which consisted in the assumption of the falsity of the thesis in question. The situation is, then, that a condition for the necessity of P (viz. the transparency of 'judged') prevents the use of P against the Identity Thesis in the way envisaged above (viz. *via* (I) and (II)).

It might be thought that P could be put to work in a different way that escapes the objection arising from the transparency of 'judged'. Could we not arrange that (2) be false (thus making α true) and (3) and (4) both true, thus making β false, and thus, as desired, getting $x \neq y$? I think it is quite clear that we cannot. For part of the *prima facie* force of the earlier method (i.e. *via* (I) and (II)) lay in the fact that no decision about the truth value of (2) was made, nor was any needed. Indeed, to have required that (2) be false, where (4) was true, would by itself have rendered the method unacceptable, since we have no guarantee that we can, given the absence of a certain brain state, also *arrange* for any mental state we like to occur. If anything, we have something verging on a guarantee of the falsity of this. Pretty obviously, one could also argue that the requirement would have been *petitio* against the Identity Thesis. It was partly in view of the absence of any such requirement of disparity in truth value between (2) and (4) that I described the conditions that *were* required as 'readily realizable'. For these conditions involve no assumptions about psychophysical correlations; they merely require that subjects make no judgment about their mental states, and be sufficiently amenable to accept the false information about their brain states that the imposing person gives them.

Thus the alternative method being considered makes unwarranted assumptions, and is also very likely question-begging. Furthermore, if the information it assumes to be in our possession, viz. information about the non-sufficiency of any mental state for any brain state, actually were in our possession, we could forget all about incorrigibility and the complications of P. We would have argument enough against the Identity Thesis.

II

In the remainder of this paper I wish to sketch what I will call the 'Objection from Location against the Identity Thesis'.[1] The

---

[1] But see J. A. Shaffer, 'Recent Work on the Mind-Body Problem', *American Philosophical Quarterly*, Vol. 2, 1965, pp. 96-8, for a quite different objection from location.

first part of the argument, A, aims at giving some reason for accepting the view that many bodily sensations are located in regions of space in just the sense in which physical bodies are so located. The second part, B, aims at showing that this fact falsifies the Identity Thesis.[1]

A

I identify and seek to meet four arguments (perhaps not entirely distinct from each other) that seem to be at work in support of the view that 'location', as applied to physical bodies and to sensations respectively, is not univocal. My thesis is that since the *onus probandi* lies on the philosopher who denies univocality, and since, according to what follows below, the relevant equivocality is unproved, univocality ought to be assumed.

The general question regarding the onus of proof in philosophy is one that has received little attention, and I do not pretend that my present claim about the onus is self-evidently correct. I can only say (for want both of space and of any adequate insight into the matter) that it seems to me to be sound procedure to assume that a term is not ambiguous until some positive reason is given for believing that it is. But it also appears that sound procedure should restrict the nature of such reason. For it might be said that the desirability of some general philosophical position, such as Physicalism or Thomism, could give a reason for deeming a particular term ambiguous, namely that univocality in that term would call in question the truth of the general position. Perhaps acceptance of a general position can reasonably yield hope, trust or faith that a desired ambiguity exists (or that an undesired argument is invalid, or that a repugnant proposition false), but short of giving up the business of philosophical criticism whenever it threatens a theory, it seems difficult to regard such acceptance as yielding a reason of the relevant kind for holding that the ambiguity in question does exist. Hence it seems that in the specific onus-principle that I enunciate above, 'some positive reason' should be understood as 'some positive reason based on suitable semantic considerations'.

---

[1] If space permitted, I would wish to add my reasons for rejecting various theories of the nature of somatic sensations which, if accepted, would allow the present objection to be by-passed. I have in mind theories such as that in Smart's *Philosophy and Scientific Realism*, Ch. 5, and that in D. M. Armstrong's *Bodily Sensations*, London, 1962. I have commented on the former in 'Sensations, Brain Processes and Colours', *Australasian Journal of Philosophy*, Vol. 41, 1963, pp. 385–93, and find related difficulties in the latter.

A quite different suggestion would be that if there were available an analysis of location claims about somatic sensation on which 'location' did appear as equivocal, and which also squared with the relevant data as well as any analysis on which the term did not appear as equivocal, then the independent desirability of Physicalism could unobjectionably lead us to prefer the former type of analysis. This does seem to be an acceptable method, and the question then is whether an analysis of the required sort is available. Quasi-behaviourist theories of location such as Baier's [1] and Taylor's [2] would be suitable, and perhaps the Identity Thesis should seek to utilize them for the purpose. I cannot enter into a discussion of these theories here, but can only record (what is obvious from the fact that I persevere with the Objection from Location) that I do not find them acceptable.

The first of the objections to univocality that I wish to consider is from phantom limbs. In view of the facts relating to these, it might be argued, it is false that all somatic sensations are spatial characteristics of some part of a human body. But the view which I wish to maintain declares that many (not all) somatic sensations are at the places they occupy, in just the sense in which neural elements (for example) are at the places they occupy. Thus, firstly, I do not wish to hold that all are. And secondly, if I did, the objection would still fail—it is consistent with my thesis that the sensations 'in' phantom limbs are not at a place occupied by any part of the body of the person who suffers, since the thesis is not that somatic sensations are spatial characteristics of bodies, but merely that they are, in large numbers, spatially located with respect to living bodies in the same sense as that in which physical bodies are located with respect to each other.

The second objection points out that medical men do not detect sensations, though they scrutinize the regions occupied by these sensations. The principle of this argument would appear to be that anything that has a position with respect to a physical coordinate system is detectable by direct sensory methods. That this principle is false can be seen from the highly indirect manner in which the position of elementary particles is determined in atomic physics. But suppose that the point is restated so that *some*

---

[1] K. Baier, 'The Place of a Pain', *Philosophical Quarterly*, Vol. 14, 1964, pp. 138–50.
[2] D. M. Taylor, 'The Location of Pain', *Philosophical Quarterly*, Vol. 15, 1965, pp. 53–62.

manner of detection by sensory methods is essential to a *locandum* having a position with respect to a physical co-ordinate system. It is clear that any such weakening is liable to the objection that *some* manner of detection by sensory methods *is* available to the neurologist; he can infer the occurrence of certain sensations from certain observed neural conditions. So that even if the weakened principle were granted, it is not clear that it would serve its purpose of allowing us to infer the equivocality of 'location'. But there is also the question why such a principle, even in its weakened form, *should* be granted. Why, without further reason, should we suppose it true or acceptable? I can only suppose that it is a rather peculiar act of faith, or a fideistic stipulation, or that it draws some sort of indirect support from the arguments that I consider next. Thus either it has no support, or else it has no more force than the arguments it indirectly leans on.

The third objection to univocality is one bound up with the question what it is that decides that a sensation *does* have a certain location. For in connection with the location of a sensation S with respect to a reference body R, we are faced with the question what it is *about* S that gives it its alleged relation to R. But the method which proceeds with this question *without further ado* is a curious one, since it ignores the fact that precisely the same question presents itself if we reflect on the location of physical bodies with respect to a reference body.

What then decides the location of sensations and of physical bodies? The obvious ambiguity of 'decides' can quickly be resolved. On the assumed view of the univocality of 'location', and in one sense of 'decides', what decides the location both of sensations and of physical bodies is *where they are*. They do not differ in this respect. Evidently the sense of 'decides' involved is rather an epistemological one; the sense of the question is 'On the strength of what marks do we assign positions to sensations and to physical bodies respectively?' G. N. Vesey[1] has drawn attention to the bearing of the Local Signs theory on this point. At times Vesey appears to be taking Lotze's theory[2] to bear directly on the question of the correct analysis of position claims about sensations, given the concept of physical position as a *datum*, but it can hardly

---

[1] In 'The Location of Bodily Sensations', *Mind*, Vol. LXX, 1961, pp. 25–35, and in *The Embodied Mind*, London, 1965.

[2] R. H. Lotze, *Outlines of Psychology* (tr. and ed. by George T. Ladd), Boston, 1886, Part I, Ch. 4.

do this, since it is a theory about the way in which a spatial world is constructed from the allegedly non-spatial raw material of visual and tactual experience. Lotze is certainly not taking the concept of physical position for granted, and then inquiring how a stimulus applied to the body is located by somatic sensation. But the claim of the theory that there is not in any sensation 'any element of actual locality, of inherent spatial order, any tone, as it were, which cries to us immediately and without further ado, "I am here", or "I am there"',[1] is probably the source of a view relevant to my present topic. For it might be said that there is no non-relational phenomenological feature of a somatic sensation that can be regarded as a mark of its location;[2] that, therefore, some other indirect secondary method must be involved in our judgments about the position of sensations; that, therefore, the sense of 'location' in which such sensations are located must be secondary and derivative; that, therefore, the thesis of univocality is false.

Yet what is it in the case of a physical *locandum* that cries, without further ado, 'I am here' or 'I am there'? In *its* case there seems to be no objection made to saying that it is in virtue of the tactually and visually perceived relationship of the physical body to the reference body that we are led to assign a particular position to the former. So far as I know, nobody supposes that the marks by which we assign physical bodies to their respective places are specifiable without the use of a relational spatial vocabulary. Yet, if I am correctly stating the third argument, it is the fact that the marks by which we assign sensations to *their* places are not specifiable without the use of a relational spatial vocabulary that is invoked in support of the view that they are not located in the sense in which physical bodies are located.

Perhaps at this point we should shift the emphasis. (Whether the upshot of doing so should be thought of as a twist to the foregoing argument, or as a new argument altogether, I shall for the moment leave undecided. But I shall call what follows 'the fourth reason'.) For while sensations can possibly be put into spatial

---

[1] W. James, *Principles of Psychology*, New York, 1890, Ch. XX, section 'Local Signs'.

[2] The argument that I am conjecturing here involves, of course, considerable departure from Lotze's theory, since on that theory there *are* suitable phenomenological differences between impressions arising from stimulation of different parts of the body surface, and it is precisely these differences that serve to establish the spatial order of the stimuli. But the non-availability of many local signs to introspection was one of the chief criticisms of the theory, so the departure would not be an unnatural one.

relations, or into some analogue of spatial relations, with *each other* (as presumably in Vesey's body *qua* sensitive), nevertheless the unacceptable consequence of the view of univocality is that if sensations, even thus located, can be put into spatial relationship *with a physical reference body*, then some sort of *rapport* can be established between the quite disparate perception modalities of sight and touch, on the one hand, and sensation perception (for the sake of a convenient phrase) on the other.[1]

What precise *rapport* is desired, and why, is a very difficult matter to specify, and the closest I can come to stating the force of the demand is in terms of the following model. Suppose two observers, who, unobserved by each other, make visual and tactual observations which reveal their environments to them. Suppose, then, that the first of them, A, selects a co-ordinate system R for spatial reference, and locates the inhabitants of his environment with respect to R. He learns that the observer B is acquainted with an environment of a certain spatial distribution and he (A) wants to know the relationship of the constituents of B's environment to R. If no communication between A and B is possible, and if, after A's initial information about B, no third parties can effect communication with both, then the question is one that A cannot, within the terms of the supposition, get the answer to. But if A can communicate with B, and be directed by B to B's environment, then he can determine where, relative to his own environment, B's lies, and he can determine this ultimately by noting, by sight and touch, the spatial relations between the environments. Now the man with somatic sensations is like A—so runs the argument—in that he is acquainted with a physical environment (in particular his own body) by sight and touch and, further, another spatial or quasi-spatial environment, viz. the distribution of his own sensations, is known to him just as the spatial environment of B is known to A (i.e. its distribution, not its relation to A's own). But whereas A *can* bring B's environment into *rapport* with his (A's) own, if he has the communication with B that allows him to bring visual and tactual perception to bear on the comprehensive environment containing both his (A's) and also B's, the man with somatic sensations is *unlike* A in this respect.

[1] Vesey, in *The Embodied Mind* (especially Chapters 4, 6, 7 and 8), is concerned with this problem of *rapport* (if not actually under this rubric). His concern however seems to be rather more epistemological than my present one, though I have little doubt he would resist the implied distinction.

He has no way of scanning, with a single sense, the comprehensive environment containing his somatic sensations (located though they may be with respect to each other) and his physical body. There is not, and could not be, such a sense as would scan the sensation, and the physical body, and note the relation of the former to the latter. Therefore the case differs from that of A and B in this; whereas A might be in a position to bring two spatial distributions into *rapport*, and can be hindered from doing so only by an accidental lack of communication with B, the man with somatic sensations could never be in the analogous position. While, therefore, the question what the spatial relationship between A's and B's environments may be is a clear one, if not actually decidable by A, the parallel question about the spatial relationships between the body and the distribution of sensations is senseless. Therefore 'location' is not univocal as applied to sensations and physical bodies respectively.

But if the argument is conceived in these terms, it is not so easy to see its force. It depends, as it stands above, on the principle that it is senseless to speak of a spatial distribution unless all of the *relata* are detectable by a single sense modality, e.g. vision *or* sensation perception. Yet this seems to me just a bizarre piece of neo-verificationism which I see no particular reason to accept. But perhaps the argument only appears to depend on such verificationism. Perhaps it really depends on what I called 'the third reason'; on the view, that is, that one requirement of univocality is that there be some non-relational phenomenological feature of sensations that enables us to locate them with reference to a physical co-ordinate system; that, failing this, the case of the man with somatic sensations cannot be regarded as comparable with the case of A, since, while A in principle has access to the observable spatial properties of B's environment that would enable him (A) to determine the relation of that environment to his (A's) own, the man who has somatic sensations can find no such marks in his somatic sensations.

But if that is what the argument depends on, then it *is* only a variation on the argument I called 'the third reason'. And I argued above that the third reason cannot be regarded as compelling.

B

This completes my discussion of the question of univocality. I now seek to apply the view I have been defending to the falsification of the Identity Thesis. For if the preceding argument is correct, then a great many bodily sensations can be specified which are not identical with any state or states of a central nervous system (hereafter 'CNS'), since they are spatially remote from those regions of bodies which are occupied by the CNSs in question.

It might be replied that this argument against the Identity Thesis fails when the distinction between 'a sensation' and 'having a sensation' is observed. It is (all) instances of the latter that are, by the Identity thesis, asserted to be identical with brain states, not instances of the former. But the argument aimed at showing that a great many bodily sensations have a physical position certainly does not show that the having of a bodily sensation has a physical position, and the objection therefore lapses.

Allowing that the *distinction* (between terms) exists, we can argue that there must also be a *difference* between any having of a sensation, on the one hand, and any located sensation on the other, for this reply to stand. For if any having of a sensation were identical with some located sensation, then the Objection from Location would still hold, since any such having of a sensation would then have acquired an unsuitable location.

How, then, is the difference to be thought of? Are havings of sensations to be regarded as complexes, of which sensations themselves are constituents? Are havings of sensations states, of which sensations are objects? Neither view is ruled out by the view that there is a distinction between 'having a sensation' and 'a sensation'. But neither seems consistent with the intentions of the Identity Thesis. Take the latter view first. Now if the Identity Thesis asserts that every such state is identical with some brain process, but makes no assertion about the sensations that figure as objects of such states, then it is freed of the Objection from Location. But on this interpretation the Identity Thesis does not support a physicalist theory of the world in the way it is usually supposed to do, namely by showing that there is nothing in the nature of mind that is inconsistent with a physicalist theory. For on this interpretation certain objects of certain mental states are not declared to be identical with any states of any CNS, viz. the somatic sensations that figure as objects of certain (cognitive) states. An Identity Thesis so weak as to be silent on the nature of such objects would hardly be worth consideration.

The former way of explaining the difference between sensations and the havings of sensations seems equally inadequate. If sensations are held to be constituents of complexes, each of which is identical with a state of some CNS, then we must again regard the unsuitable locations of many sensations as inconsistent with the identification. This holds, since, on the Identity Thesis, every such complex has a physical location, namely, in some region of a CNS. But if some constituent of such a complex is spatially remote from any such region, then the complex is not fully located in any such region, but is spread over a wider region (one as extensive as a human body, or even more so).

If the foregoing really are consequences of invoking the distinction between 'having a sensation' and 'a sensation', then it seems that if the Identity Thesis is to be maintained against the Objection from Location, and if this is to be done by leaning on the notion 'having a sensation', then the latter will have to be treated as unanalysable, and 'a sensation' will have to be treated as no distinct (semantic) constituent. To adapt an example of Quine's, 'a sensation' is on this view no more a (semantic) element of a complex 'having a sensation' than 'rat' is a (semantic) element of a complex 'refrigeration'. The point can be illustrated in this way, but there is a striking disanalogy between the cases, for 'rat' is a semantic element (of English) in its own right, whereas if it were allowed that, in a similar sense, 'a sensation' is a semantic element in its own right, then the present reply to the Objection from Location would be given up. Presumably, then, the point should rather be made by saying that 'a sensation' is no more a component of a complex 'having a sensation' (or better 'having-a-sensation', or better still 'havingasensation') than 'efrig' is a component of a complex 'refrigeration'. But still the analogy is imperfect, since 'refrigeration' is not unanalysable. Let us say, for the sake of argument, that 'yellow' is unanalysable, and then the point could be made by saying that 'a sensation' is no more a component of a complex 'havingasensation' than 'yel' is a component of a complex 'yellow'. Now on this view there ought to be as many true propositions about sensations as there are about yels, namely none. But that is false. For there are many true propositions relating to sensations, declaring of them, for example, that they have such and such spatial locations, that they are pleasant, or not pleasant, or neutral, that they are more or less intense. Thus the analogy with 'yel' and 'yellow' fails. Even if it is (somehow) true, then, that 'havingasensation' is an *unanalysable* term, there is nevertheless a term, 'a sensation', which, even if no more (semantically) a component of 'havingasensation' than 'rat' is (semantically) a component of 'refrigeration', is such as to warrant examination by a physicalist theory of the world. For the term is true of some things, and an Identity Thesis so weak as to be silent on the nature of such things would hardly be worth consideration.

10

D. H. MUNRO

MILL'S THIRD HOWLER

I

It used to be said that, in the fourth chapter of his *Utilitarianism*, Mill made three glaring howlers: he confused 'desired' with 'desirable'; he maintained that 'all desire the happiness of all' follows from 'each desires his own happiness'; he failed to distinguish a means to happiness from a part of happiness. Comparatively recently, Mill has been defended on the first two charges,[1] but, so far as I know, not on the third. Yet this third argument is, I believe, at least equally defensible. Moreover a consideration of Mill's views on this matter raises some quite central questions in ethics.

Let me first state the charge against Mill in the words of the most vehement of his accusers, G. E. Moore.[2]

'But now let us return to consider another of Mill's arguments for his position that "happiness is the sole end of human action". Mill admits, as I have said, that pleasure is not the only thing we actually desire. "The desire of virtue", he says, "is not as universal, but it is as authentic a fact, as the desire of happiness." And again, "Money is, in many cases, desired in and for itself". These admissions are, of course, in naked and glaring contradiction with his argument that pleasure is the only thing desirable, because it is the only thing desired. How then does Mill even attempt to avoid this contradiction? His chief argument seems to be that

---

[1] See James Seth, 'The Alleged Fallacies in Mill's *Utilitarianism*', *Philosophical Review*, Vol. XVII, 1908; E. W. Hall, 'The "Proof" of Utility in Bentham and Mill', *Ethics*, Vol. IX, 1949; D. D. Raphael, 'Fallacies in and about Mill's Utilitarianism', *Philosophy*, Vol. XXX, 1955; R. F. Atkinson, 'J. S. Mill's "Proof" of the Principle of Utility', *Philosophy*, Vol. XXXII, 1957.

[2] G. E. Moore, *Principia Ethica*, 1903, s. 43. Henry Sidgwick makes essentially the same point against Mill (though he thought the confusion due to 'a mere looseness of phraseology, venial in a treatise aiming at a popular style') in *Methods of Ethics*, 7th ed., Book I, Ch. VII, note to the last sentence of s. 1. This note does not appear in editions before the sixth.

"virtue", "money" and other such objects, when they are thus
desired in and for themselves, are desired only as "a part of happiness". Now what does this mean? Happiness, as we saw, has been
defined by Mill, as "pleasure and the absence of pain". Does Mill
mean to say that "money", these actual coins, which he admits to
be desired in and for themselves, are a part either of pleasure or of
the absence of pain? Will he maintain that those coins themselves
are in my mind, and actually a part of my pleasant feelings? If this
is to be said, all words are useless: nothing can possibly be distinguished from anything else: if these two things are not distinct,
what on earth is? We shall hear next that this table is really and
truly the same thing as this room; that a cab-horse is in fact indistinguishable from St Paul's Cathedral; that this book of Mill's
which I hold in my hand, because it was his pleasure to produce it,
is now and at this moment a part of the happiness which he felt
many years ago and which has so long ceased to be. Pray consider
a moment what this contemptible nonsense really means. "Money",
says Mill, "is only desirable as a means to happiness." Perhaps
so; but what then? "Why," says Mill, "money is undoubtedly
desired for its own sake." "Yes, go on", say we. "Well," says Mill,
"if money is desired for its own sake, it must be desirable as an
end-in-itself; I have said so myself." "Oh," say we, "but you also
said just now that it was only desirable as a means." "I own I did,"
says Mill, "but I will try to patch up matters, by saying that what is
only a means to an end, is the same thing as a part of that end.
I daresay the public won't notice." And the public hasn't noticed.
Yet this is certainly what Mill has done. He has broken down the
distinction between means and ends, upon the precise observance
of which his Hedonism rests.'

Having heard counsel for the prosecution, let us now put in as
Exhibit A the passage from Mill (or part of it) which provoked
this tirade.

'The principle of utility does not mean that any given pleasure, as
music, for instance, or any given exemption from pain, as for
example health, is to be looked upon as means to a collective
something termed happiness, and to be desired on that account.
They are desired and desirable in and for themselves; besides
being means, they are part of the end. Virtue, according to the
utilitarian doctrine, is not naturally and originally part of the end,

but it is capable of becoming so; and in those who love it disinterestedly it has become so, and is desired and cherished, not as a means to happiness, but as a part of their happiness.'[1]

That there is some looseness in Mill's language can hardly be denied. (He was, after all, writing a semi-popular article for *Fraser's Magazine*.) If happiness or 'pleasure' is, as Moore certainly thought it was, a 'state of mind', it is hard to see how music, or health, or money, or virtue, could be a part of it. The obvious conclusion would be that we want to listen to music because listening to it produces a plesasurable state of mind, to have money because it can be spent on things whose possession produces a pleasurable state of mind, and so on. Music, money and the rest would be means to pleasure, not parts of it. Yet Moore's own treatment of pleasure is not free from absurdity. If pleasure is a state of mind, it is hard to see how he can talk of 'pleasure, of which we never were and never could be conscious' (*Principia Ethica*, Section 52). Nor is it much better to talk, as he also does, about consciousness of pleasure as existing by itself. Pleasure is, after all, pleasure in something: it is not a mere thrill or twinge. To go walking for pleasure is not to go walking in order to feel a particular physical sensation called 'pleasure'. It is, rather, to go walking not in order to get to a particular place, not in order to be healthy, but simply because one likes walking. To do something for pleasure is, in short, to do it for its own sake, as an end and not as a means.

One's pleasure, or happiness, then, can be regarded as just the sum of those things one does for their own sake: the sum of one's ends. It is in this sense that listening to music, or being healthy, can be part of one's happiness. To do something as a means to happiness, on the other hand, is to do it not for its own sake but because it leads to something that is part of one's happiness: buying a record, for example, as distinct from listening to it.

But if anything one wants for its own sake is part of one's happiness, what becomes of the assertion that 'there is really nothing desired except happiness'?[2] Is it not quite empty? Apparently one can desire anything, and anything that one does desire is thereby part of one's happiness.

---

[1] *Utilitarianism*, Everyman edition, p. 34.
[2] *Op. cit.*, p. 45. Mill also says that 'pleasure and freedom from pain are the only things desirable as ends' (p. 6).

Here one must remember that behind what Mill is saying there is quite an elaborate psychological theory: the associationism of David Hartley and James Mill. In essentials, associationism is not very different from Pavlov's conditioning, with which we are nowadays much more familiar. Consider, then, one of Pavlov's dogs. He may be said to have certain 'natural' desires: for food, bodily comfort and so on. Suppose that he has been conditioned to expect a bell to ring before food appears. (For the dog, the bell is *associated* with food.) Pavlov, of course, was mainly interested in the fact that the dog could be induced to salivate, at least for a time, by the bell alone, without the food. But one can imagine a situation in which the dog might be said to want the bell as well as the food. He might be trained, for example, not to eat unless the bell were rung; or might spontaneously show signs of uneasiness when food appeared without the bell. Pets, as well as children, are sometimes reluctant to eat unless they get their food in the familiar dish, or from the familiar source. (Actually, of course, it does not matter for the argument whether this is true of dogs or not: men do behave like this, and it is the parallel with men that really concerns us.)

Suppose, then, that a dog does show signs of being completely at ease only when he hears the bell at the same time as he gets the food. Suppose, too, that it is not too anthropomorphic to say that the dog wants (or desires) both bell and food. Does he desire the bell merely as a means to food? Certainly he would not have come to want the bell at all if it had not been associated with food. Moreover, if the association were completely broken, he would, no doubt, no longer want the bell. On the other hand, he can hardly be said to want the bell only as a means if he continues to want it even when he has got the food. There is point in saying that the bell is part of his happiness, is itself one of the things he wants, 'disinterestedly, for their own sake'. We can say of it what Mill said of virtue:

'Virtue . . . is a good of this description. There was no original desire of it, or motive to it, save its conduciveness to pleasure, and especially to protection from pain. But through the association thus formed, it may be felt a good in itself, and desired as such with as great intensity as any other good.'[1]

[1] *Op. cit.*, p. 35.

N

According to Hartley,[1] men, like Pavlov's dogs, originally desired only physical pleasures: such things as food, comfort, or copulation. Like the dogs, they come to desire other things they associate with these. They can be trained to make these associations; but they can hardly help making some anyway, through the ordinary accidents of daily living. Where man differs from the other animals is in the immense richness and complexity of the associations he forms. He looks before and after, and pines for what is not: anticipation and memory transform and enrich his pleasures. As Hartley puts it, a new and distinct kind of pleasure and pain arises immediately out of the purely physical pleasures and pains. These are the pleasures and pains of imagination.

Nor is this all. Hartley's whole system depends on an elaborate hierarchy of pleasures, such that each grade is intrinsically more pleasant than the grade below it. Further, he says that the pleasures of each grade, above the first, are factitious. This means that they are derived by association from the grade below. The very lowest pleasures, then, the pleasures of sense, are the only original pleasures: but this does not mean that they are more real or more solid than the pleasures of the higher grades. It is a peculiarity of man that he is capable of refining the pleasures of sense, and as they become more refined they also become more pleasant.

How do the pleasures of sense generate intellectual pleasures? Hartley does not simply mean that we derive pleasure from remembering the pleasures of sense after they have vanished, or from anticipating them before they come. He means that the sensory pleasures are associated with their concomitants, so that the concomitants alone will evoke the idea of the original pleasure. But the idea of a sensation is, for Hartley, itself a sensation. There is no need to go into his theory of 'vibratiuncles', beyond saying that it depends on the contemporary distinction between impressions and ideas. An impression is essentially a vibration of the nerve centres: an idea is a minute vibration, differing from the impression only in vividness. Every impression, then, gathers round it in the course of experience a cluster of minor sensations, individually minute but collectively powerful. It follows that, in man, the simplest physical sensation is transformed, sometimes beyond recognition. The pleasures of eating, for example, are originally no doubt much the same in man as in the animals. But men eat in

[1] David Hartley, *Observations on Man, His Frame, His Duty, and His Expectations*, 2 vols, London, 1749. Esp. Vol. I, Ch. IV, and Vol. II, Ch. III.

company. Food, then, becomes associated with the idea of pleasant and relaxed conversation among one's friends. It is associated also with such concomitants as fine table linen, handsome plate and the like. The associations here are reciprocal. In part, table talk and table linen are pleasant because they are associated with food: but they have further associations, direct or indirect, with other original sources of pleasure. One can put this by saying that they suggest, in general, companionship and wealth: each of which is a means to the gratification of very many desires. In generating the intellectual pleasures, the pleasures of sense are themselves, as it were, swamped. Eating can never again be for a civilized man the narrow physical sensation it is for an animal. The most obvious example is sexual pleasure. It can hardly be doubted that the relations between men and women in civilized societies do derive their peculiar flavour from the knowledge, at the back of our minds, of the possibility of the physical pleasure of mating. But the pleasure of, let us say, a social evening in mixed company is not in any obvious sense physical at all. Similarly the physical act itself, when it does occur, is very much enriched by the wealth of associations which, in our culture at least, cluster round it. If your mind is full of the phrases of mediaeval chivalry, or of *Romeo and Juliet*, or of D. H. Lawrence, or even the latest love lyric from Tin Pan Alley, you simply do not have the same experience when you mate as your primitive ancestors had.

We can now see what Hartley means when he says that the intellectual pleasures are necessarily more pleasant than the pleasures of sense. Man leads a richer and fuller life than the animals simply because they are restricted to the narrow core of purely physical experience, which in man becomes overlaid with successive layers of mental experience. But it would seem, then, that Hartley does not quite mean what we naturally take him to mean. He is not simply saying that you will derive more pleasure, in the long run, from a disinterested love for your friends than from gluttony. He is saying that a large part of what we think of as the pleasures of the table is derived from, and made possible by, the disinterested love of one's friends. This changes the whole moral problem. It is not simply a question of choosing between alternatives. The hedonic calculus is usually thought of as a kind of graded catalogue of pleasures, useful if we find ourselves in the position of having to choose between pleasure A and pleasure B. We refer to the catalogue, discover that A is marked at ten units and *B* at nine, and make our choice accordingly. This is not what Hartley means when he puts the intellectual pleasures above the pleasures of sense. There is no question of rejecting one in favour of the other. Asceticism is self-stultifying, since the intellectual pleasures themselves need to be based on the pleasures of sense. But it is important that the pleasures of sense should be of the kind that makes the enriching process possible. Here again sex provides the most obvious example. Hartley would certainly have said that a monogamous marriage provides the best framework within which the pleasures of mere lust may be enriched and enhanced. Whether or not he is right, it is easy to see what he meant.

We can now, I think, see clearly what Hartley means by his hierarchy of pleasures. It is not merely that pleasures of the higher grades are more pleasant than an equal quantity of those of lower grades. The point is rather that pleasures of the lower grade should be subordinated to those of the higher grade: that is to say, the controlling factor must always be whether or not the lower grade pleasure leaves room for development into a higher pleasure. The ultimate justification for this is still quantity of pleasure; but we must not think of pleasures as competing against each other for our consideration, like so many candidates in a parliamentary election. Pleasures are not isolated or mutually exclusive units: they are bound up with one another (and with pains) in various ways. The problem is to integrate them so that they do not conflict. For Hartley as for some modern psychologists, the good life is the integrated life.

If *Utilitarianism* is read with Hartley in mind, one suspects that Moore missed the whole point of what Mill was saying. James Mill had pleaded for a system of education that would lead the pupil to associate his own happiness with the general happiness. 'Not only', said his son, 'does all strengthening of social ties, and all healthy growth of society, give to each individual a stronger personal interest in practically consulting the welfare of others; it also leads him to identify his *feelings* more and more with their good, or at least with an even greater degree of practical consideration for it. He comes to think of himself as a being who *of course* pays regard to others.'[1]

For a utilitarian, virtue is the desire to promote the general happiness. This can become an end in itself (and so part of one's

[1] *Op. cit.*, p. 30.

own happiness), Mill suggests, because one can (and, in a society to some extent must) come to associate one's own happiness with the general happiness in the way that Pavlov's dog associates the satisfaction of his hunger with the ringing of the bell.

But, it may be retorted, all this may perhaps explain or even excuse Mill's confusions; it does not make them any the less confusions. Hartley's psychology is, after all, out-dated now. Mill is not to be blamed if the psychology of his day was inadequate; but, even if he was not the fool that Moore thought him, there is no reason to suppose that he was right.

The main lesson that Mill learned from Hartley, however, is not in conflict with the findings of later psychologists. Human pleasures have a biological basis; but biological needs may be satisfied in a variety of ways. The food that delights a cannibal may disgust a European to the point where his body, as well as his mind, rejects it: he may spew it up when told what he has eaten. This may apply not only to human flesh, but to the flesh of puppies, or even to slugs and snails. Men find pleasure in eating, no doubt, because of a need for nourishment; but quite nourishing food may please some men but not others, and some food may please very much and nourish very little.

In the light of all this, it is too simple to say, with Moore, that there is a clear distinction between a means to happiness and a part of happiness. If you want a child to be happy one of the things you will do is to see that he is well nourished. If there were no connection between eating and nourishment he would probably not get pleasure from eating; but the pleasure he does take in eating is not just pleasure in anything that nourishes him. It is pleasure in certain kinds of food prepared and eaten in certain ways.

Biological needs, in short, give rise to secondary or acquired needs; once acquired, secondary needs may be as important (as much part of happiness) as the biological needs from which they are derived. Secondary needs 'are not naturally and originally part of the end, but are capable of becoming so'.

Self-interest may be regarded as the satisfaction of all a man's needs, whether biological or acquired. The important point for Mill is that one man's interests need not inevitably conflict with those of other men. Whether they do or not will depend largely on the nature of his secondary needs; even the biological needs themselves are modified by the secondary needs. If interests need not clash, it follows that self-interest and morality need not clash either.

II

This leads me to the second thesis of this paper: which is that Mill's arguments have implications that go beyond associationism or even utilitarianism. The relation between self-interest and morality has more than merely historical interest. We are no longer happy to talk with Bishop Butler of the 'faculties in the human soul' of cool self-love, benevolence, and conscience;[1] but if we ask, with Professor Baier,[2] what are good reasons for acting, the answer is that my enjoying something is a good reason, that the fact that others enjoy something is also a good reason, and that, in addition to these, there are moral reasons. Clearly this is simply Butler rephrased. Butler said that conscience had a natural supremacy; Baier that it is 'a rule of reason' that moral reasons take precedence over the other two. But it is certainly not absurd to ask why. Why is it rational to subordinate self-interest to morality? Is it enough to answer: 'It just is'?

Hobbes's answer, it will be remembered, was that moral rules state the way in which men must behave if society is to be possible. It is rational to obey them, because without society no one has much chance of gratifying any of his desires. The individual, then, accepts as his aim, not 'self-interest' simply, but a compromise between his own interests and those of everybody else. He accepts the compromise because half a loaf is better than no bread. Accepting the compromise implies that he feels obliged to subordinate his own interests to the compromise, when they conflict. This, of course, is not inconsistent with regarding the compromise as a means to serving his own interests, in the long run. To take a rough parallel: the aim of a business man is to make money, to have a substantial credit balance in the bank. To do this he may find it necessary to spend a good deal of money, perhaps to have an overdraft. In a sense, spending money is in direct conflict with having it: the larger the expenditure, the smaller the credit balance. But spending money may be a means to making it, nonetheless.

Business expenses are, of course, different from personal expenses. The business man wants money so that he can spend it. He may spend money on his business premises simply as a means to making money: the money he spends on his own house he spends

[1] Joseph Butler, Sermon I (Upon Human Nature), in *Works*, ed. by S. Halifax, Edinburgh, 1804, Vol. 2.

[2] K. Baier, *The Moral Point of View*, Ithaca, New York, 1958, Chs 4–7.

for the sake of having the house. According to Hobbes, we obey moral rules only as a means: in order to induce others to obey them too. Having others obey them is our reward; obeying them ourselves is the price we pay. The obvious objection is that we do not think of morality like this. We want to do the right thing for the sake of doing it; we want to *be* good blokes, decent chaps, and not just to make others believe that we are. It would seem to follow from Hobbes's account that it is more rational to be a successful hypocrite than a genuinely good man.

It is here that Hartley (or Pavlov, or at least the notion of training) comes in. If society depends on a general acceptance of the compromise, society will take pains to inculcate in each new generation the importance of accepting it. To anyone so trained, the compromise will not be thought of *as* a compromise, but simply as the right thing to aim at. Moreover he will feel uneasy at the prospect of attaining his purely personal ends in a way that would run counter to the compromise, much as our hypothetical dog feels uneasy at getting food when no bell has rung. In Mill's words, he comes to think of himself as a being who *of course* pays regard to others. Conformity with morality, with what Hobbes calls the laws of nature, has become a part of his happiness and not just a means to it.

It is true, of course, that the distinction between one's own interest and the interest of others now becomes blurred. If one's happiness consists in whatever one desires as an end, and if, as a result of conditioning or forming certain 'associations', one comes to desire that others shall attain their ends too, then their happiness becomes part of one's own happiness. But, of course, ends may conflict. Morality is largely a matter of adopting a settled policy of preferring one type of end to another, when such conflicts occur. Anyone raised in a Hobbist society will have been trained to prefer the compromise between interests ('the greatest happiness of the greatest number') to his own interest considered in isolation, much as a dog may be trained not to eat the food in front of him until he hears the bell.

In this way, Butler's three parts of human nature, or Baier's three types of reason for action, all fall into place. Men have desires, try to attain certain ends. Attaining them might be called self-interest, in its broadest sense. There are, however, two qualifications, each of which leads to a narrowing of the term. In the first place, since individual ends may conflict, there is room for

Butler's distinction between gratifying particular desires ('passions' or 'affections') and gratifying as many as possible, or perhaps the most central ones ('cool self-love'). Secondly, one may desire that others shall gratify *their* desires: either because of some natural 'sympathy' with one's fellows, or because, as a member of a society, one has learned to associate one's own well-being with that of others. (His mother's smiles and frowns are to an infant what the bells and flashing lights were to Pavlov's dogs.) These second-order desires for the happiness of others, though, in Mill's sense, a part of one's own happiness, may be distinguished from one's first-order desires. This gives us a narrower sense of self-interest, in which it is contrasted with benevolence. These two types of desire may conflict: as members of a society, we have been training to aim at that compromise between our own interests and those of others, a compromise which, according to Hobbes, is embodied in the social mores. Our conditioned acceptance of the compromise is what Butler calls conscience, and some other philosophers the moral sense. Mill also refers to it as the internal sanction.

In one way, the Butler-Baier account fits in well enough with the hedonic calculus. The individual, faced with a moral decision, is supposed to consider the consequences of his proposed actions, in terms of pleasure and pain, for all affected by it. Let us suppose that he decides that it will cause x units of pleasure to himself and y units of pain to someone else. If x is greater than y, he should do the action; if x is less than y, he should not. (This is a simplification, since he should consider the action, not in isolation, but along with the available alternative actions open to him; but we may ignore this complication at the moment.)

Now it is clear that this account presupposes Baier's three rules of reason, granted that 'moral reasons' are analysed as a utilitarian would analyse them. That the action causes pleasure to me is a reason for doing it; that it causes pain to another is a reason for not doing it; that it causes more pleasure than pain on balance is a reason for doing it. The third of these is the basic principle on which all more specific 'moral reasons' depend. The third is also the decisive consideration: in Baier's terms, moral reasons override both the others. This gives us a fourth principle: viz. that the third principle is the decisive one. This fourth principle is, of course, the utilitarian 'greatest happiness' principle.

Each of the four can be regarded as just brute facts, which can only be accepted. For Butler they are facts of human nature; for Baier 'rules of reason', i.e. basic postulates which we do in fact adopt in moral argument, and which it would be irrational not to adopt: parallels to the traditional logician's 'laws of thought'. For Sidgwick, they are 'intuitions'.

Up to a point, Mill's account is not very different from these. It is perhaps closest to Butler's. Certainly, it is a fact of human nature that the pursuit of pleasure and the avoidance of pain is a powerful (and ultimately the sole) motive. It is also a fact of human nature that we pay regard to the internal sanction. In Mill's own words) 'Its binding force consists in the existence of a mass of feeling which must be broken through in order to do what violates our standard of right, and which, if we do neverthess violate that standard, will probably have to be encountered afterwards in the form of remorse.'[1]

Where Mill differs is that he is not content to take either conscience or the utilitarian standard itself simply as an ultimate, admitting of no explanation. We acquire this 'mass of feeling' as the result of conditioning. It follows that 'the actual standard of right and wrong' to which it attaches itself will depend on the social mores, and vary as they vary. This would seem to make for a purely conventional morality, and to be inconsistent with utilitarianism. But the mores adopted by a society are not entirely arbitrary. They originate in the need to reconcile the conflicting interests of individuals. While this leaves room for a good deal of variation, Hobbes was probably right in maintaining that there are certain indispensable rules which must be followed (his 'laws of nature') if there is not to be an intolerable amount of internal friction. Hobbes may, indeed, have exaggerated the extent to which lack of equality, justice and the rest will lead to actual social disintegration. There have been quite stable societies built round the institution of slavery, for example. In such a society a man may very well feel quite genuine guilt and remorse at treating a slave as an equal. On the other hand, even a slave society will need, in at least some of its institutions, to lay down principles to some extent inconsistent with the institution of slavery: for example, that rewards should depend on what a man can help, and not on accidents of birth. It is inconsistencies of this kind that make moral reform possible. The moral reformer seizes on some principle already accepted in at least some social institu-

[1] *Op. cit.*, p. 26.

tions, and applies it to other institutions in the same society. Consequently it is possible for the individual conscience to be socially acquired without reflecting uncritically the conventions of the society. Moreover, since any society is bound to aim at establishing at least a minimum of peace and internal harmony, Mill can argue, at least plausibly, that the standards of right and wrong inculcated by society will tend towards the greatest happiness of the greatest number: that is to say, the maximum possible internal harmony. Society may not lay this down explicitly; but when the codes of behaviour it does inculcate are reflected on and made consistent, the utilitarian formula may very well result.

If we now ask why anyone should be moral—i.e. should subordinate self-interest to the general happiness—the answer is fairly clear. It is not quite Hobbes's answer. It is not that one does what is right merely as a means to getting what one wants for oneself. What one wants is that one should have one's personal desires gratified in a way sanctioned by morality—i.e. in a way that also conduces to the general happiness. To have them gratified in a way that would run counter to the general happiness would make one uneasy and dissatisfied, in exactly the way that a man or a woman imbued with the tradition of romantic love might be dissatisfied with mere sexual gratification without the 'falling in love' he (or, in our culture, perhaps especially she) has learned to associate with it. No doubt the 'romance' without any sexual gratification, ever, would also cease to satisfy; and so would the austere pursuit of the general happiness to the complete exclusion of one's own. But it is not the case that the one is sought as a means to the other: the two have become inseparably associated.

This account at least has the advantage of not making either conscience, or the standards by which it operates, simply an ultimate mystery, as both Baier and the intuitionists do, in their separate ways. It is true that Baier qualifies his position by making quite substantial concessions to Hobbes, but he still seems to think that at least the universalizability principle is somehow ultimate.[1] And when Baier tries to show that anyone who disregards his rules of reason is 'simply mad', it is significant that he considers only the first rule (about one's own enjoyment) in any detail.[2] Not to regard one's own enjoyment as *a* good reason for action does seem irrational. If we substitute 'happiness' for

[1] Baier, *op. cit.*, pp. 191 *et seq.* and pp. 314–15.
[2] *Ibid.* p. 302.

'enjoyment', and, with Mill, regard happiness as simply a composite name for those ends we do actually aim at, we may even be contradicting ourselves if we say that we do not have a good reason to attain those ends. It is by no means so obvious that it is irrational (as distinct from selfish or immoral) not to include among our ends the happiness of others, or the state of affairs in which everyone attains as much happiness as possible.

In short, Mill was right to regard the relation between self-interest and utility (the standard of right and wrong) as crucial. It is usually said that in his attempt to reconcile the two he fell into quite elementary confusions. My contention has been that this is unjust. But it is not merely a matter of rehabilitating Mill's reputation. The question still remains, and is still crucial. Whether or not Mill was wholly right, a solution along his general lines would seem to be at least as promising as any other as yet put forward.

11

G. SCHLESINGER

THE PASSAGE OF TIME

I

It has been persuasively argued in the past that it is absurd to refer to time as if it were something flowing, advancing or moving. If such talk made sense, one could very well ask how fast time moved, how many hours, for instance, did it take for the last hour to pass by? Consequently, philosophers concluded that anyone attempting to measure the rate at which time progresses must be hopelessly confused. But to try and attribute movement to time, without it having any specifiable speed, does not improve the situation either. For there could be no other way of attributing sense to such talk—it has been claimed—but by postulating a super-time in terms of which ordinary time could be thought of as flowing in the same way as water flows down the river in terms of normal time. The introduction of such an extraordinary entity into our physics, however, would not only be completely unjustified but would prove quite useless too. For as soon as we have explained the flow of ordinary time in terms of super-time, we are back where we began, at once wishing to talk about the passage of super-time itself. Thus immediately we require a still higher-order time and are involved in an infinite regress.

It has not been denied, of course, that our desire to picture time as marching on relentlessly has deep roots in habits of thought, universally shared, about such temporal relationships as: *before*, *after*, *past*, and *future*. Accordingly, it is suggested that in our thought all event-clusters formed by simultaneous events are arranged in a series built by the uniquely ordering relationship 'earlier than' or 'later than'. The position of every event cluster on the beam representing the series is eternally fixed. The present, on to which everyone's conscious self is anchored, however, constantly changes its position on this beam. Clusters of events which lie far ahead are approached by the travelling present, are passed, and then left further and further behind in the past. But what the anti-passage-of-time philosophers argue is that in spite of its attractiveness this is a profoundly wrong picture. If it were to be taken seriously, then the movement ascribed to the present must be the process of its covering a distance—temporal distance that is—in a given time, where 'time' must be referring now to some additional, extra-temporal time!

It should be noted that anti-passage-of-time philosophers do not wish to deny movement in general. They talk freely, like everyone else, about the progress of processes *in* time and assign a rate to every such progress which itself may have a rate of change in time. They are even prepared to talk about the progress of time as *defined by a specific clock* and only object to talking about the progress of time itself, conceived as existing apart from and in addition to the movements of all the clocks in nature. Indeed, by clearly understanding why the former talk is permissible we see exactly why the latter talk is absurd.

Every movement, or more generally every physical process, consists of stages which are formed by couples of events. Consider the process consisting in a pail of water heated on the stove. We regard a stage in this process: the event consisting in the water reaching a certain temperature, an event which may be coupled with the simultaneous event of a clock-hand coinciding with a certain point on a given clock dial. Two such stages are required before one can determine the rate of the water's rise in temperature in terms of the time defined by the movement of the clock hand of our chosen clock. The same event couples may, of course, also serve to determine the rate of the clock in terms of the progress of the water's rise in temperature. One process is to be called the complementary of the other. To use the previous picture: in every process, two lines out of the bundle of lines representing the temporal world are involved. Each line is formed by a series of events of a certain kind. In our example the first line L is formed by events E_1, E_2, E_3, etc., which are the events consisting in the water reaching temperatures θ_1, θ_2, θ_3, etc. The second line L' is formed by events E_1', E_2', E_3', etc. which are the events consisting in the clock-hand coinciding with points p_1, p_2, p_3, etc., on the dial. The value of the ratio of an interval on L divided by a corresponding interval on L' is the rate of progress of the clock represented by L—in this case the temperature clock. Corresponding intervals, of course, are intervals cut off by two event couples which are simultaneous. The reciprocal of this ratio gives the rate of progress of the complementary process, namely, the advance of the dial clock in terms of temperature intervals given by the warming water.

It is clear that anything not made up of a succession of event couples, the first member of which is independent and distinguishable from the second, can neither have a rate of progress nor be a process. The so-called journey of the present along the bundle of lines formed by all the event series lacks this essential feature of all processes. The coincidence of the present with a specific cross-cut of the beam consisting of the succession of event clusters cannot be coupled with any other event, since there are no other events that are not already lying on one of the lines comprising the beam.

And it will obviously not do to say that the coinciding of the present with point t_1 on line L' should be coupled with the simultaneous event of its resting at t_1' on L' present at t_2 on L with present at t_2' on L', and so on. This would be a completely redundant and futile exercise not capable of yielding the process of time's passage. All that we would be doing is coupling t_1, t_2, etc., on L to t_1', t_2', etc., respectively on L'. But this series of event couples has already been accounted for. It represents the process consisting in the series of events E_1, E_2, etc., occurring at points t_1, t_2, etc., on L, coupled with events E_1', E_2', etc. occurring at t_1', t_2', on L', which is the process consisting in the rise of temperature and its complementary, the process of the dial clock's running. In order to obtain an extra process which could be regarded as that of time's progress, we should need in addition to the event of the present reaching a given set of points on all the lines formed by the various successions of events, that the present also reach a point on an extra line not formed by events. This seems absurd.

It may be noted in passing that anti-time-flow philosophers are not in the least perturbed by the fact that in special relativity theory we do speak of time passing at different rates in different systems. It is easily seen that such talk need not be taken literally. All that is being claimed in relativity physics is that when one inertial system is in motion relative to another then all *physical processes* in the former system slow down relative to measurements made in the latter. The fact that this is normally expressed by relating t in one system to t' in the other does not amount to a claim that time itself passes at different rates in the two systems. Since time itself is not the sort of thing to which one can meaningfully attribute the property of passing, its 'rate of passage' cannot differ in different systems. t and t' do not stand for *time itself* but for intervals of *time as defined* by the progress (with certain corrections added) of some physical process designated as our standard. The formula relating t with t' is a brief way of indicating how the movements of all clocks in one system are related to the movements of various other clocks in the second system.

Further probing shows, however, that the foregoing analysis is not a sufficiently penetrating one. Consequently the view which rules out talk about time's flow as absurd, and which is based on this analysis, is unwarranted.

II

A crucial step toward gaining a deeper insight into the nature of time is to inquire whether there is any way to determine which intervals along the bundle of lines representing the various successions of events are to be regarded as of equal length. On a superficial view, it may seem that this is an entirely arbitrary matter of choice. If we so wished, we could treat the series of events consisting of drops of water escaping a given water clock as lying along a line divided into equal segments by the fall of each individual drop, and thus as our standard criterion by which the length of all other intervals on the other lines in the bundle are to be measured. If we adopt this view then, of course, we shall maintain that all one can say about a given clock A is that it gains time, or loses time, relative to clock B, but that there is nothing in objective reality which in any way is indicative whether A *really* keeps time more accurately than B or vice versa. But this is not quite so. It is not merely a matter of convention, physicists tell us, that we should regard water clocks as being very inaccurate timekeepers, whereas mechanical clocks may be looked upon as considerably more accurate devices for measuring time. Or that the spinning earth, though much more accurate than both, is still far inferior to atomic clocks. If physicists were to decide arbitrarily, for instance, that the rotation of the earth is a perfectly regular clock this would result in our having to assume that a great number of physical laws are far more complicated than hitherto believed. The choice of the clock which is to serve as the standard, and hence is to measure the varying amount of irregularities possessed by other clocks, is determined by our desire to make physics as simple as possible. While the question which clock is to be our standard may be settled by choice, the question which of these choices will yield maximum simplicity is no longer a matter of choice. Consequently, the whole of physics, combined with the simplicity-maximization principle, creates a clock which serves as our standard, and the rate of which may or may not correspond to that of an actual physical clock.

Thus, if we confine our considerations to any given line we will not be able to discern any marks on it which divide it into what, for objective reasons, should be regarded as equal segments. But with a combined look at all the lines, there emerges a succession of intervals—which may be made as short as we desire, and thus form a new line (to be denoted L^t) lying alongside all the other lines consisting of all the event successions of the universe—which are for sound reasons to be regarded as of equal length.

Accordingly, it might conceivably be argued, the progress of any physical process may be measured not only in terms of intervals given by some physical clock, but also in terms of intervals provided by time itself. The reason, it could be said, is that we have, after all, an extra line—namely L^t—which we said was essential for this purpose. The two lines to be employed for expressing the rate of progress of the clock represented by L in terms of time are L and L^t. Intervals on the former divided by corresponding intervals on the latter give us the required rate of progress. The reciprocal value of this rate gives us the rate of progress of the complementary process, namely, the progress of time in terms of intervals given by the clock represented by L.

For example, Smith may boast of a very fine watch which he says gains no more than three seconds in every twenty-four hours. He makes his claim on the basis of a careful comparison of his watch with the clock by which the BBC keeps time. Upon further probing, he would admit that his statement is not completely accurate, for even that clock does not keep perfect time. Upon careful investigation of all the clocks involved, and making the correct adjustments, it may turn out that the correct thing to say is that Smith's clock gains 2·997 seconds every twenty-four hours or, what is more likely, 2·997 during the *last* twenty-four hours, whereas in the course of the twenty-four hours before, it was gaining 0.001 second more, or less (since usually mechanical clocks are not only inaccurate, they are also non-uniformly so). Consequently, one straight-forward answer to the question: How fast is time moving? is: It progressed exactly twenty-four hours while Smith's clock progressed twenty-four hours and $2 \cdot 997$ seconds.

It would be wrong to object that we were not compelled to introduce an extra line to be the bearer of the equal intervals which emerge through a consideration involving the whole of physics—that these intervals could be marked out upon the already existing lines. It would be wrong because one could counter this by saying that it is sufficient to have the *possibility* of an extra line in order to lend intelligibility to the talk about time's progress. And if it were objected that we are precluded from marking out the equal intervals on anything but the existing lines, since we lack an extra series of actual events which are not already represented by one of those lines, the reply is a simple one. It is, that what emerges through the combination of the laws of physics is a genuinely new series of events, namely: E_1^t, which is the event consisting in *time* having a value t_1^t, E_2, which is the event consisting in *time* having a value t_2, etc. Admittedly, when it is stated that time by clock C is t_1 we are referring to something that can be read off straight from a dial and are thus speaking of a directly observable event. Not so when we are referring to E_1^t. But in the bundle of lines which constitute the temporal world there are many lines that are formed by events to which we have no direct access except through observations remotely connected to them by theories. In science we confer full status upon theoretical events, and L^t represents a succession of such events.

An objection which seems more serious concerns the extraordinary nature of this new clock. It seems to be an essential feature of every clock that its rate need not remain constant but may vary relatively to the rates of other clocks. In other words, it is possible that clock C should slow down or speed up relatively to all other clocks while they maintain their rates relatively to each other. Our new clock seems to lack this characteristic property of clocks. It plainly makes no sense to say that while all the physical clocks in the universe remain unchanged, time has doubled or halved its previous rate. The very fact that the rate at which time itself is supposed to move cannot be read off from any dial or inferred from any specific phenomenon, but is determined by all processes combined, guarantees that when all these processes remain unchanged time cannot change its rate either. Conversely, when the rate of clocks undergoes a uniform variation (as in the case of relative motion where the clocks of one system all go at a

o

different rate from that of the clocks in the system which is in motion relative to it) time undergoes the same variation. This argument provides a strong reason for saying that all those lines which really represent clocks are divided into intervals whose values are logically independent of one another. L^t is not such a line since its intervals cannot conceptually be separated from those on the other lines. Consequently, the right thing to say is, after all that from all the laws of physics and the simplicity-maximization principle there emerges not yet another line, but only a set of equal intervals to be marked out upon the existing lines. In the next section we shall see how to meet this objection.

III

Let q_t stand for the amount to which all those physical quantities which are functionally time-dependent grow in time t. These quantities will include the various distances covered by bodies whose movement is governed by different laws; the number of particles emitted by substances decaying in accordance with various time-dependent laws; the amount of heat, electric charge or mass gained or lost by various systems, etc. The amount q_t is given by the general equation

$$q_t = a_0 + a_1 t + a_2 t^2 + \ldots + a_n t^n + \ldots (T)$$

to any desired degree of approximation, provided we adjust appropriately the co-efficients a_1, a_2, etc.

For example: the distance covered by light in vacuum is a growing quantity q_t. In order to obtain the value of this distance from equation (T) at any time t, we put all the co-efficients as equalling zero except a_1, which equals c.

In order to obtain the value of the distance fallen by a particle subject to the earth's gravity alone, near its surface, we put all the co-efficients as zero except a_2, which equals $1/2g$.

In order to obtain the value of the displacement of an oscillating particle from its equilibrium position whose movement is governed by the law $d = K \sin (nt)$ we put a_0, a_2, a_4, etc. as zero and

$$a_1 = K_n, \quad a_3 = -\frac{Kn^3}{3!}, \quad a_5 = +\frac{Kn^5}{5!}, \quad a_7 = -\frac{Kn^7}{7!} \text{ etc.}$$

Suppose that one day we discover another region of space (region R) where every physical process progresses at half the rate at which a process of its kind progresses in normal space (region N). For example: while in normal space the distance travelled by light in vacuum in one second is c units, in region R it is only $c/2$ units; while the distance fallen near the surface of a planet with earth's mass and radius is, in normal space, in one second, $1/2g$ units, it is $1/8g$ in region R; while the displacement of an oscillating particle from its equilibrium position whose movement is governed by the law $d = K \sin{(nt)}$ is K units in normal space, it is $\dfrac{K}{\sqrt{2}}$ units in R-space, etc.

It should be noted that no difference between the two spaces becomes evident with respect to processes whose amount of progress is given by equation (T)—no difference except to an observer who is in a position to watch both regions of space simultaneously.[1]

The experience of those, however, whose observations are confined to region R will be identical with the experience of those whose observations are confined to normal space.[2] For just as in our space the quantity c (the distance covered by light in one second) corresponds to the quantity $1/2g$ (the distance travelled during that period by a freely falling body in the vicinity of an earth-like planet) so it does in region R. (Except, of course, that in our region of space both quantities are reached in one second by our scale of time while in R-space the same is reached in two seconds on the same time scale—to which, by definition, those whose observation is confined to R have no access.) And just as in region R, $c/2$ corresponds to $1/8g$, so in our space (in half a second on our time scale) $c/2$ is reached when $1/8g$ is reached.

Judging by the behaviour of all the q_ts alone, the situation can

[1] Some may feel uneasy about the complications which affect an observer simultaneously surveying both spaces. Is part of his body in R and part of his body in N? Then the biochemical processes in one half of his body proceed at a different rate from those in the other, giving rise to a very unfamiliar situation. Is he fully immersed in one space? What would his observations be like of objects, reflecting light, which abruptly change velocity as they cross the boundary between the spaces? But such worries can be avoided. It suffices if the observer sends across the border to region R a number of physical systems such as a decaying nucleus, a heat radiating body, and a leaking condenser, and examines these upon their return—say after an hour—and notes that the number of particles escaped, the heat and charge loss, amount to what they normally amount to, in half an hour. Thus all we need is an observer who can compare processes in the two spaces, but not necessarily at the time they occur.

[2] At any rate with respect to q_t-type quantities, but not necessarily with respect to others, as will be seen later.

be described in two different ways. According to one description, in region R, unlike region N where q_t is given by (T), the equation relating q_t with t is:

$$q_t = a_0 + \frac{a_1}{2}t + \frac{a_2}{2^2}t^2 + \frac{a_3}{2^3}t^3 + \ldots + \frac{a_n}{2^n}t^n \qquad (T')_A$$

and according to the other description in region R,

$$q_t = a_0 + a_1(t/2) + a_2(t/2)^2 + a_3(t/2)^3 + \ldots + a_n(t/2)^n \qquad (T')_B$$

Clearly, equation $(T')_A$ and $(T')_B$ are identical. But this does not mean, of course, that descriptions A and B are identical and therefore interchangeable. The two descriptions are identical only so far as growing or waning quantities q_t are concerned, but with respect to innumerably many other parameters they are not.

Consider the following example: there are two identical, frictionless, horizontal, centripetal machines in each of which a particle of mass m is attached at one end of a spring with modulus of elasticity λ, the other end of which is fixed at the centre of the circle along which the mass moves with constant speed. One machine is in region N and its counterpart is in region R; both masses are made to travel at a uniform velocity along a circular path of radius r. The distance covered by the rotating mass is a q_t-type of quantity, and its value in N is obtained from (T) by putting all coefficients zero except a_1 which equals $\sqrt{Fr/m}$, remembering that $F = ms^2/r$. On the other hand, a glance at (T') shows that the corresponding distance travelled by the mass in region R is $\sqrt{(Fr/m)}/2$. How do we explain this? How is it that the spring expands by the same amount through the force generated by a speed $s/2$ in R as it expands by the force generated by s in N?

There are two distinct explanations, depending on whether we adopt description A or B. If we adopt the former we commit ourselves to the view that all the clocks in R run at half the rate they run in N because innumerably many constants of nature have different values in R from those in N. The relevant constant in our case is a_1, which is $\sqrt{Fr/m}$ whose value is halved in R, either because $F_R = F_N/4$, i.e. $\lambda_R = \lambda_N/4$ where λ_R and λ_N are the moduli of elasticity of the spring in R and N respectively (assuming that $F = \lambda x$ extension), or because $m_R = 4m_N$. Clearly, either the fact that the modulus of elasticity of a spring decreases, or that the mass of a body increases, when moving from N to R, explains why at half the speed in R we should have the same extension as in N.

If, however, we adopt description B, we hold that none of the laws or constants of nature varies from region to region. In R, just as in N, the spring will expand to a length r if and only if the speed of the rotating mass is s. But we must not forget that according to B in region R not only the clocks, but time also, runs at half the rate it runs in region N. Consequently, in terms of the time system which prevails in R, the mass at the end of the spring—which appears to be moving at $s/2$ relative to the clocks in N—is really moving at speed s.

Thus description A and B are fundamentally different from one another. According to A, in R all clocks run at halved rates—because of the changed physical constants—but not time, which retains the same rate in R as in N. According to B, however, both time and clocks go more slowly in R than in N. The objection of the last section is thus seen to disappear. Time—which we have identified with the clock which emerges when the principle of the maximization of simplicity is applied to the laws of physics governing processes—is logically separable from other clocks. It may vary its rate together with them, as in R according to B, or it may not do so, as is the case according to description A.

The possibility of there being innumerably many phenomena tending to determine whether to maintain description A or B will not be disputed. To such phenomena belong those in which the physical constants represented by our earlier $a_1, a_2, \ldots$, etc. are involved and not the variable represented by t. Suppose region R was discovered in the days of the caloric theory of heat, a theory according to which heat was a massless, invisible and odourless substance. On crossing the border from N to R the absolute temperature of all bodies might be found to drop by 75 per cent. The hypothesis that $m_R = 4m_N$—which is in accordance with description A but not with B—explains now two diverse phenomena. It explains the difference in the behaviour of the centripetal machine in the two regions and also the seeming disappearance of heat on entering R. Since temperature $\theta = \dfrac{H}{m \, x \, \text{specif. heat,}}$

on a fourfold increase in mass, H has to be spread over four times as much mass in R bringing about a 75 per cent decrease in θ.

INDEX

DATE DUE

2-3			
GAYLORD			PRINTED IN U.S.A.